BAD MACHINERY

THE CASE OF THE SIMPLE SOUL

By
John Allison

Edited by
James Lucas Jones & Ari Yarwood

Designed by
Jason Storey

Colour Assists by
Adam Cadwell

Oni Press, Inc.
publisher, Joe Nozemack
editor in chief, James Lucas Jones
v.p. of business development, Tim Wiesch
director of sales, Cheyenne Allott
director of publicity, John Schork
editor, Charlie Chu
associate editor, Robin Herrera
production manager, Troy Look
senior designer, Jason Storey
inventory coordinator, Brad Rooks
administrative assistant, Ari Yarwood
office assistant, Jung Lee
production assistant, Jared Jones

Oni Press, Inc.
1305 SE Martin Luther King Jr. Blvd.
Suite A
Portland, OR 97214

onipress.com
badmachinery.com

Become our fan on Facebook: facebook.com/onipress
Follow us on Twitter: @onipress
onipress.tumblr.com

ISBN: 978-1-62010-193-3
eISBN: 978-1-62010-194-0

Library of Congress Control Number: 2012953355

Bad Machinery Volume Three: The Case of the Simple Soul, December 2014. Published by Oni Press, Inc. 1305 SE Martin Luther King Jr. Blvd., Suite A, Portland, OR 97214.

First Edition: December 2014

20 19 18 17 16 15 14 13 12 11 10 9 8 7 6 5 4 3 2 1

Printed in China.

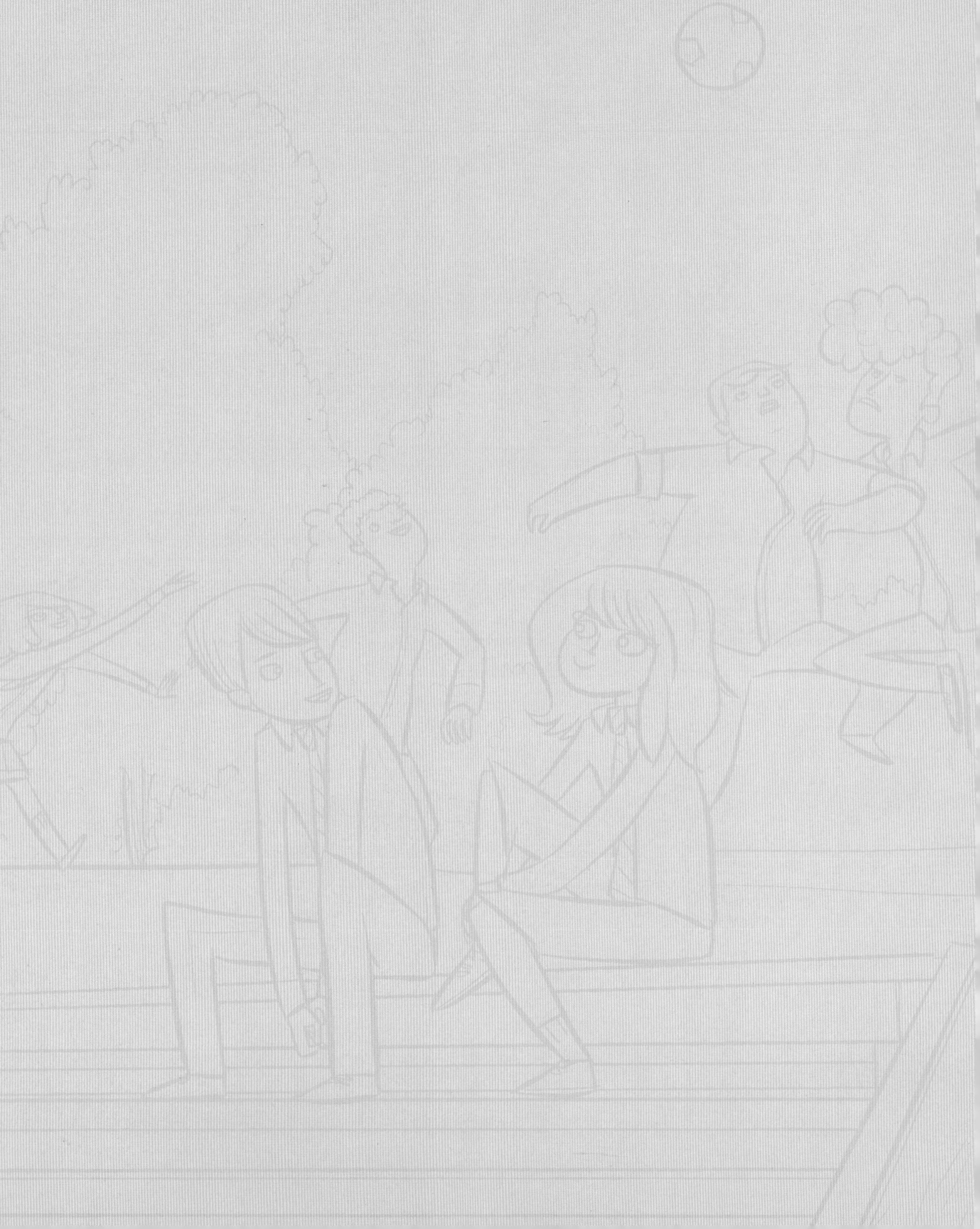

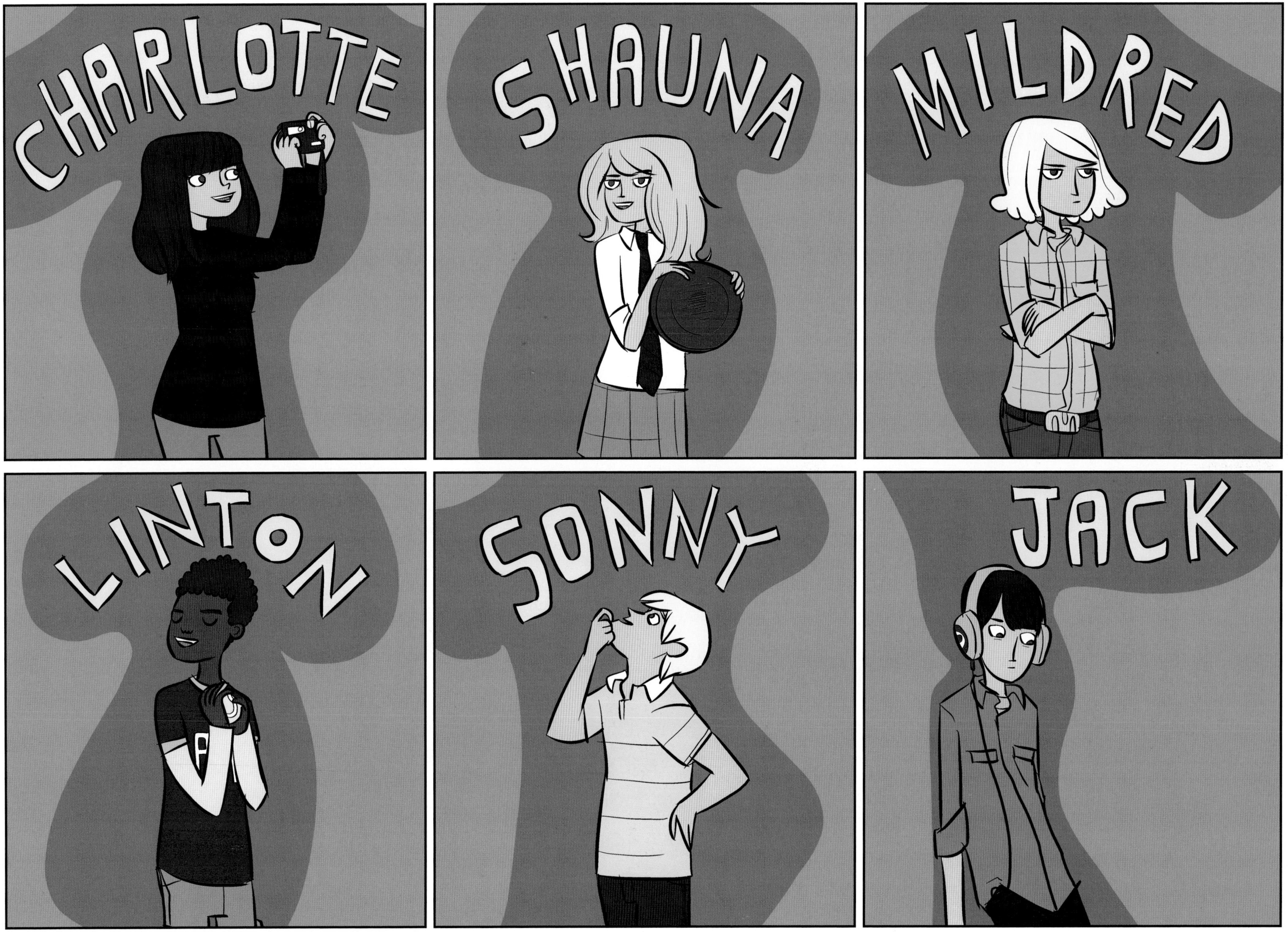
CHARLOTTE
SHAUNA
MILDRED
LINTON
SONNY
JACK

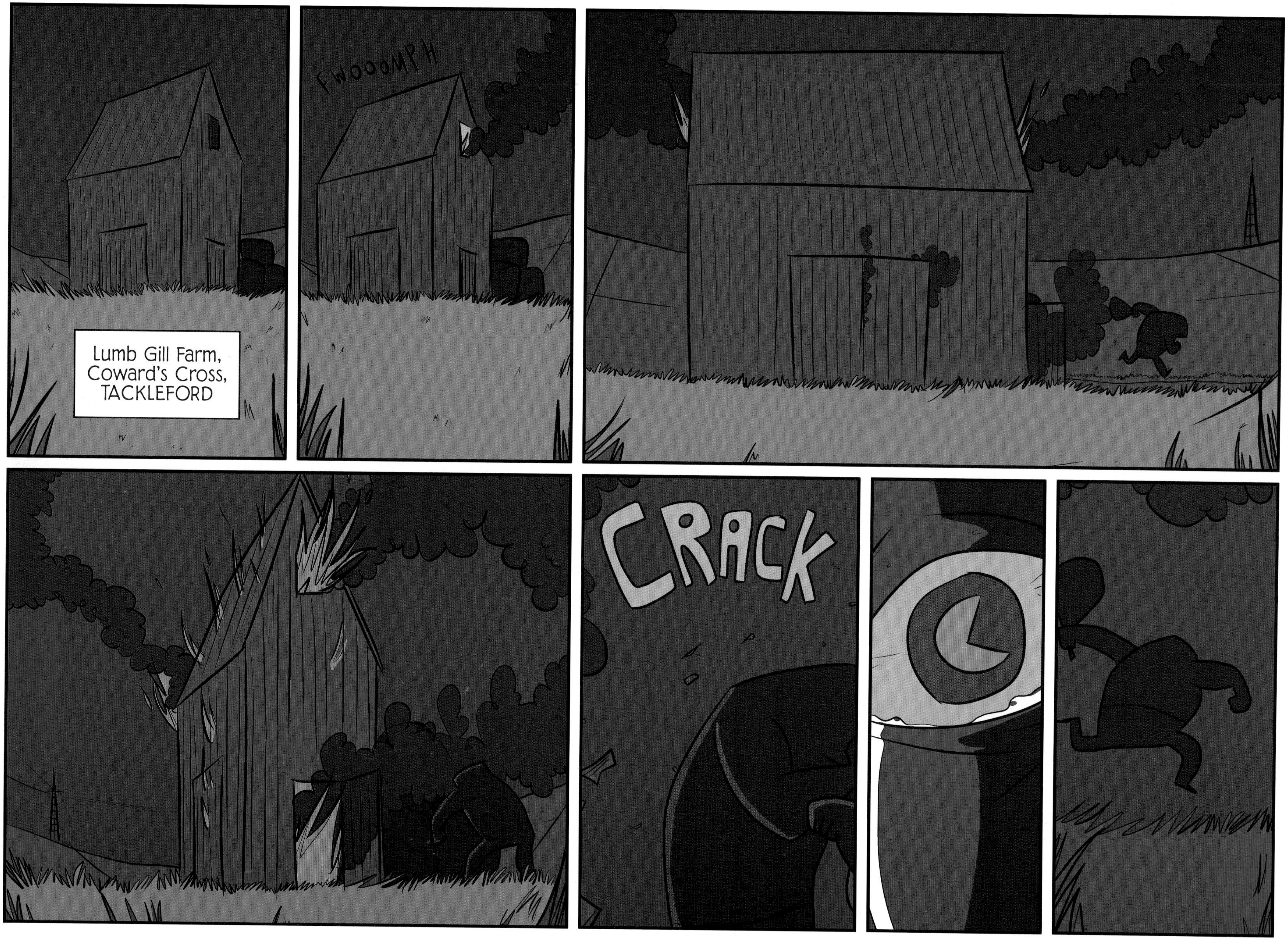
Lumb Gill Farm,
Coward's Cross,
TACKLEFORD
FWOOOMPH
CRACK

Tackleford Mummy

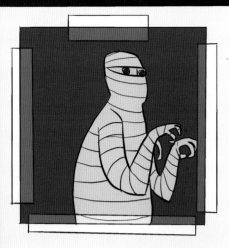

Museum menace. Average member of staff unabel to repel using gift shop contents. Slightly murderess.

Jerry the cyclops

Fearsome looking but his lack of depth perceptien and phisycal fitness mean he is NON-THRETTENING.

Giant bee

Does it make giant honey?

NOT SURE.

Local cyborg

Not billionaire playboy as suspected, just an idiot with a soldering iron and too much spare time.

House of evil

On no account put your hand through the letter box.

Wee folk

Almost too wee!

Reminder: watch where you are walking.

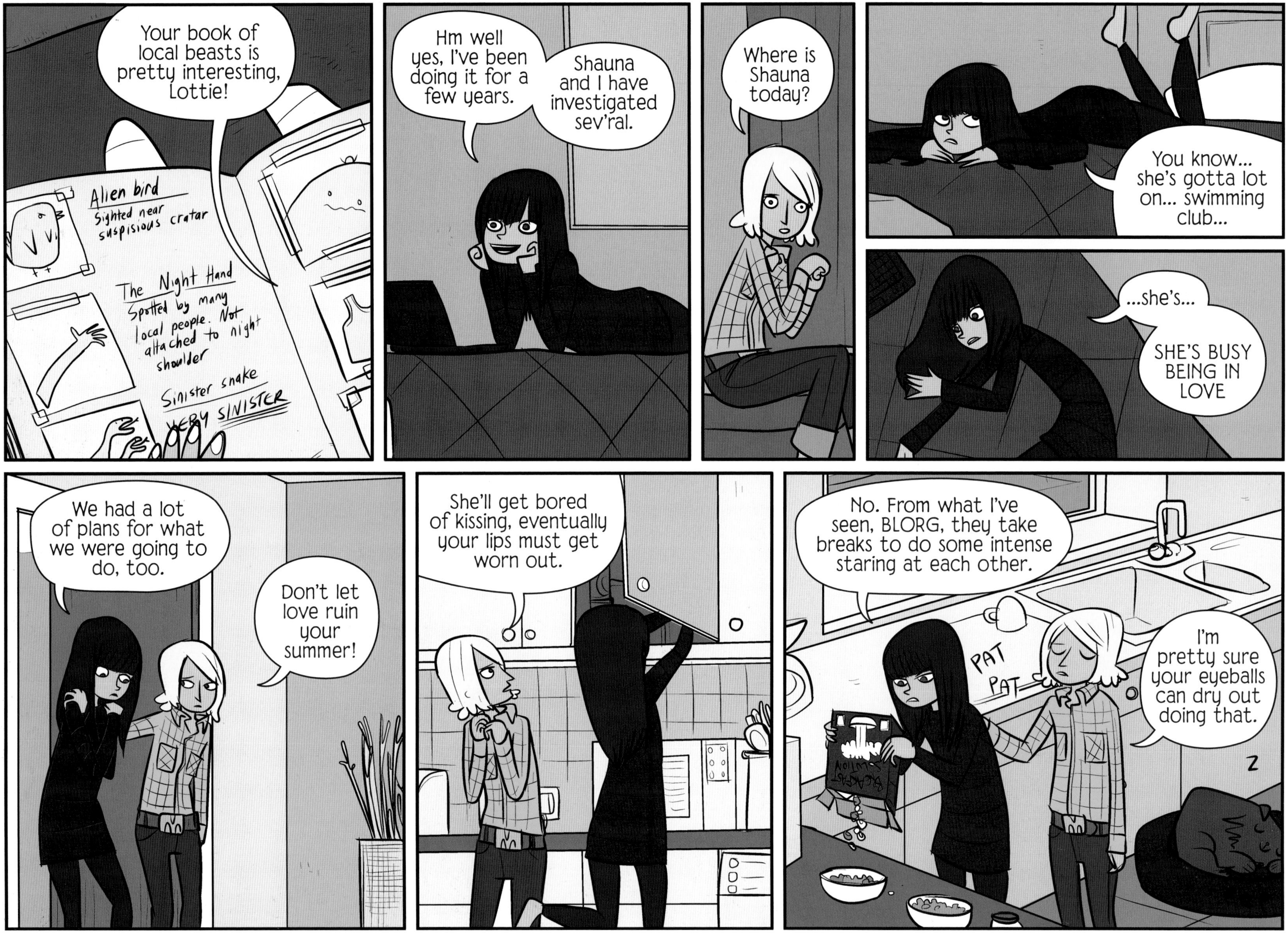
Your book of local beasts is pretty interesting, Lottie!
Alien bird
Sighted near suspisious cratar
The Night Hand
Spotted by many local people. Not attached to night shoulder
Sinister snake
VERY SINISTER
Hm well yes, I've been doing it for a few years.
Shauna and I have investigated sev'ral.
Where is Shauna today?
You know... she's gotta lot on... swimming club...
...she's...
SHE'S BUSY BEING IN LOVE
We had a lot of plans for what we were going to do, too.
Don't let love ruin your summer!
She'll get bored of kissing, eventually your lips must get worn out.
No. From what I've seen, BLORG, they take breaks to do some intense staring at each other.
PAT
PAT
I'm pretty sure your eyeballs can dry out doing that.
Z

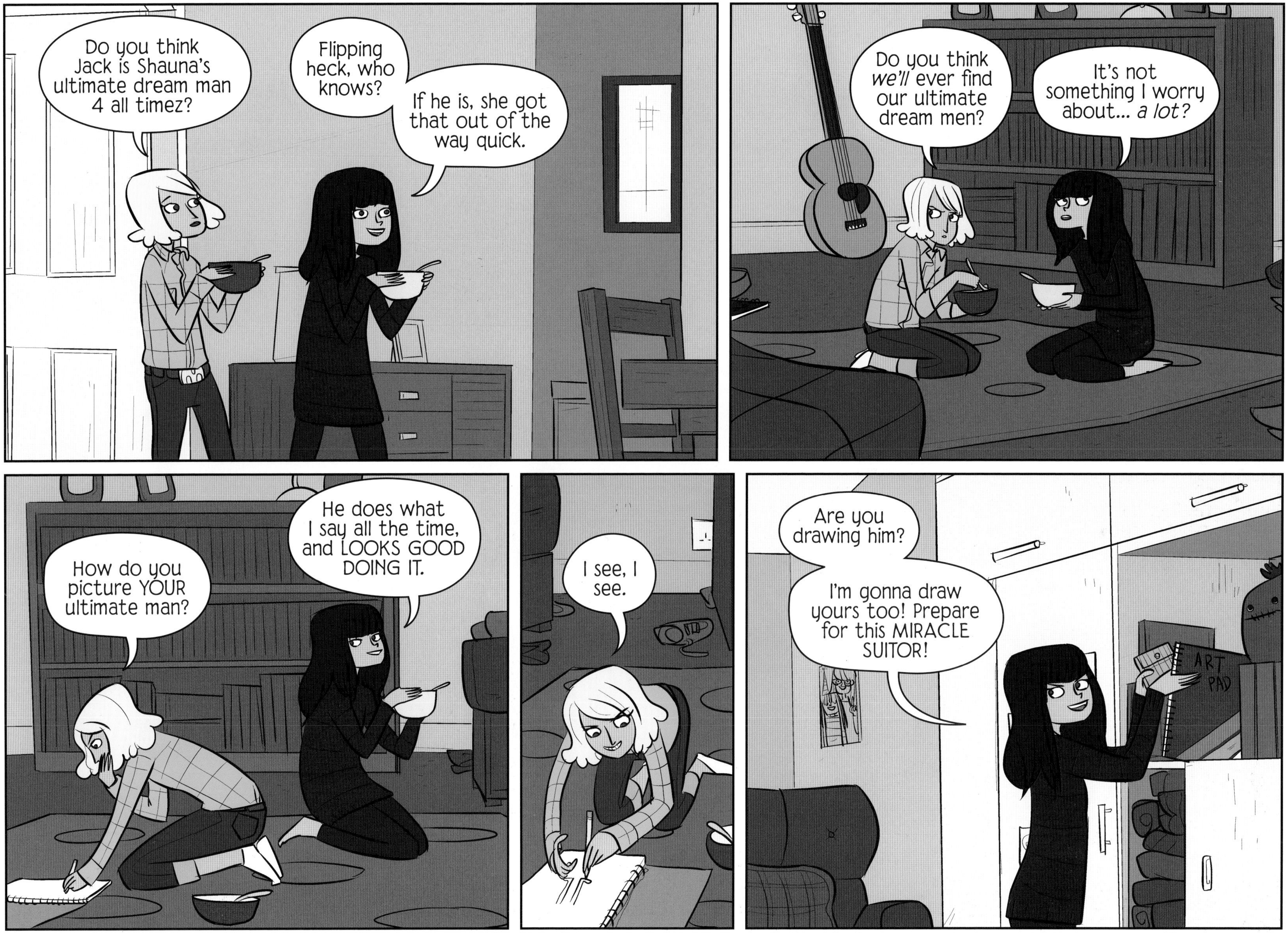
Do you think Jack is Shauna's ultimate dream man 4 all timez?
Flipping heck, who knows?
If he is, she got that out of the way quick.
Do you think *we'll* ever find our ultimate dream men?
It's not something I worry about... *a lot?*
How do you picture YOUR ultimate man?
He does what I say all the time, and LOOKS GOOD DOING IT.
I see, I see.
Are you drawing him?
I'm gonna draw yours too! Prepare for this MIRACLE SUITOR!
ART PAD

All right, I'm done.
Me too. SHOW!
HAHAHA HAH HA HAHA HA!
AAAARGH! HA HA HA HA HA!
CHARLOTTE'S IDEAL DREAM MAN by MILDRED
fashion hair
Handsome Moustache
Bare chest
for combat
musculre
weapons
small kilt
Paul Warrior
Mildred's ideal dream man by Charlotte
Hi honey IM home
Also hes' a werewolf
MOON
Kiss my hairy face baby
WAG
buisness dollars
Posy
Michael Harbottle
I CAN'T BREATHE
"FOR COMBAT"!!!
These are exciting men. Too exciting.
It seems pretty obvious to me that one day they'll meet...
...and *fight to the death.*

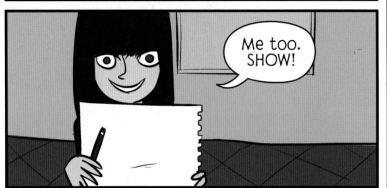

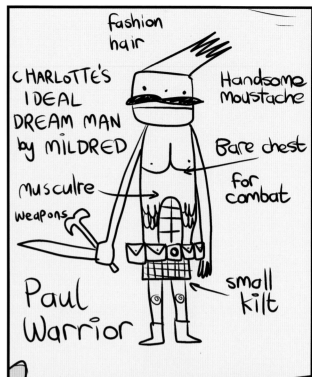

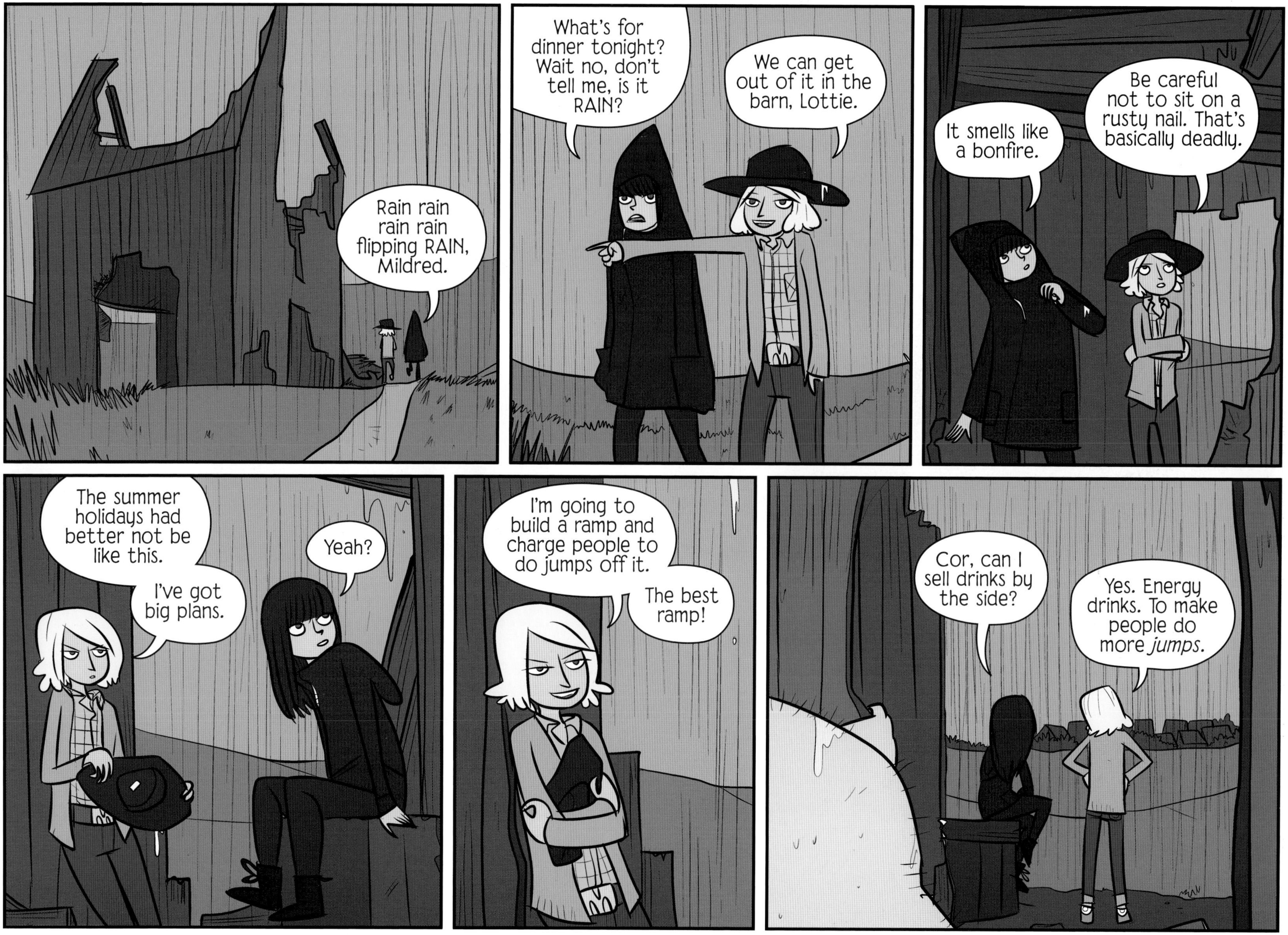
Rain rain
rain rain
flipping RAIN,
Mildred.
What's for
dinner tonight?
Wait no, don't
tell me, is it
RAIN?
We can get
out of it in the
barn, Lottie.
It smells like
a bonfire.
Be careful
not to sit on a
rusty nail. That's
basically deadly.
The summer
holidays had
better not be
like this.
I've got
big plans.
Yeah?
I'm going to
build a ramp and
charge people to
do jumps off it.
The best
ramp!
Cor, can I
sell drinks by
the side?
Yes. Energy
drinks. To make
people do
more *jumps*.

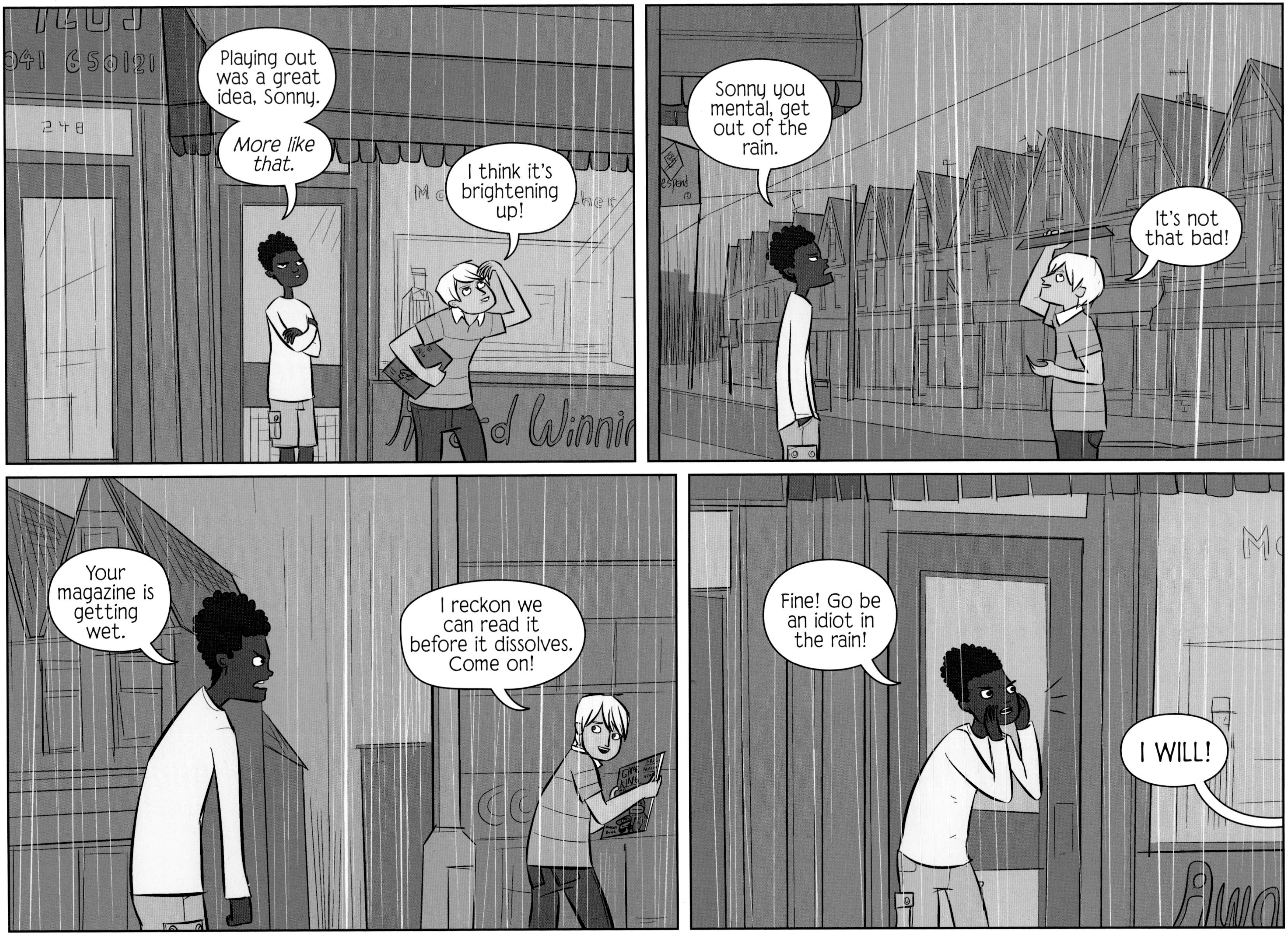
Playing out was a great idea, Sonny.
More like that.
I think it's brightening up!
Sonny you mental, get out of the rain.
It's not that bad!
Your magazine is getting wet.
I reckon we can read it before it dissolves. Come on!
Fine! Go be an idiot in the rain!
I WILL!

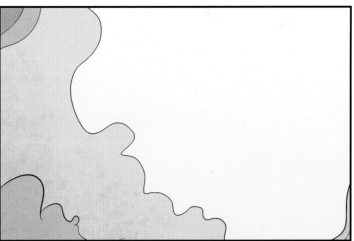

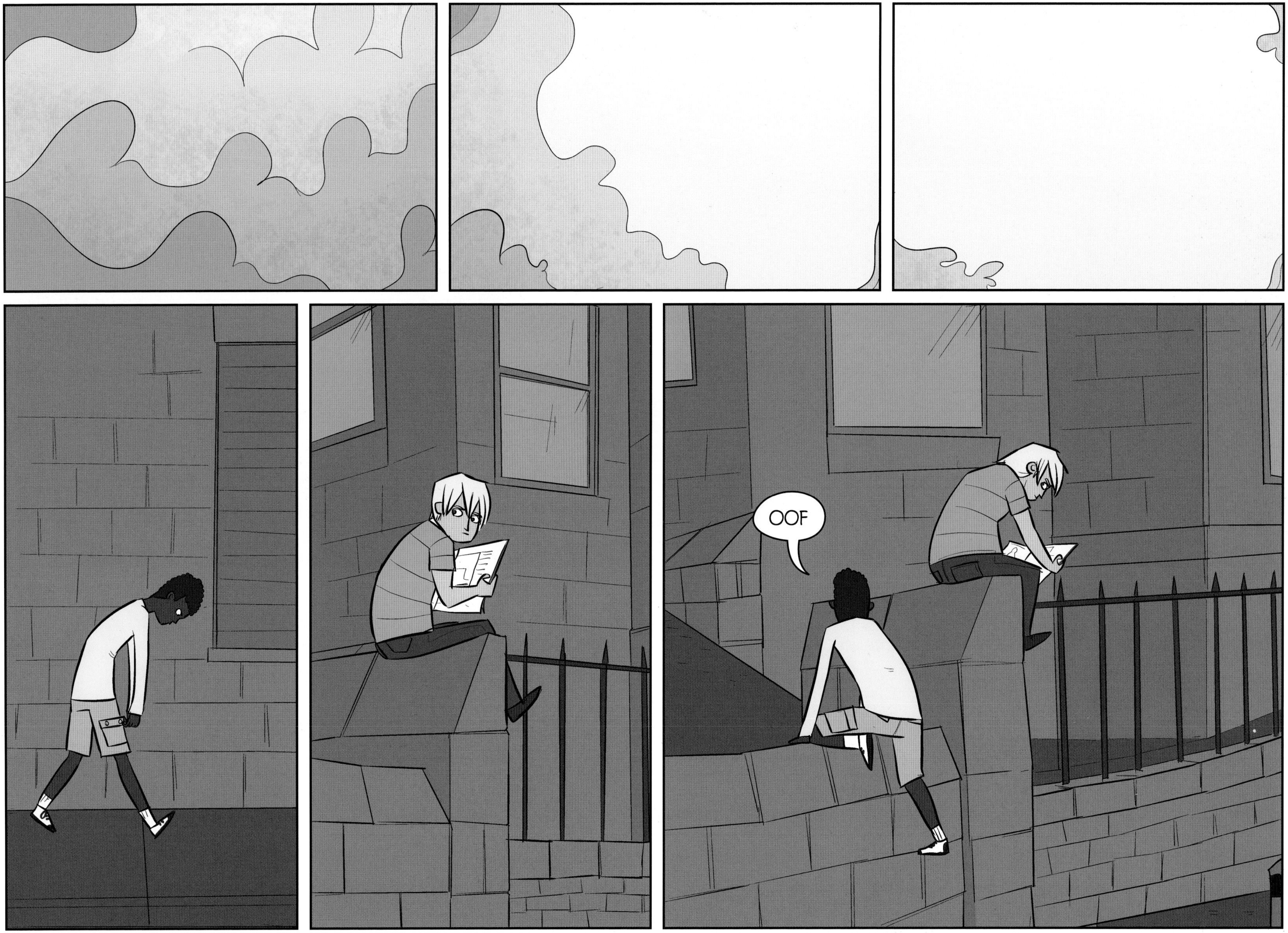
OOF

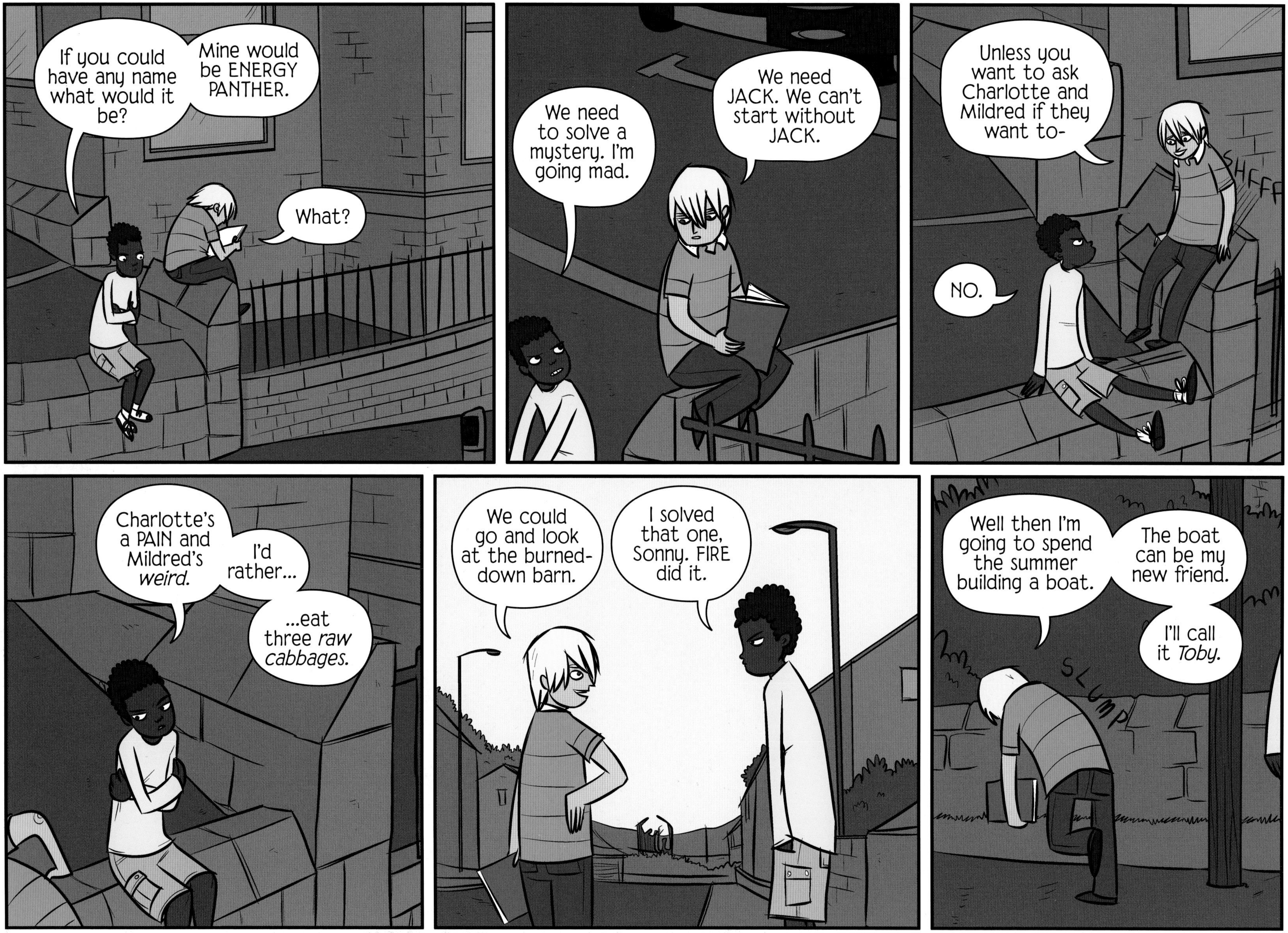
If you could have any name what would it be?
Mine would be ENERGY PANTHER.
What?
We need to solve a mystery. I'm going mad.
We need JACK. We can't start without JACK.
Unless you want to ask Charlotte and Mildred if they want to-
SHFFF
NO.
Charlotte's a PAIN and Mildred's *weird.*
I'd rather...
...eat three *raw cabbages.*
We could go and look at the burned-down barn.
I solved that one, Sonny. FIRE did it.
Well then I'm going to spend the summer building a boat.
The boat can be my new friend.
I'll call it *Toby.*
SLUMP

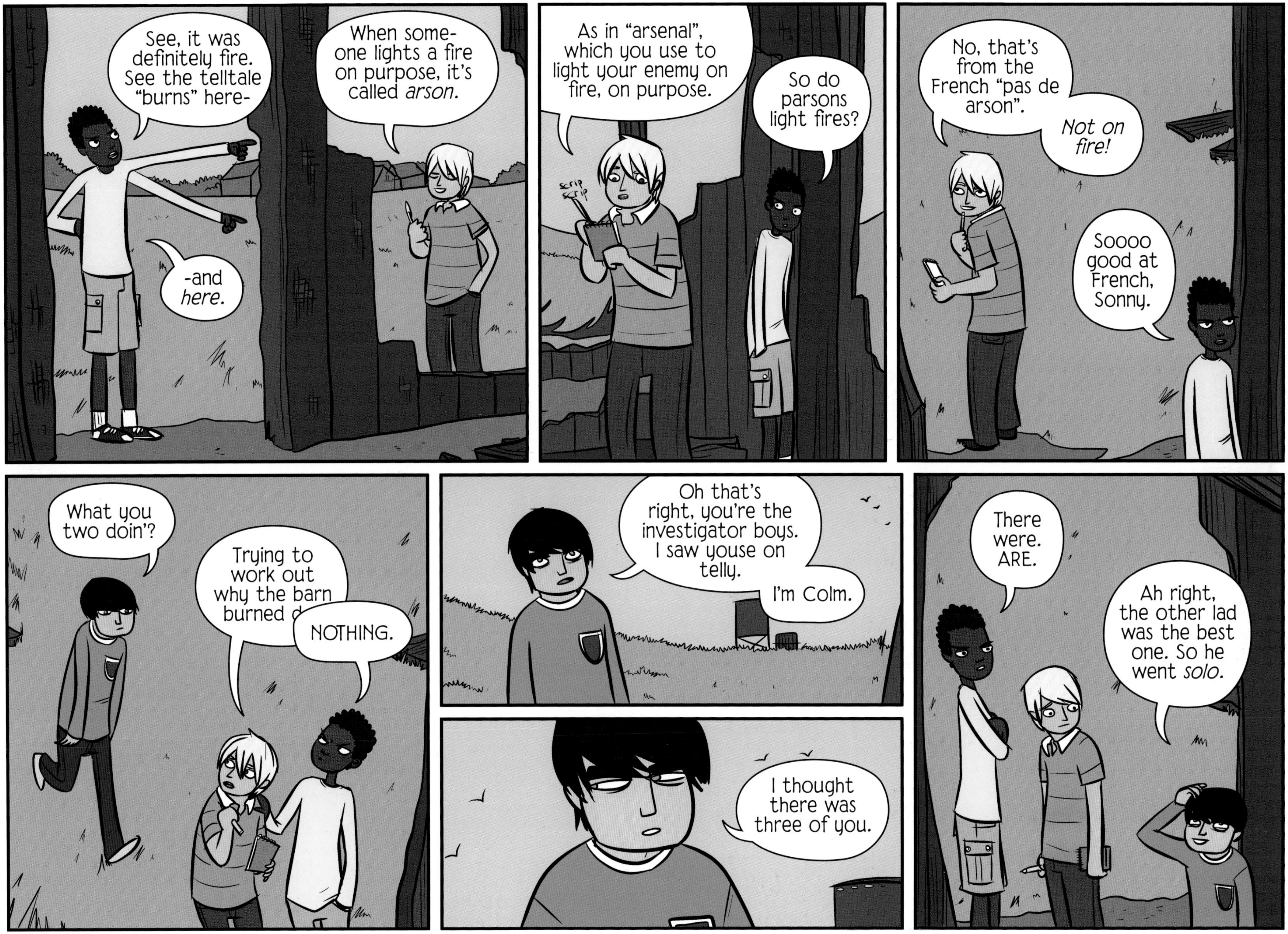
See, it was definitely fire. See the telltale "burns" here-
-and *here.*
When some-one lights a fire on purpose, it's called *arson.*
As in "arsenal", which you use to light your enemy on fire, on purpose.
scrip scrip
So do parsons light fires?
No, that's from the French "pas de arson".
Not on fire!
Soooo good at French, Sonny.
What you two doin'?
Trying to work out why the barn burned d
NOTHING.
Oh that's right, you're the investigator boys. I saw youse on telly.
I'm Colm.
I thought there was three of you.
There were. ARE.
Ah right, the other lad was the best one. So he went *solo.*

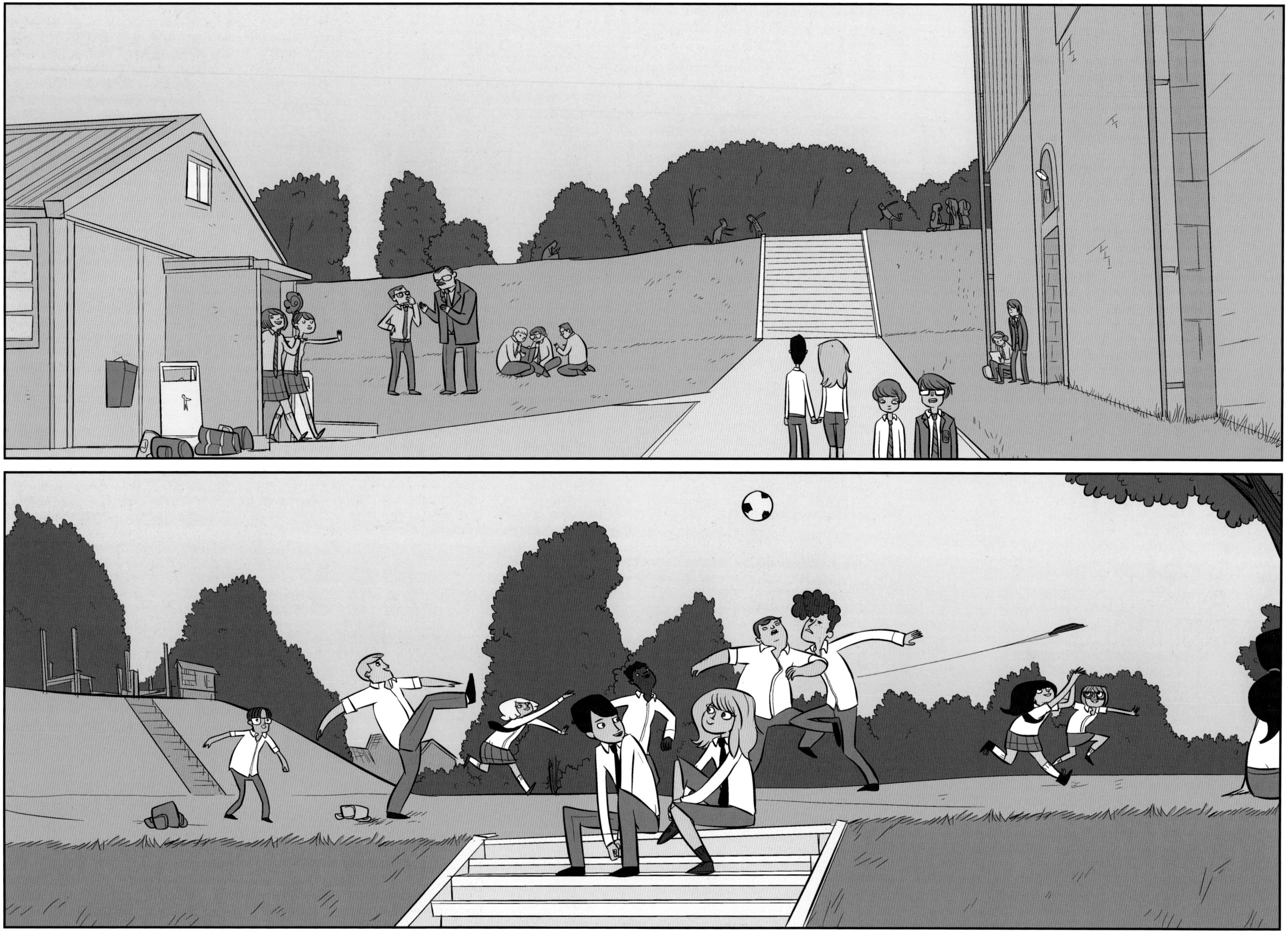

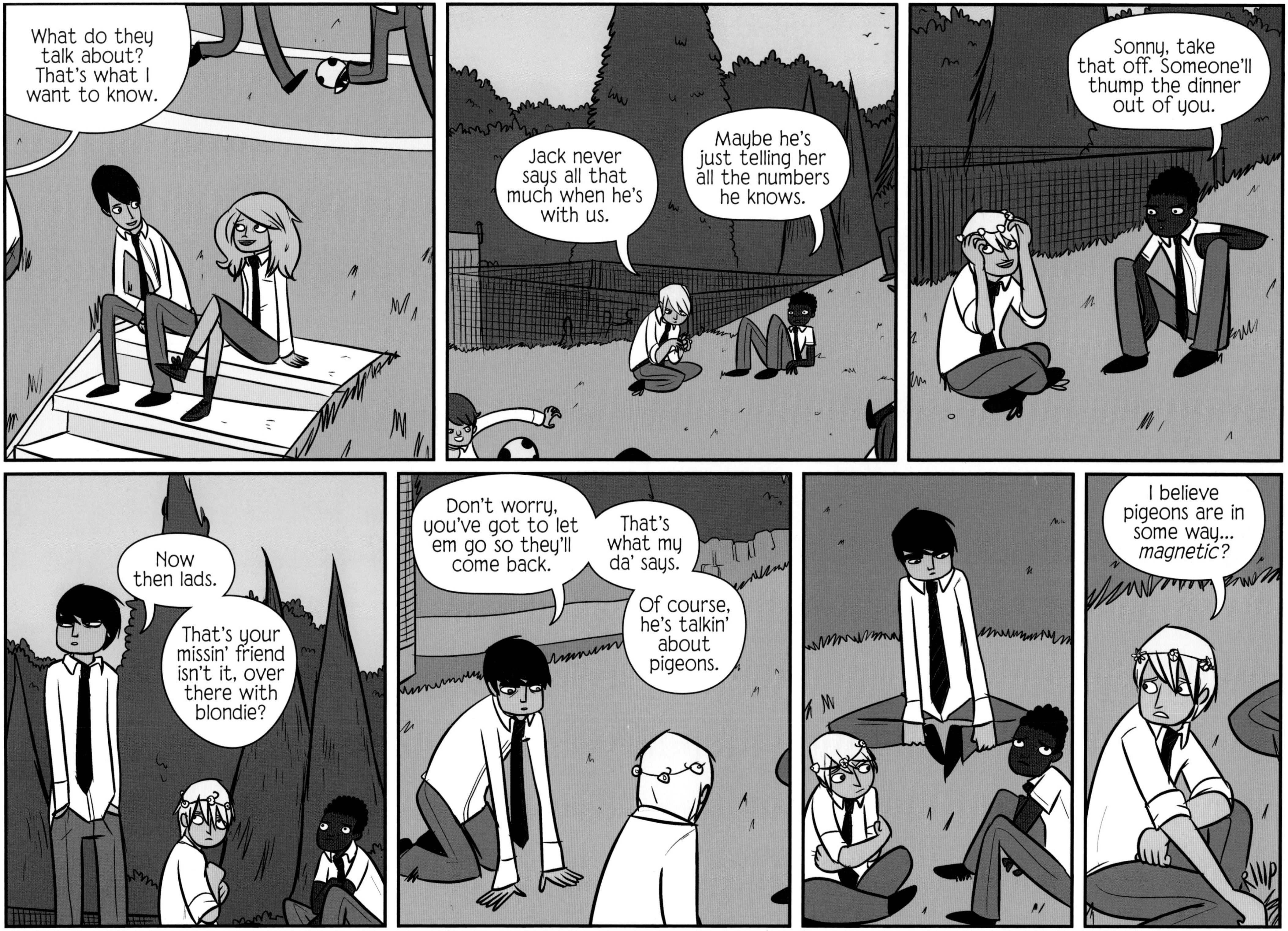
What do they talk about? That's what I want to know.
Jack never says all that much when he's with us.
Maybe he's just telling her all the numbers he knows.
Sonny, take that off. Someone'll thump the dinner out of you.
Now then lads.
That's your missin' friend isn't it, over there with blondie?
Don't worry, you've got to let em go so they'll come back.
That's what my da' says.
Of course, he's talkin' about pigeons.
I believe pigeons are in some way... *magnetic*?

Bad Machinery, Volume Three

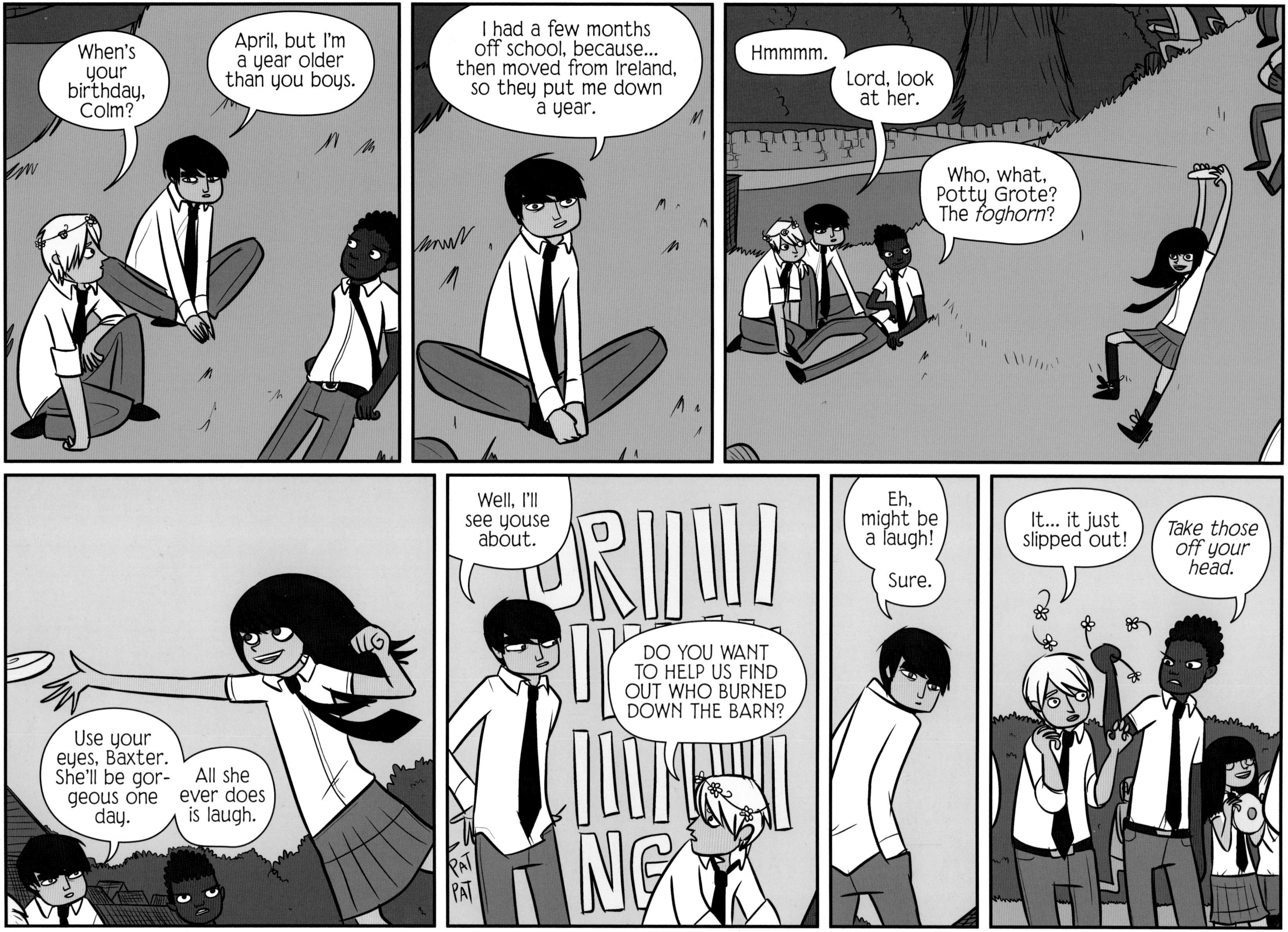
When's your birthday, Colm?
April, but I'm a year older than you boys.
I had a few months off school, because... then moved from Ireland, so they put me down a year.
Hmmmm.
Lord, look at her.
Who, what, Potty Grote? The *foghorn*?
Use your eyes, Baxter. She'll be gor-geous one day.
All she ever does is laugh.
Well, I'll see youse about.
DRIIIIIIIIIIIIIIIIIING
PAT PAT
DO YOU WANT TO HELP US FIND OUT WHO BURNED DOWN THE BARN?
Eh, might be a laugh!
Sure.
It... it just slipped out!
Take those off your head.

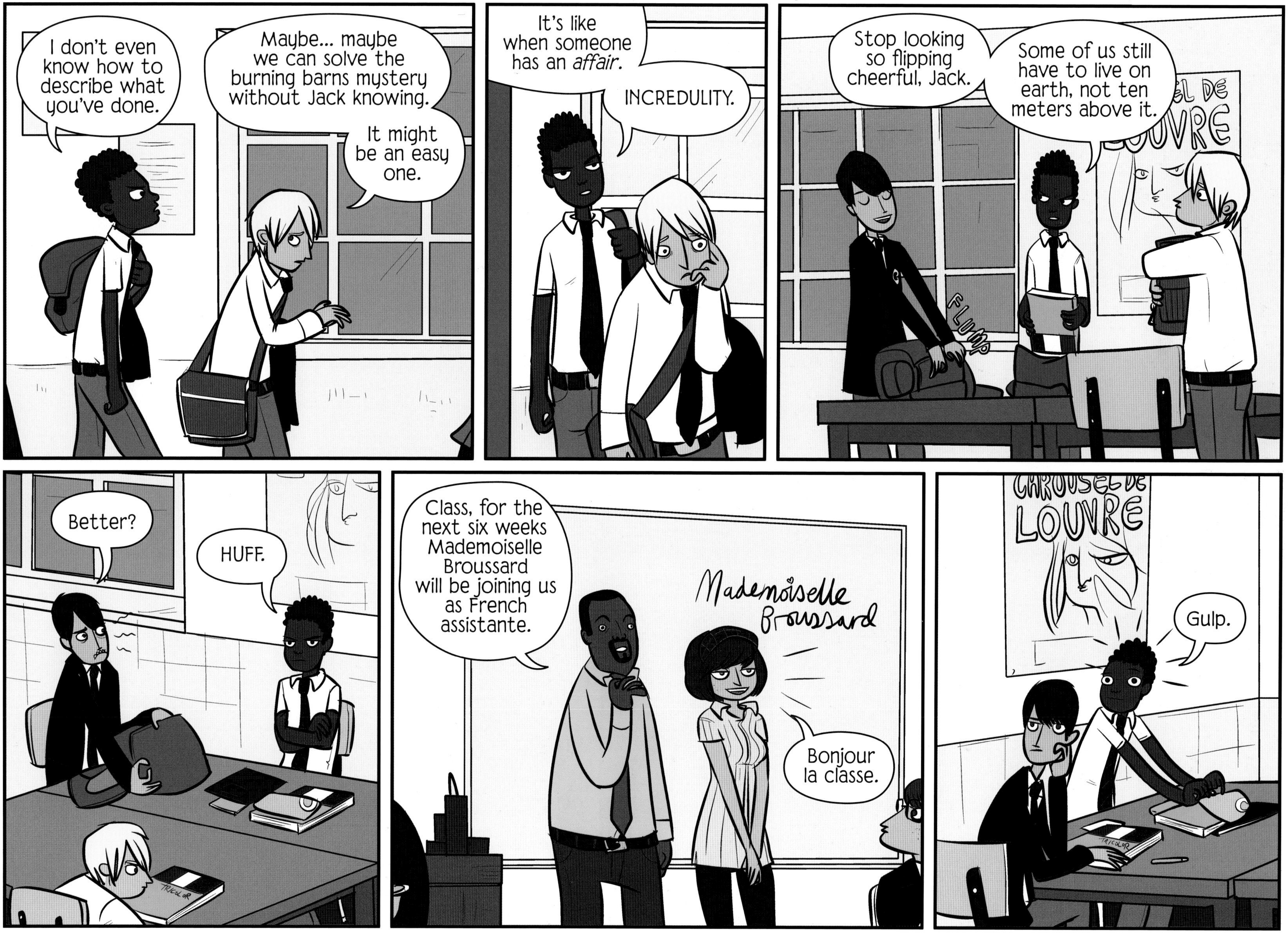
I don't even know how to describe what you've done.
Maybe... maybe we can solve the burning barns mystery without Jack knowing.
It might be an easy one.
It's like when someone has an *affair*.
INCREDULITY.
Stop looking so flipping cheerful, Jack.
Some of us still have to live on earth, not ten meters above it.
FLUMP
Better?
HUFF.
Class, for the next six weeks Mademoiselle Broussard will be joining us as French assistante.
Mademoiselle Broussard
Bonjour la classe.
CARROUSEL DE LOUVRE
Gulp.

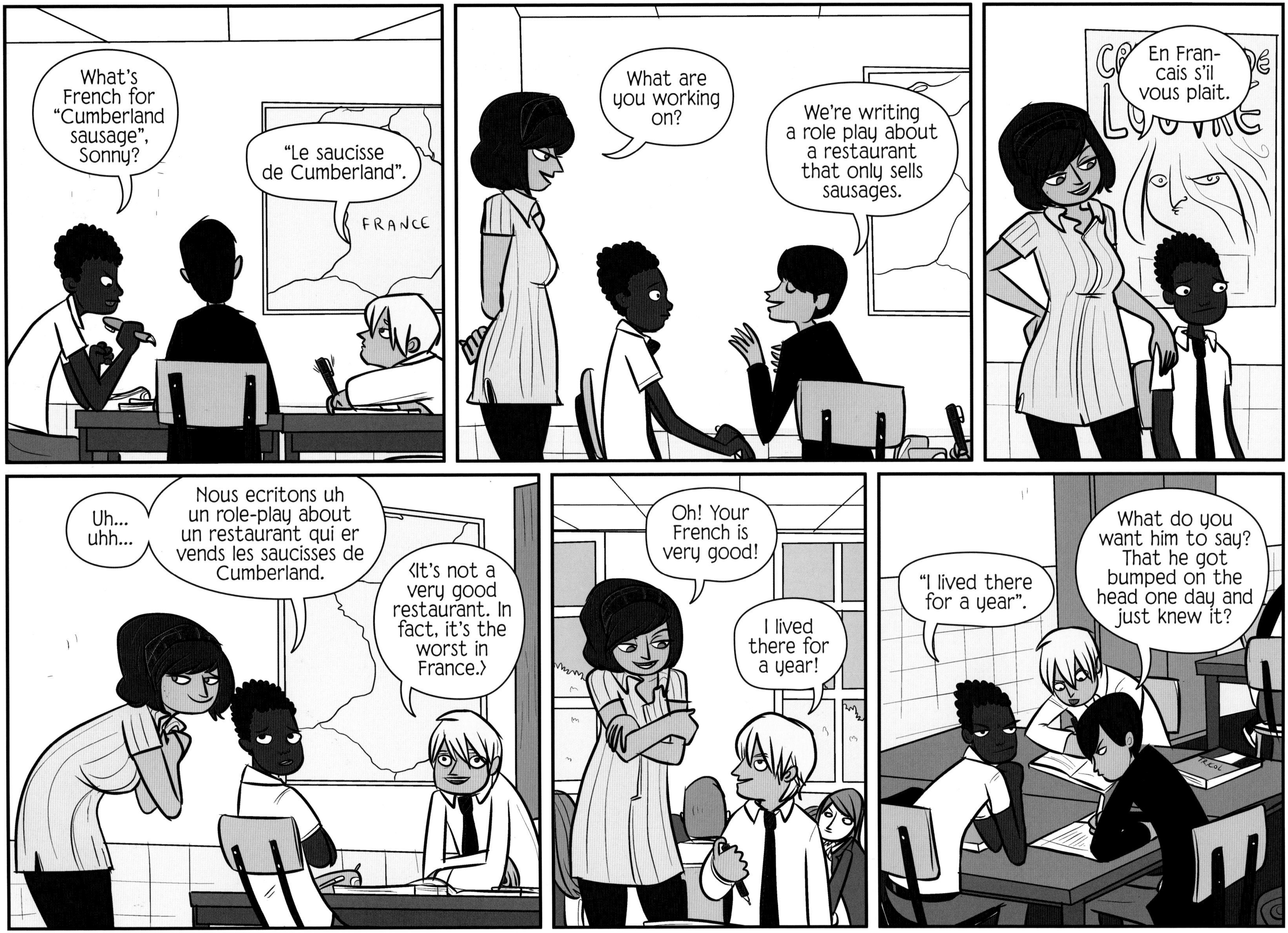
What's French for "Cumberland sausage", Sonny?
"Le saucisse de Cumberland".
FRANCE
What are you working on?
We're writing a role play about a restaurant that only sells sausages.
En Francais s'il vous plait.
Uh... uhh...
Nous ecritons uh un role-play about un restaurant qui er vends les saucisses de Cumberland.
‹It's not a very good restaurant. In fact, it's the worst in France.›
Oh! Your French is very good!
I lived there for a year!
"I lived there for a year".
What do you want him to say? That he got bumped on the head one day and just knew it?

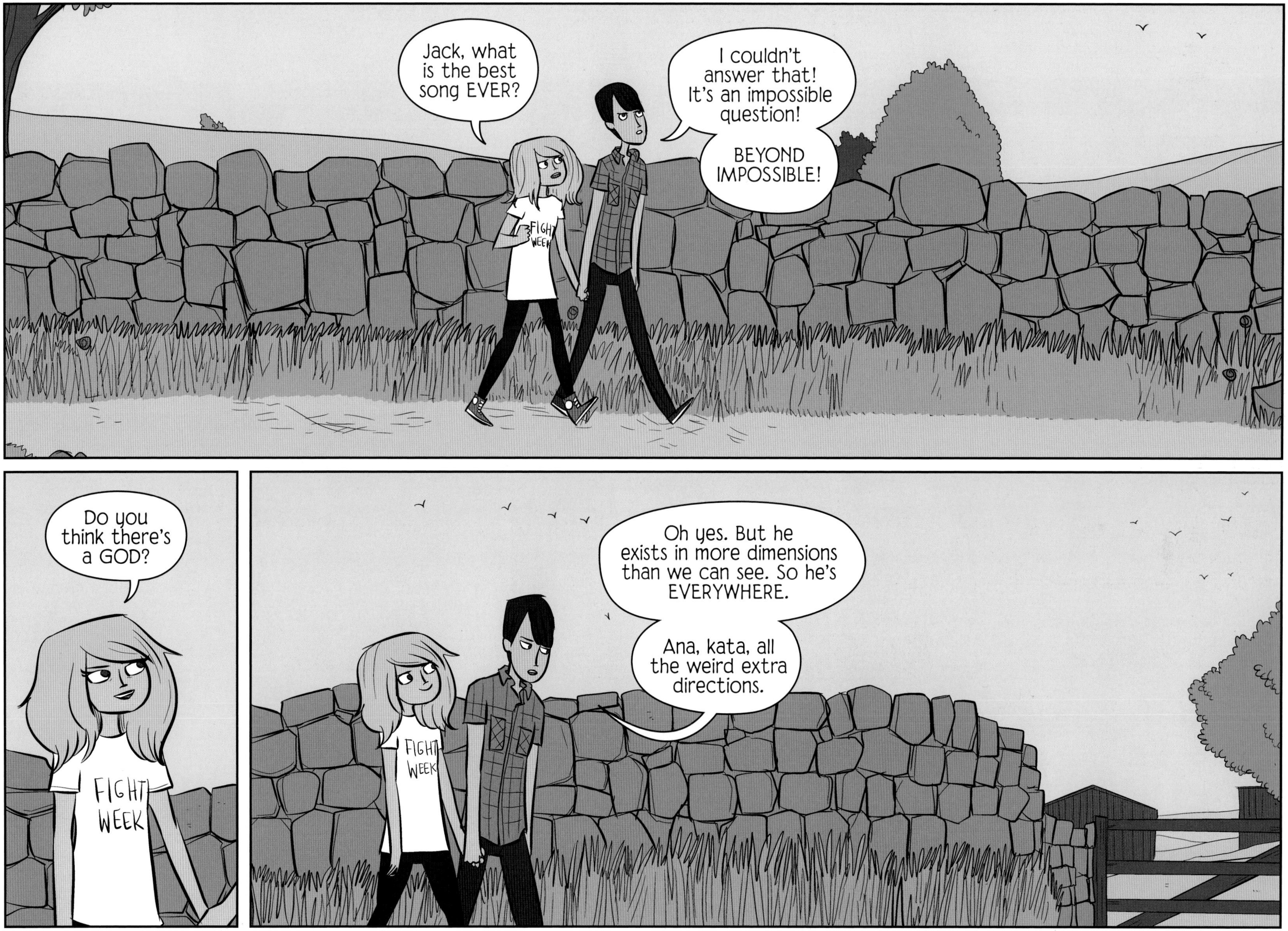
Jack, what is the best song EVER?
I couldn't answer that! It's an impossible question!
BEYOND IMPOSSIBLE!
FIGHT WEEK
Do you think there's a GOD?
FIGHT WEEK
Oh yes. But he exists in more dimensions than we can see. So he's EVERYWHERE.
Ana, kata, all the weird extra directions.
FIGHT WEEK

Bad Machinery, Volume Three

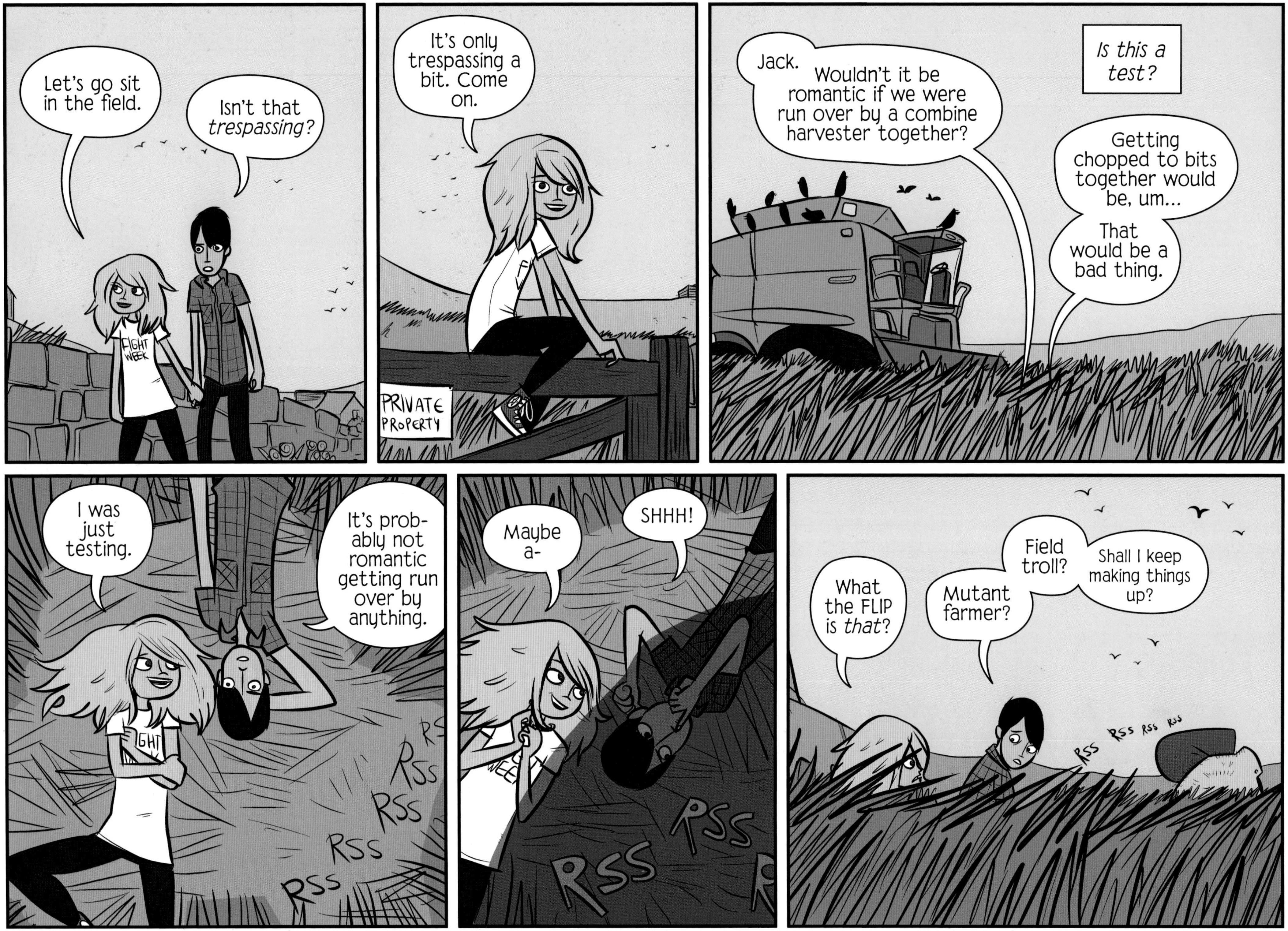
Let's go sit in the field.
Isn't that *trespassing*?
FIGHT WEEK
It's only trespassing a bit. Come on.
PRIVATE PROPERTY
Jack.
Wouldn't it be romantic if we were run over by a combine harvester together?
Is this a test?
Getting chopped to bits together would be, um...
That would be a bad thing.
I was just testing.
It's probably not romantic getting run over by anything.
RSS RSS RSS RSS
Maybe a-
SHHH!
RSS RSS
What the FLIP is *that*?
Mutant farmer?
Field troll?
Shall I keep making things up?
RSS RSS RSS RSS

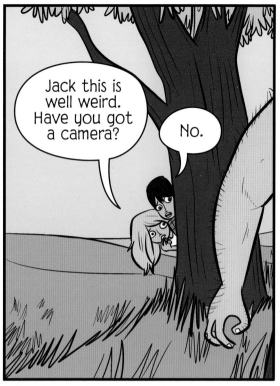

Jack this is well weird. Have you got a camera?

No.

Is this a new local beast? A secret creature?

It's not hiding very well if it is.

DID IT SEE US?

I don't know!

Oh! It's gone. We should—

Shauna, I thought we agreed no mysteries, just a nice summer.

Just you and me.

Yeah... yeah, but that was exciting, wasn't it?

Feel my heart beating!

I've always found sitting down exciting.

Maybe that's just how I am.

You should have a go at it, maybe.

Lots of different chairs to try.

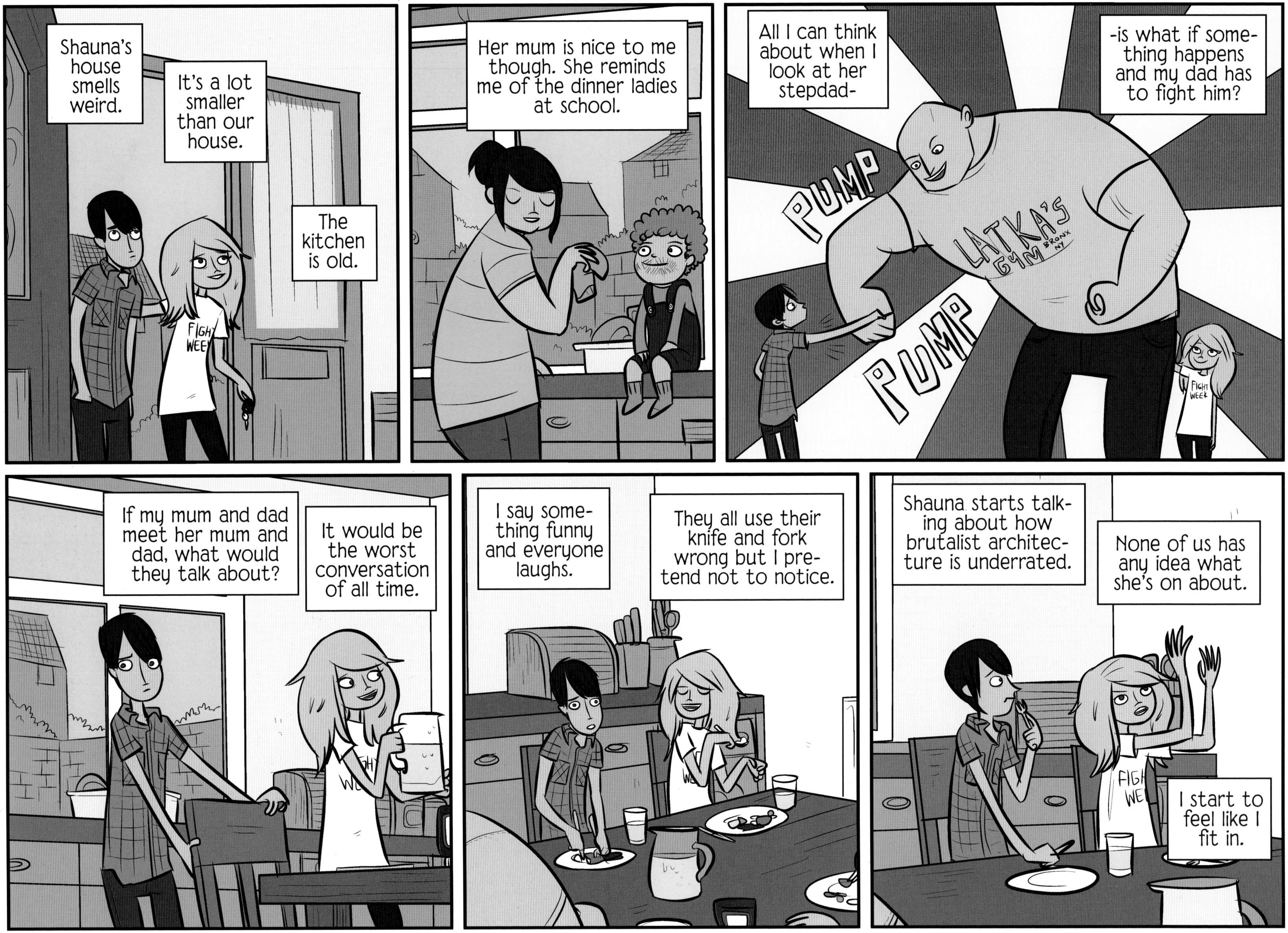
Shauna's house smells weird.
It's a lot smaller than our house.
The kitchen is old.
Her mum is nice to me though. She reminds me of the dinner ladies at school.
All I can think about when I look at her stepdad-
-is what if something happens and my dad has to fight him?
PUMP
LATKA'S GYM BRONX NY
PUMP
FIGHT WEEK
If my mum and dad meet her mum and dad, what would they talk about?
It would be the worst conversation of all time.
I say something funny and everyone laughs.
They all use their knife and fork wrong but I pretend not to notice.
Shauna starts talking about how brutalist architecture is underrated.
None of us has any idea what she's on about.
I start to feel like I fit in.

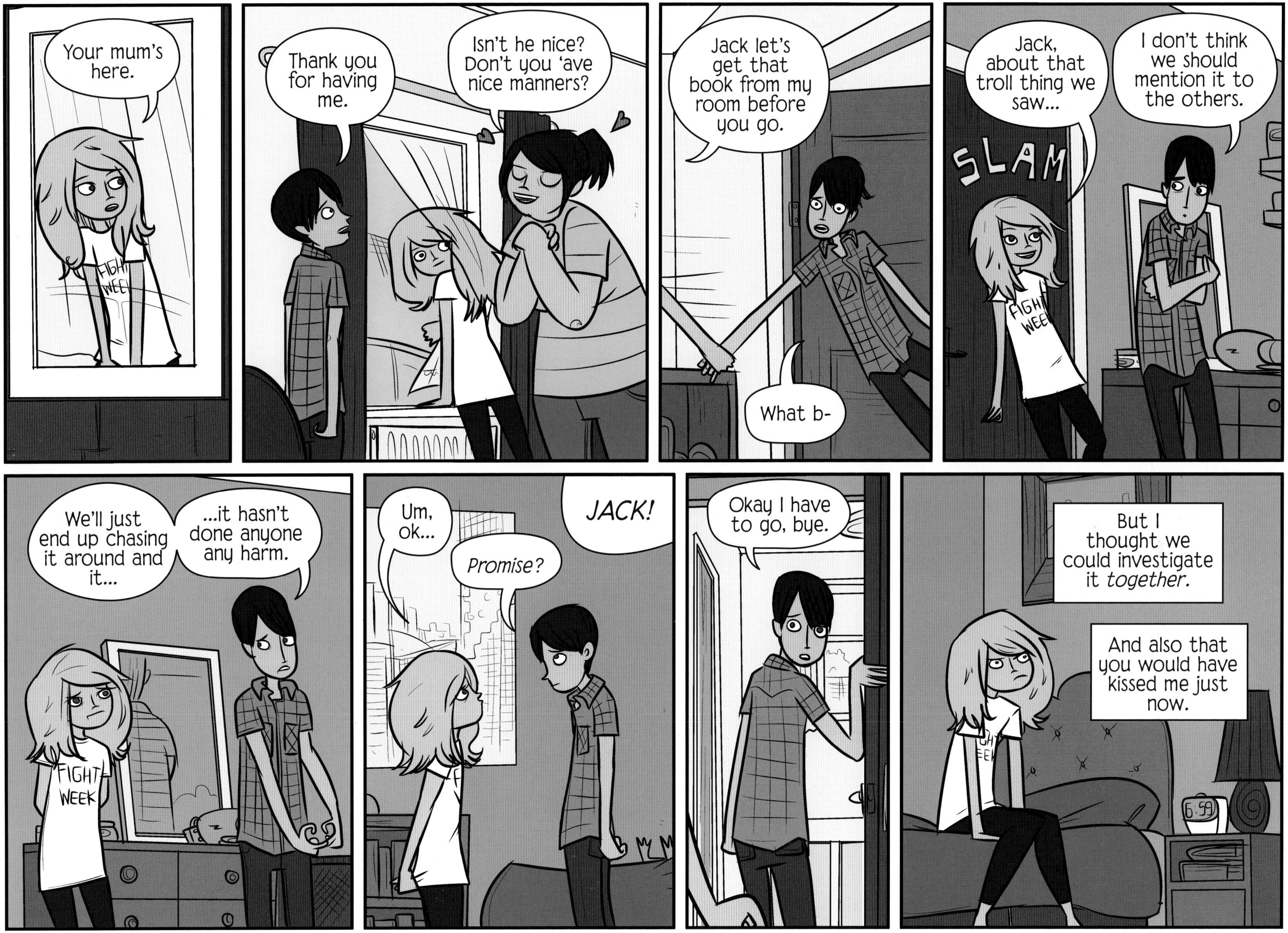

Your mum's here.
Thank you for having me.
Isn't he nice? Don't you 'ave nice manners?
Jack let's get that book from my room before you go.
What b-
SLAM
Jack, about that troll thing we saw...
I don't think we should mention it to the others.
We'll just end up chasing it around and it...
...it hasn't done anyone any harm.
Um, ok...
Promise?
JACK!
Okay I have to go, bye.
But I thought we could investigate it *together.*
And also that you would have kissed me just now.

Bad Machinery, Volume Three

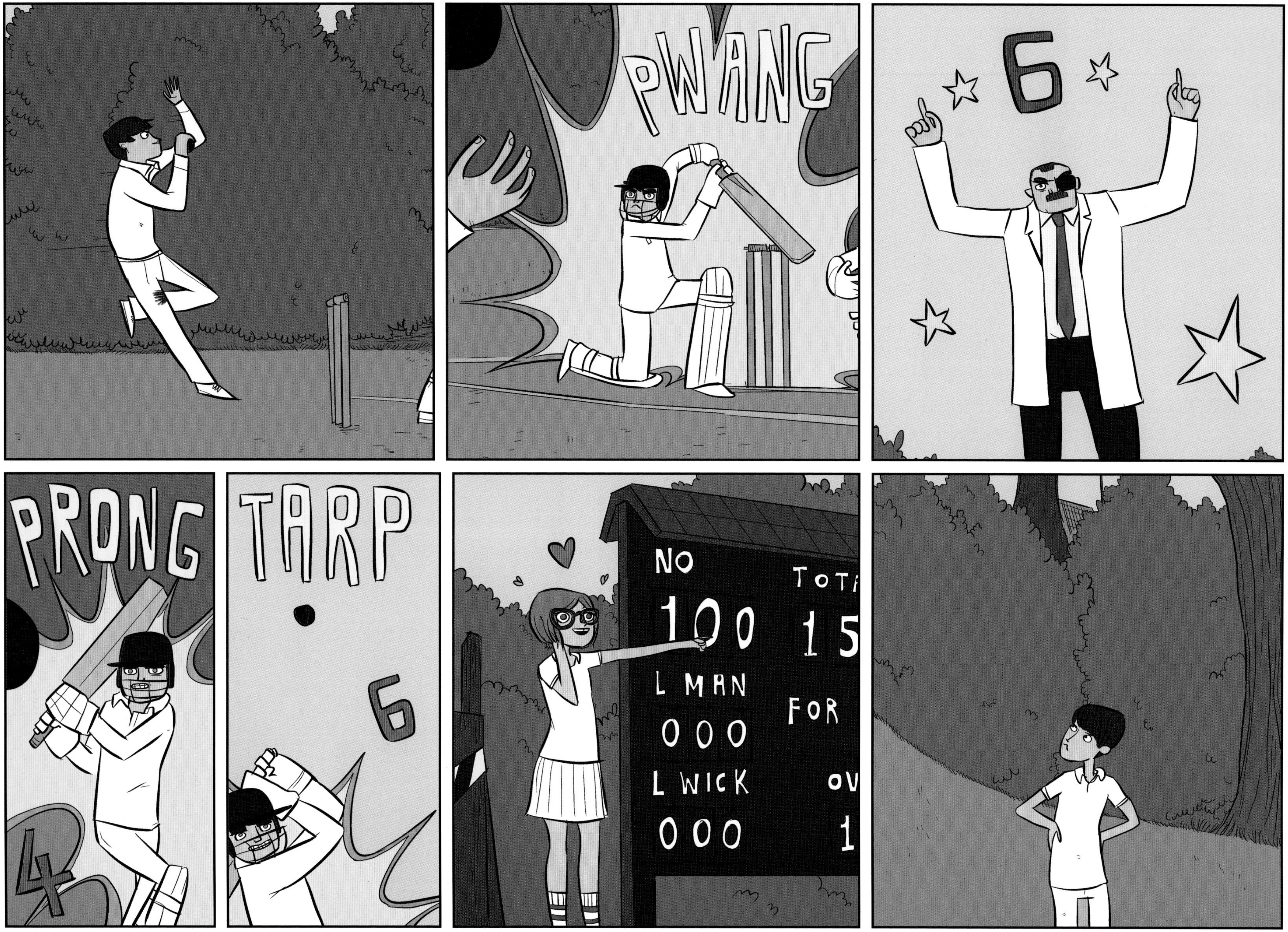
PWANG
6
PRONG
4
TARP
6
NO
100
15
L MAN
FOR
000
L WICK
000
1

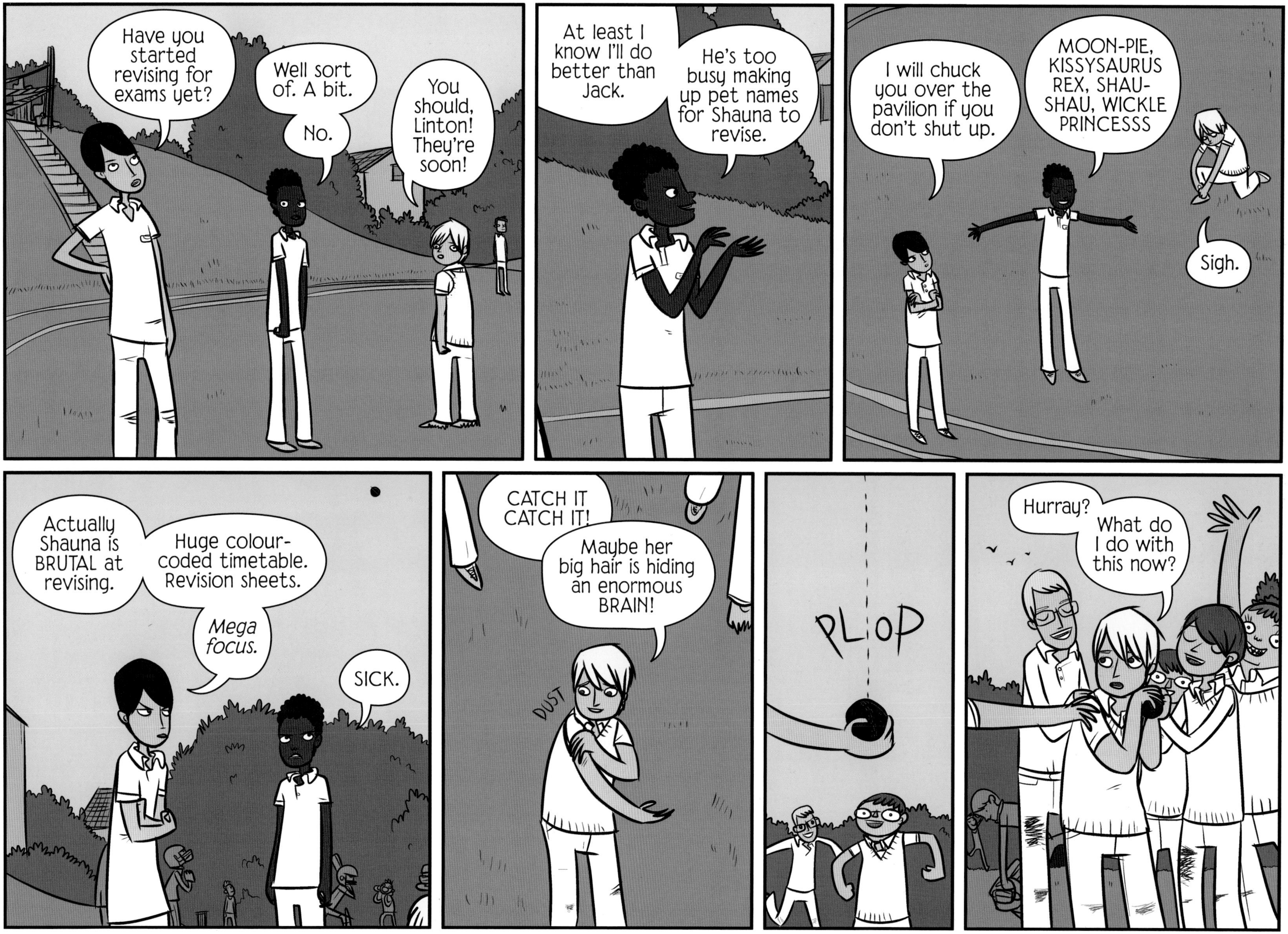
Have you started revising for exams yet?
Well sort of. A bit.
No.
You should, Linton! They're soon!
At least I know I'll do better than Jack.
He's too busy making up pet names for Shauna to revise.
I will chuck you over the pavilion if you don't shut up.
MOON-PIE, KISSYSAURUS REX, SHAU-SHAU, WICKLE PRINCESSS
Sigh.
Actually Shauna is BRUTAL at revising.
Huge colour-coded timetable. Revision sheets.
Mega focus.
SICK.
CATCH IT CATCH IT!
Maybe her big hair is hiding an enormous BRAIN!
DUST
PLOP
Hurray?
What do I do with this now?

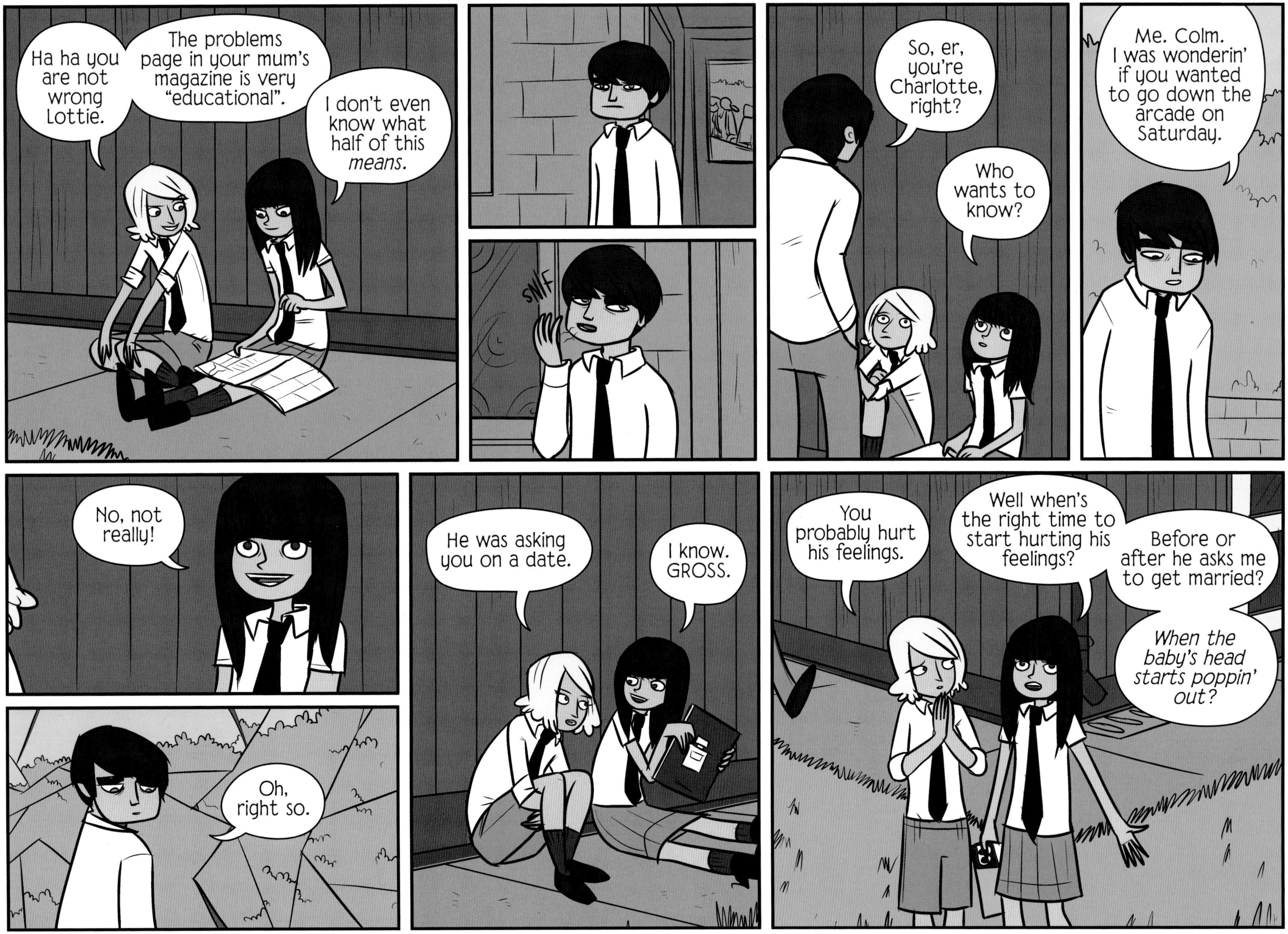
Ha ha you are not wrong Lottie.
The problems page in your mum's magazine is very "educational".
I don't even know what half of this *means.*
SNIF
So, er, you're Charlotte, right?
Who wants to know?
Me. Colm. I was wonderin' if you wanted to go down the arcade on Saturday.
No, not really!
Oh, right so.
He was asking you on a date.
I know. GROSS.
You probably hurt his feelings.
Well when's the right time to start hurting his feelings?
Before or after he asks me to get married?
When the baby's head starts poppin' out?

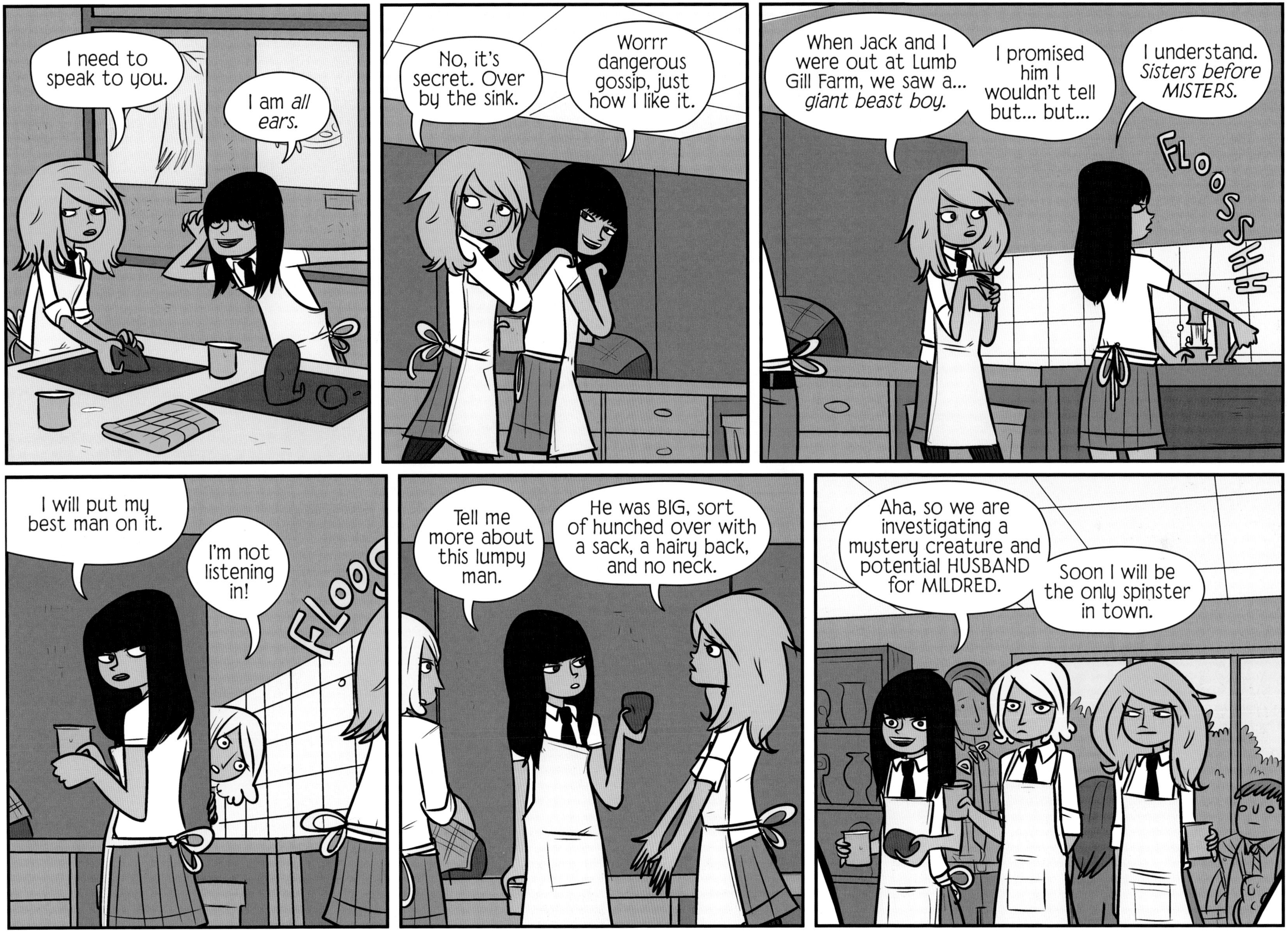
I need to speak to you.
I am *all ears.*
No, it's secret. Over by the sink.
Worrr dangerous gossip, just how I like it.
When Jack and I were out at Lumb Gill Farm, we saw a... *giant beast boy.*
I promised him I wouldn't tell but... but...
I understand. *Sisters before MISTERS.*
FLOOSSHH
I will put my best man on it.
I'm not listening in!
FLOOS
Tell me more about this lumpy man.
He was BIG, sort of hunched over with a sack, a hairy back, and no neck.
Aha, so we are investigating a mystery creature and potential HUSBAND for MILDRED.
Soon I will be the only spinster in town.

Bad Machinery, Volume Three

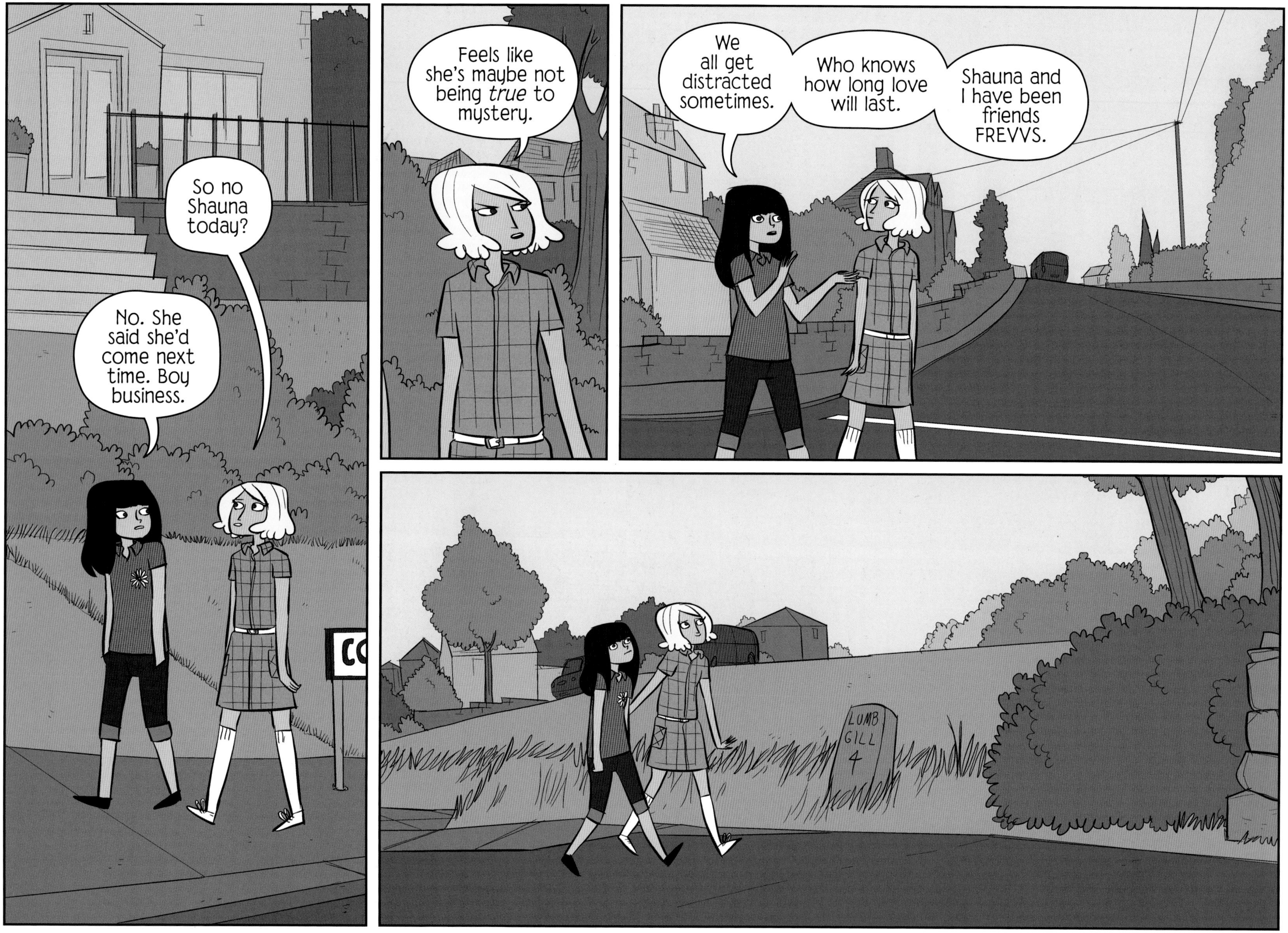
So no Shauna today?
No. She said she'd come next time. Boy business.
Feels like she's maybe not being *true* to mystery.
We all get distracted sometimes.
Who knows how long love will last.
Shauna and I have been friends FREVVS.
LUMB GILL 4

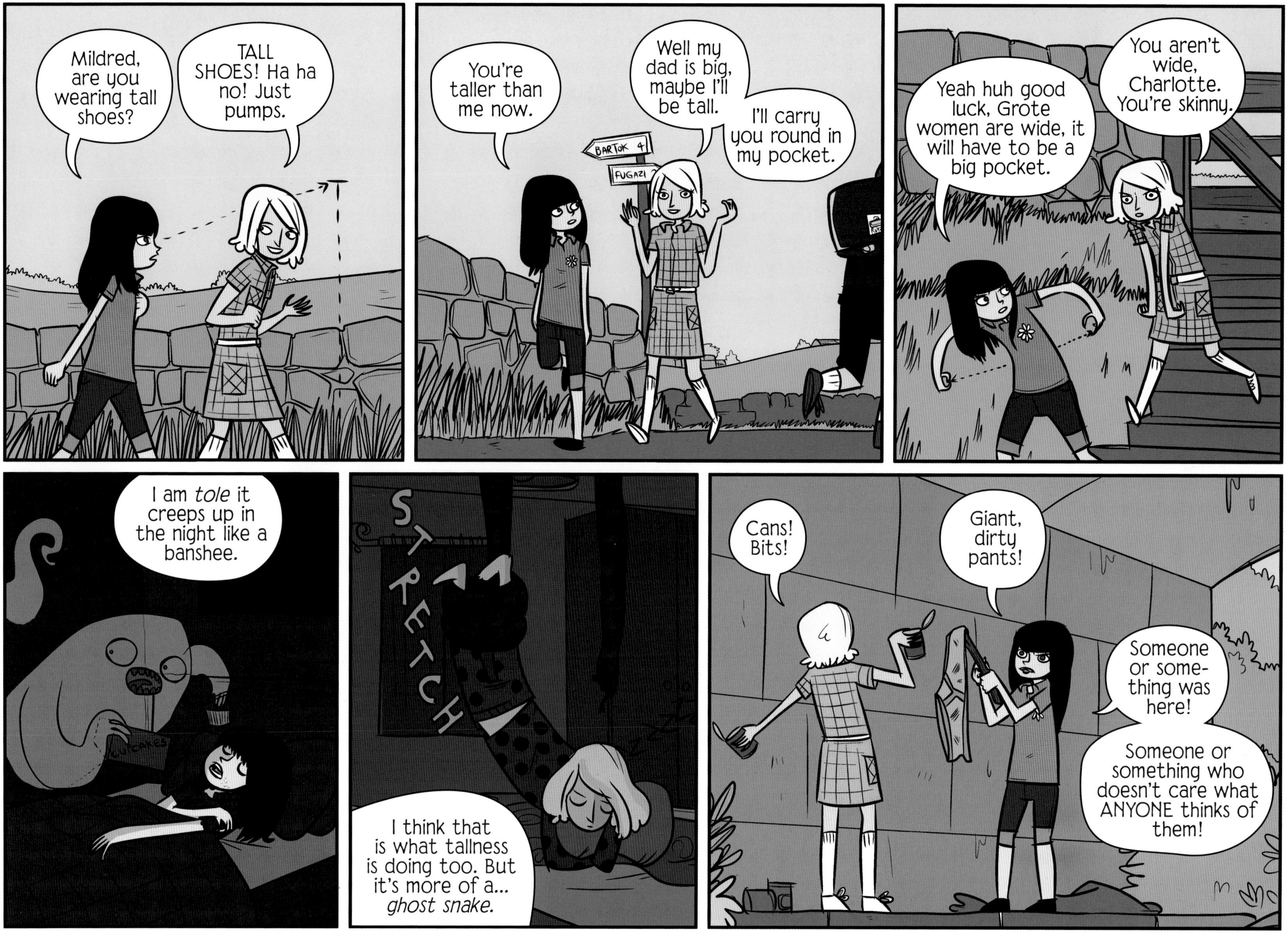
Mildred, are you wearing tall shoes?
TALL SHOES! Ha ha no! Just pumps.
You're taller than me now.
Well my dad is big, maybe I'll be tall.
I'll carry you round in my pocket.
BARTOK 4
FUGAZI
Yeah huh good luck, Grote women are wide, it will have to be a big pocket.
You aren't wide, Charlotte. You're skinny.
I am *tole* it creeps up in the night like a banshee.
CUPCAKES
STRETCH
I think that is what tallness is doing too. But it's more of a... *ghost snake*.
Cans! Bits!
Giant, dirty pants!
Someone or something was here!
Someone or something who doesn't care what ANYONE thinks of them!

Lottie put down the pants! HIDE! HIDE!

Oh my god.

Oh my god.

OH MY GOD

Oh my *days* Mildred I have never seen such a beast.

Really? COR.

Look at his hairy back! The hairiest!

I'm noting it down.

Perhaps this is how he catches his lunch... or just keeps clean.

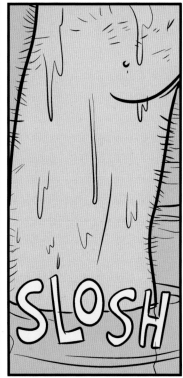

SLOSH

Cover my eyes, I've frozen in fear!

He is not a trunks wearer, this is *clear*.

Whoa. Are those features *normal*?

WE MAY NEVER KNOW.

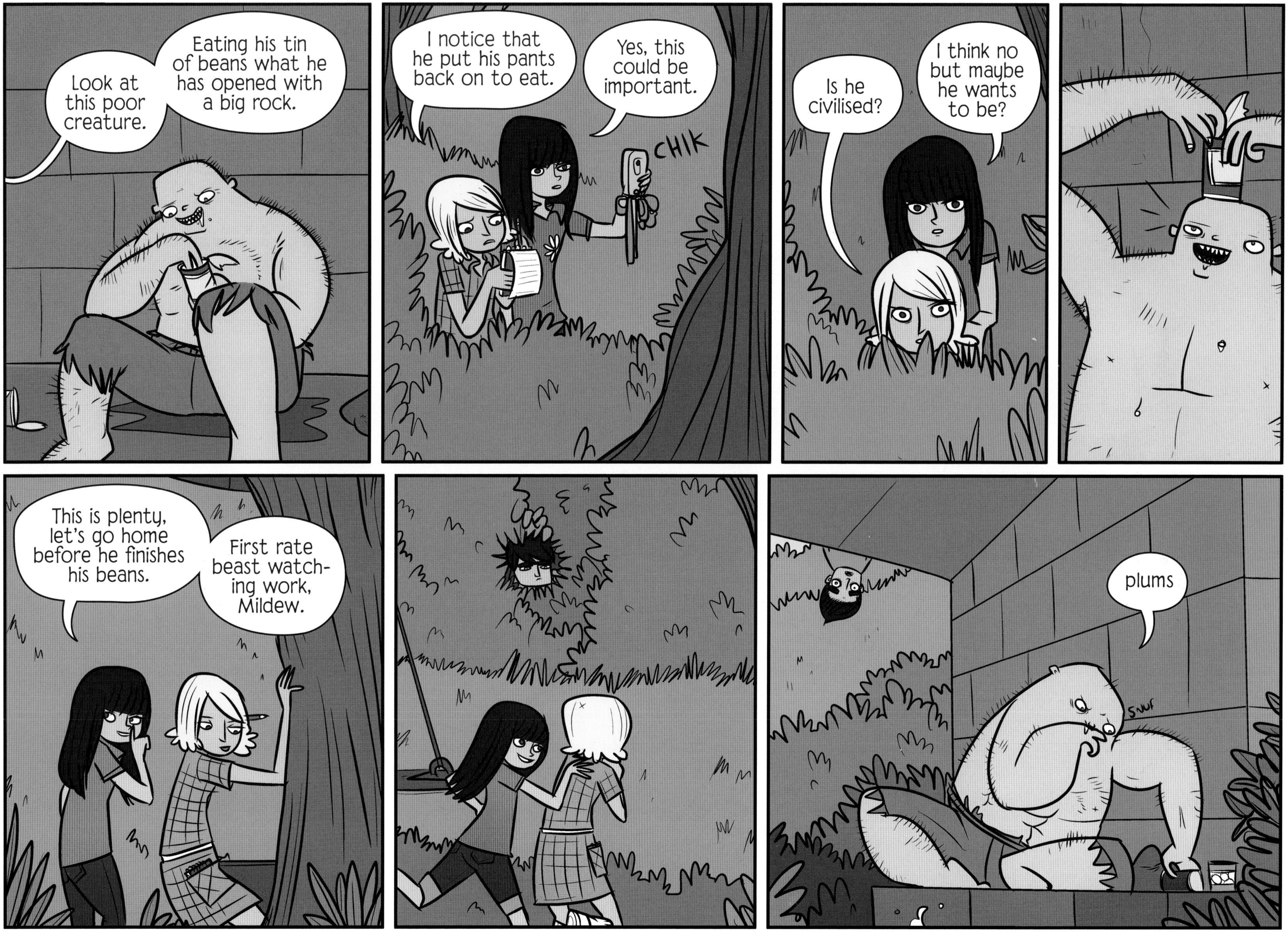
Look at this poor creature.
Eating his tin of beans what he has opened with a big rock.
I notice that he put his pants back on to eat.
Yes, this could be important.
CHIK
Is he civilised?
I think no but maybe he wants to be?
This is plenty, let's go home before he finishes his beans.
First rate beast watching work, Mildew.
plums
snuf

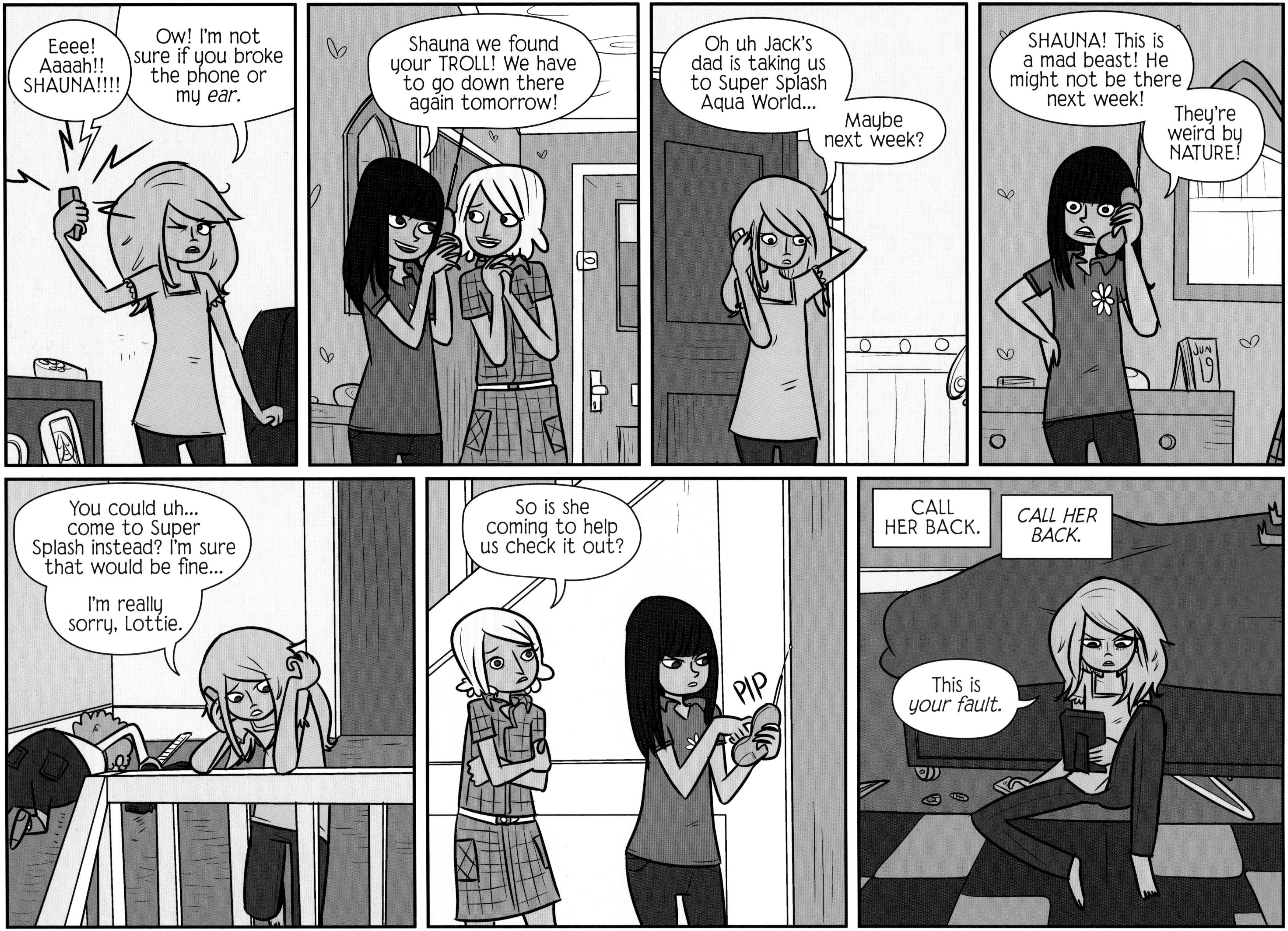
Eeee! Aaaah!! SHAUNA!!!!
Ow! I'm not sure if you broke the phone or my *ear.*
Shauna we found your TROLL! We have to go down there again tomorrow!
Oh uh Jack's dad is taking us to Super Splash Aqua World...
Maybe next week?
SHAUNA! This is a mad beast! He might not be there next week!
They're weird by NATURE!
JUN 19
You could uh... come to Super Splash instead? I'm sure that would be fine...
I'm really sorry, Lottie.
So is she coming to help us check it out?
PIP
CALL HER BACK.
CALL HER BACK.
This is *your fault.*

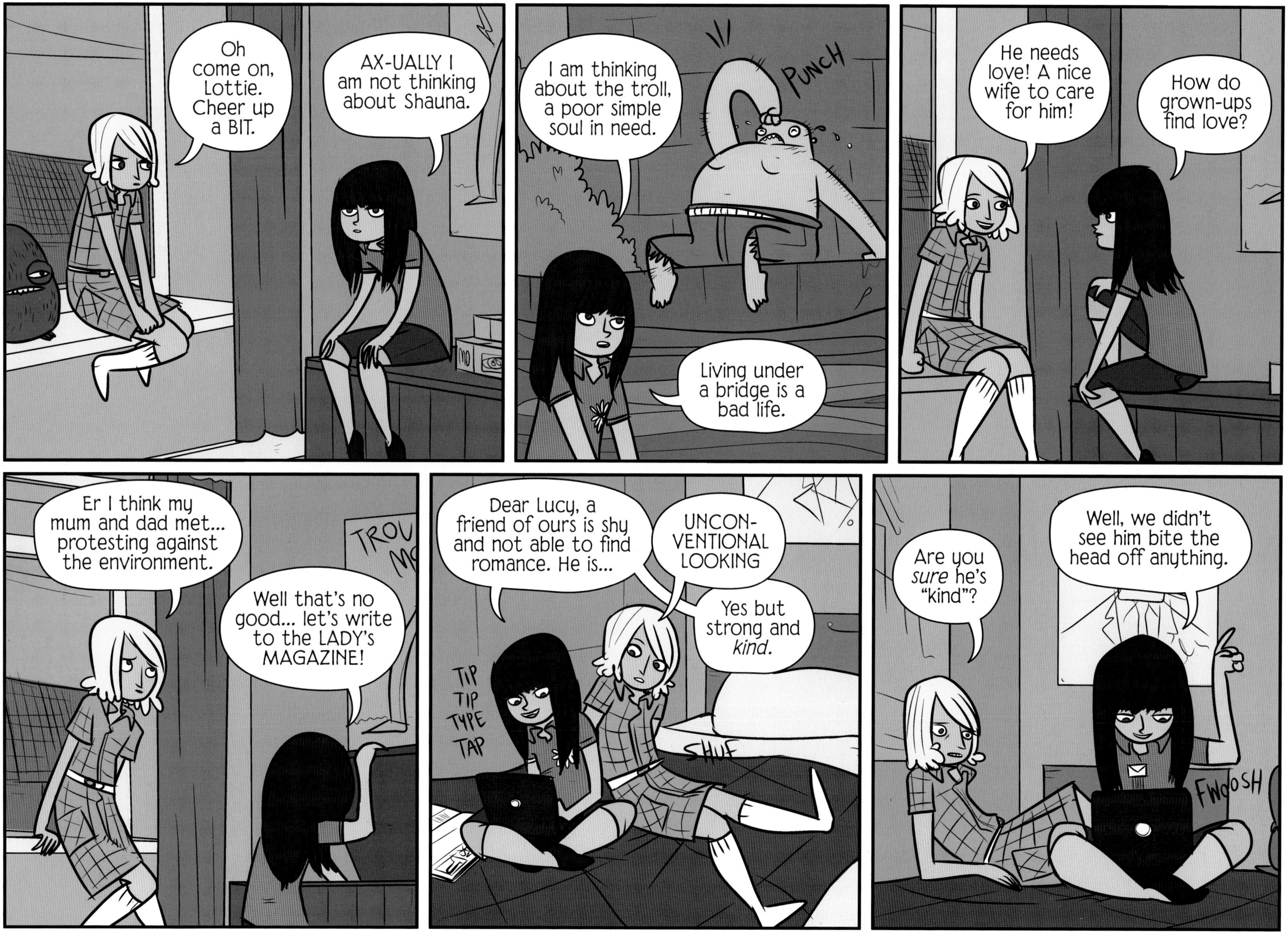
Oh come on, Lottie. Cheer up a BIT.
AX-UALLY I am not thinking about Shauna.
I am thinking about the troll, a poor simple soul in need.
PUNCH
Living under a bridge is a bad life.
He needs love! A nice wife to care for him!
How do grown-ups find love?
Er I think my mum and dad met... protesting against the environment.
Well that's no good... let's write to the LADY's MAGAZINE!
Dear Lucy, a friend of ours is shy and not able to find romance. He is...
UNCON-VENTIONAL LOOKING
Yes but strong and *kind*.
TIP TIP TYPE TAP
SHUF
Are you *sure* he's "kind"?
Well, we didn't see him bite the head off anything.
FWOOSH

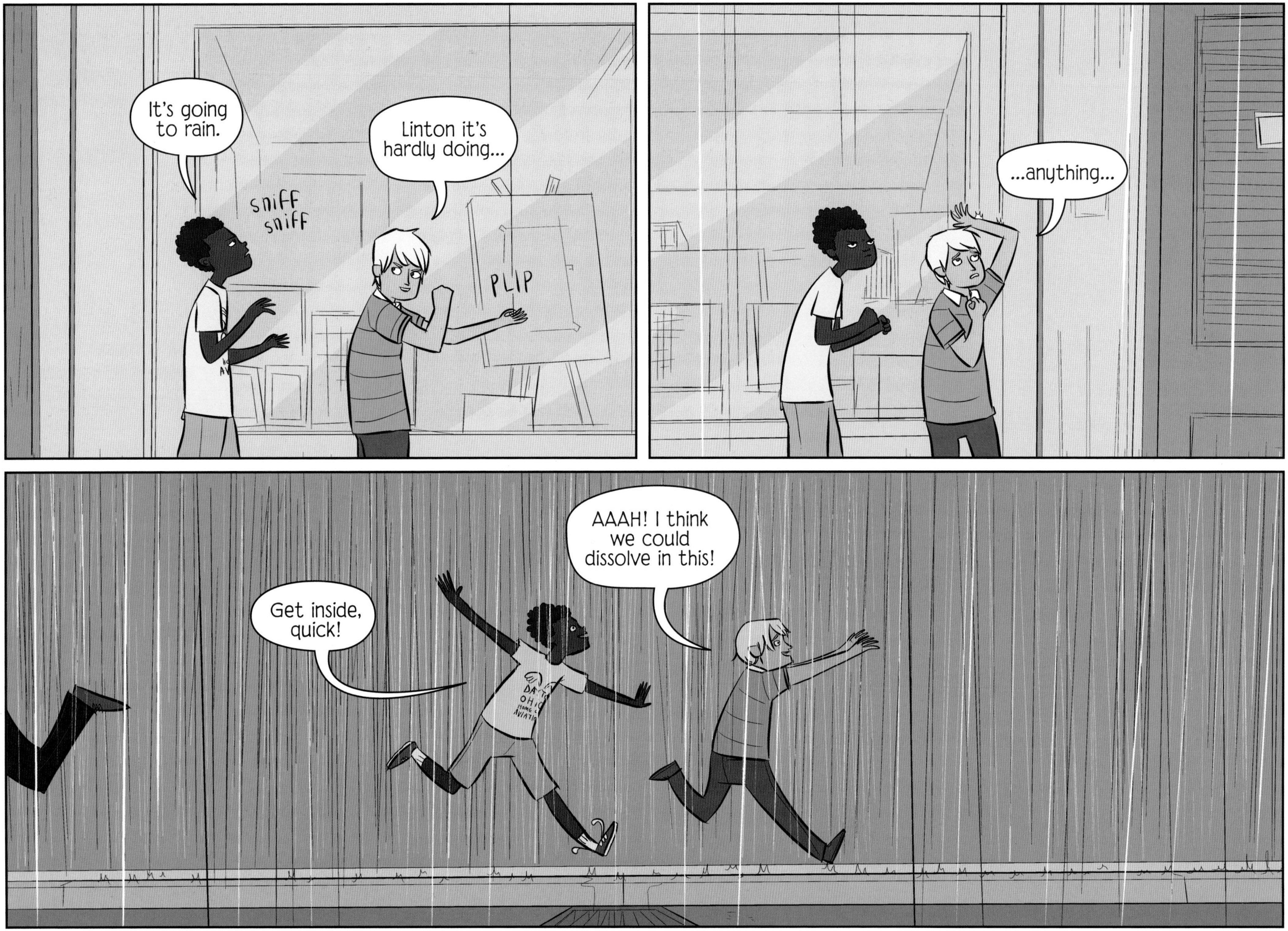
It's going to rain.
sniff sniff
Linton it's hardly doing...
PLIP
...anything...
AAAH! I think we could dissolve in this!
Get inside, quick!

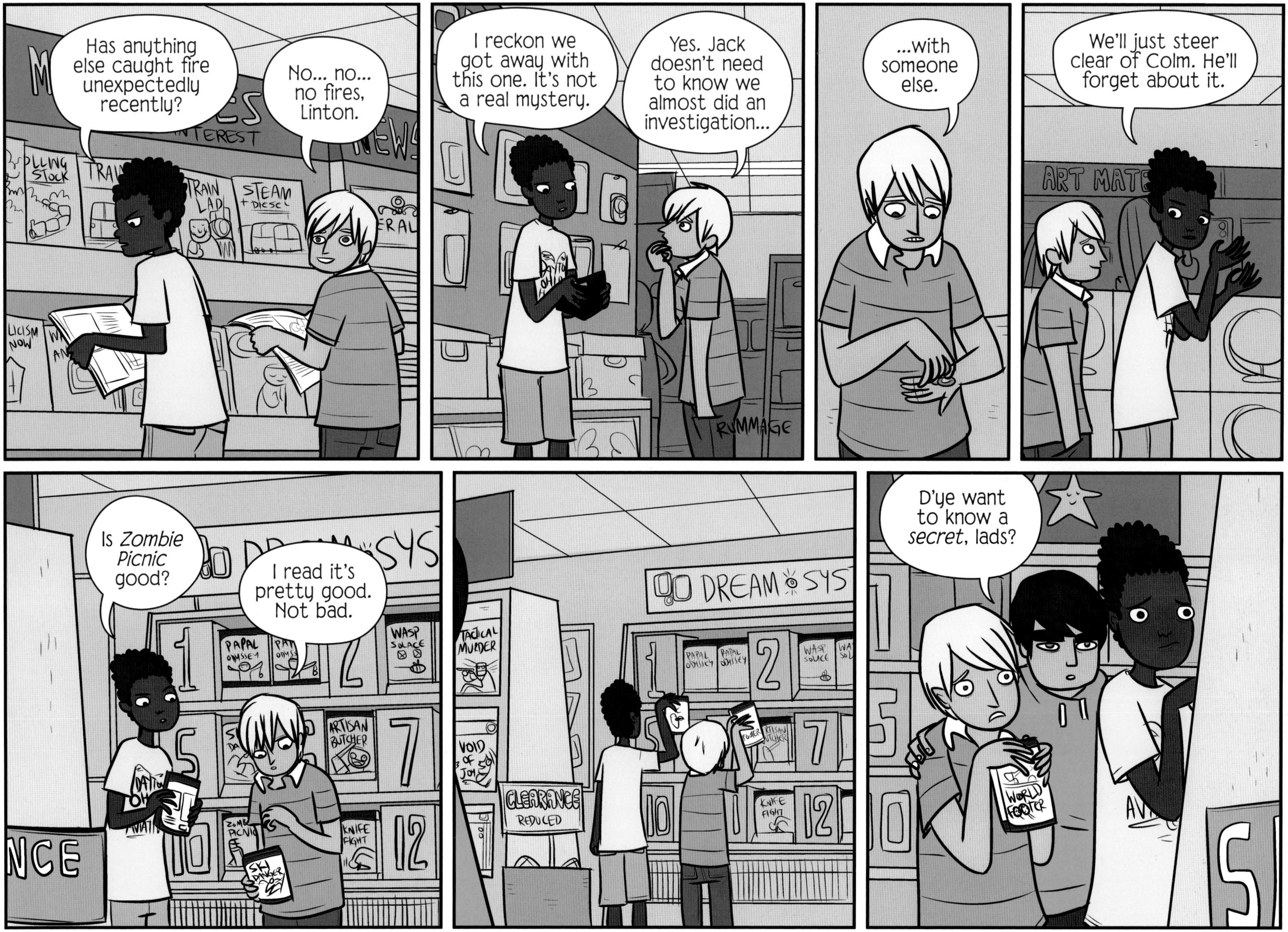
Has anything else caught fire unexpectedly recently?
No... no... no fires, Linton.
I reckon we got away with this one. It's not a real mystery.
Yes. Jack doesn't need to know we almost did an investigation...
RUMMAGE
...with someone else.
We'll just steer clear of Colm. He'll forget about it.
ART MATE
Is *Zombie Picnic* good?
I read it's pretty good. Not bad.
DREAM SYS
WASP SOLACE
ARTISAN BUTCHER
KNIFE FIGHT
CLEARANCE
REDUCED
D'ye want to know a *secret*, lads?

Bad Machinery, Volume Three

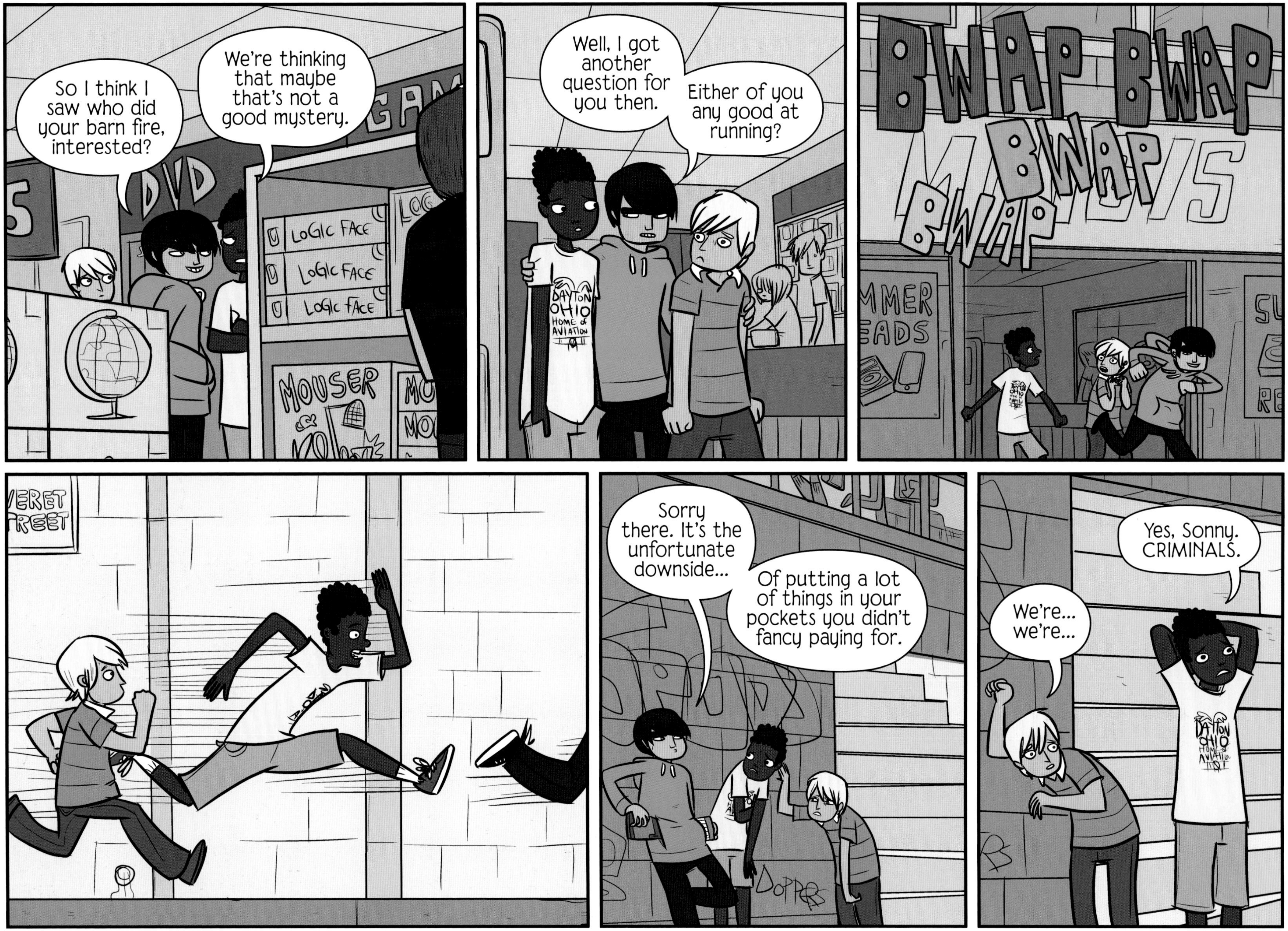
So I think I saw who did your barn fire, interested?
We're thinking that maybe that's not a good mystery.
Well, I got another question for you then.
Either of you any good at running?
BWAP BWAP
BWAP
BWAP
Sorry there. It's the unfortunate downside...
Of putting a lot of things in your pockets you didn't fancy paying for.
We're... we're...
Yes, Sonny. CRIMINALS.

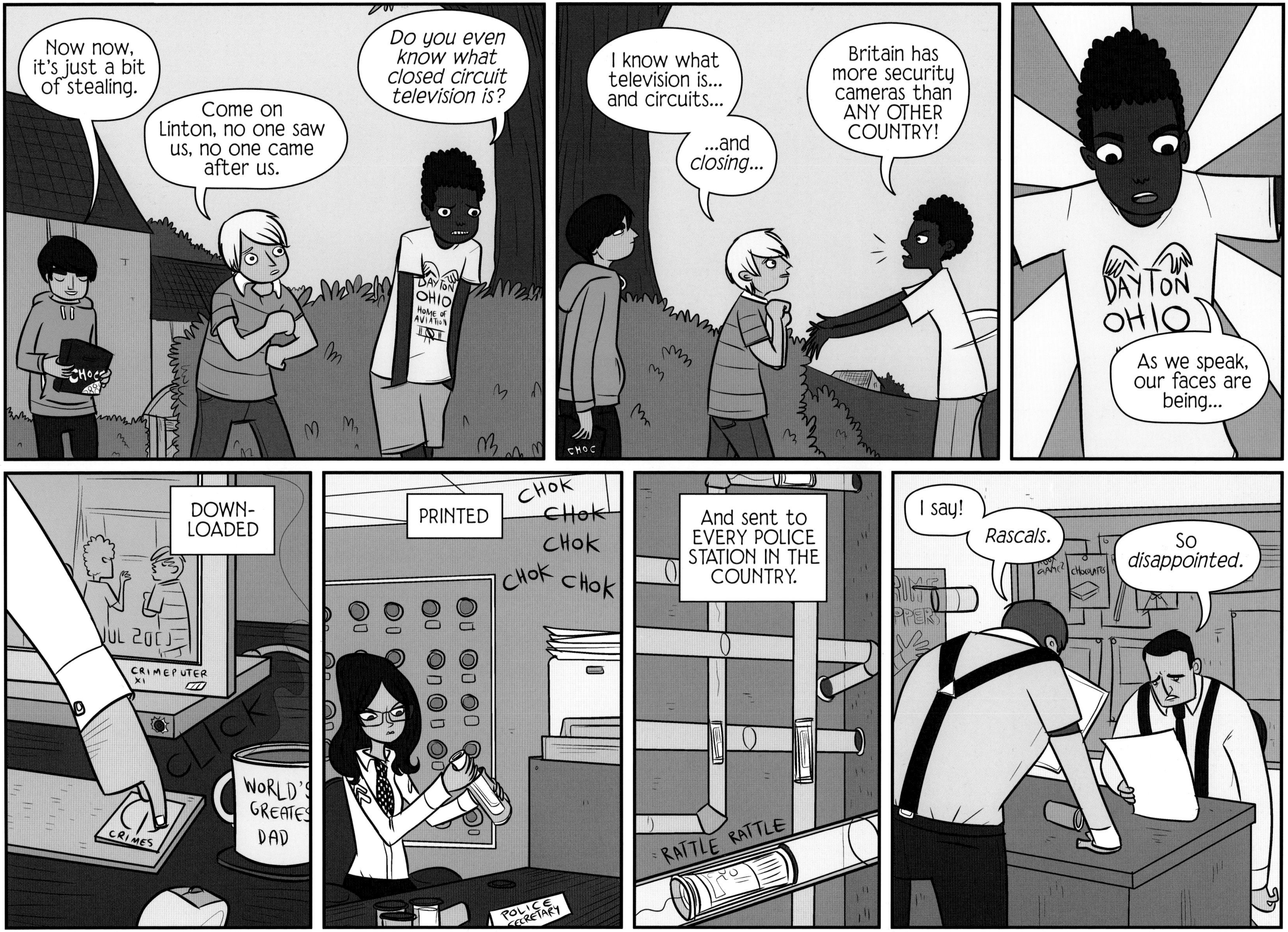

Now now, it's just a bit of stealing.
Come on Linton, no one saw us, no one came after us.
Do you even know what closed circuit television is?
DAYTON OHIO HOME OF AVIATION
I know what television is... and circuits...
...and *closing...*
Britain has more security cameras than ANY OTHER COUNTRY!
DAYTON OHIO
As we speak, our faces are being...
DOWN-LOADED
CRIMEPUTER XI
CLICK
CRIMES
WORLD'S GREATES DAD
PRINTED
CHOK CHOK CHOK CHOK CHOK
POLICE SECRETARY
And sent to EVERY POLICE STATION IN THE COUNTRY.
RATTLE RATTLE
I say!
Rascals.
So *disappointed.*

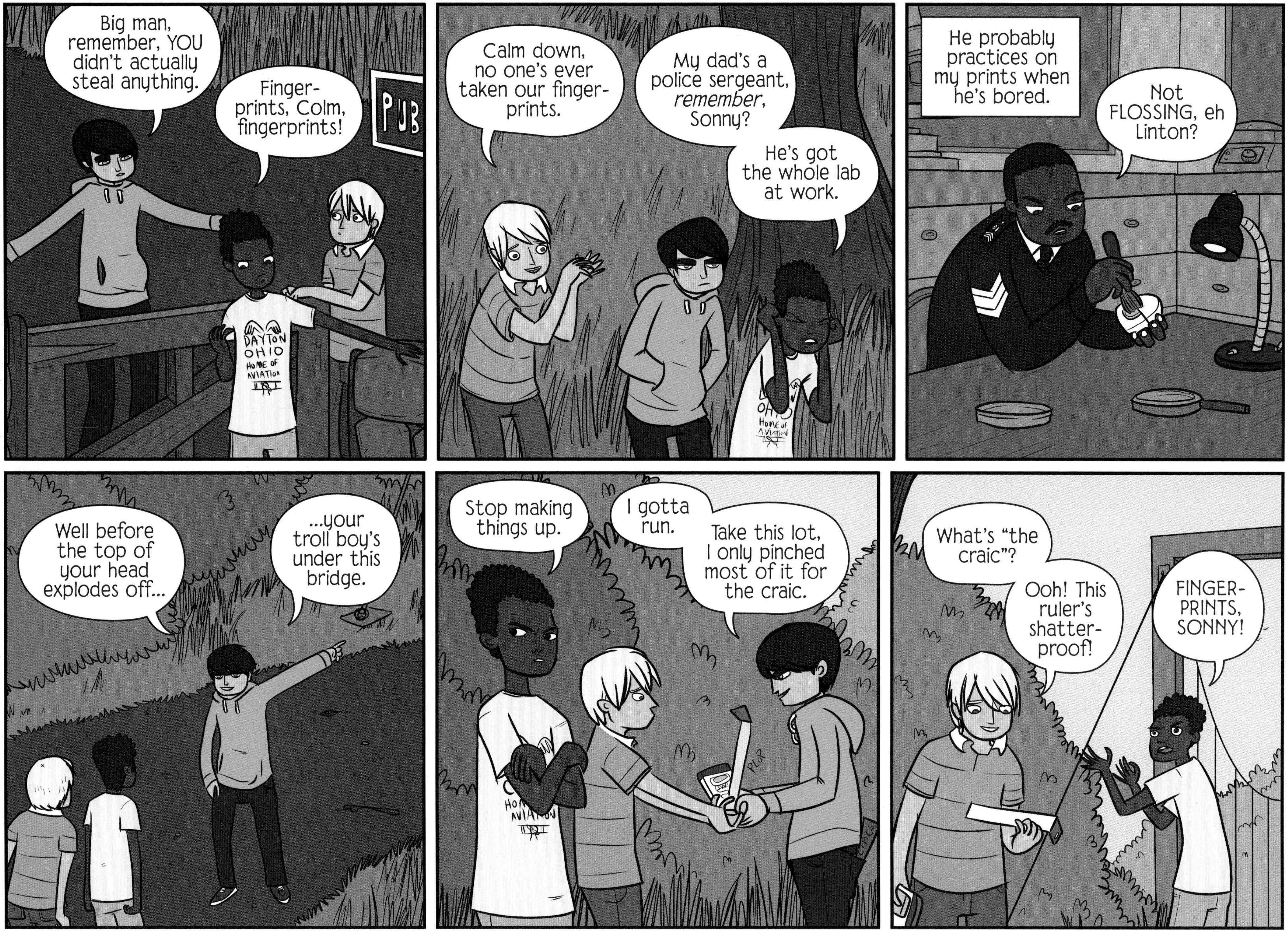
Big man, remember, YOU didn't actually steal anything.
Finger-prints, Colm, fingerprints!
PUB
DAYTON OHIO HOME OF AVIATION
Calm down, no one's ever taken our finger-prints.
My dad's a police sergeant, *remember*, Sonny?
He's got the whole lab at work.
He probably practices on my prints when he's bored.
Not FLOSSING, eh Linton?
Well before the top of your head explodes off...
...your troll boy's under this bridge.
Stop making things up.
I gotta run.
Take this lot, I only pinched most of it for the craic.
PLOP
What's "the craic"?
Ooh! This ruler's shatter-proof!
FINGER-PRINTS, SONNY!

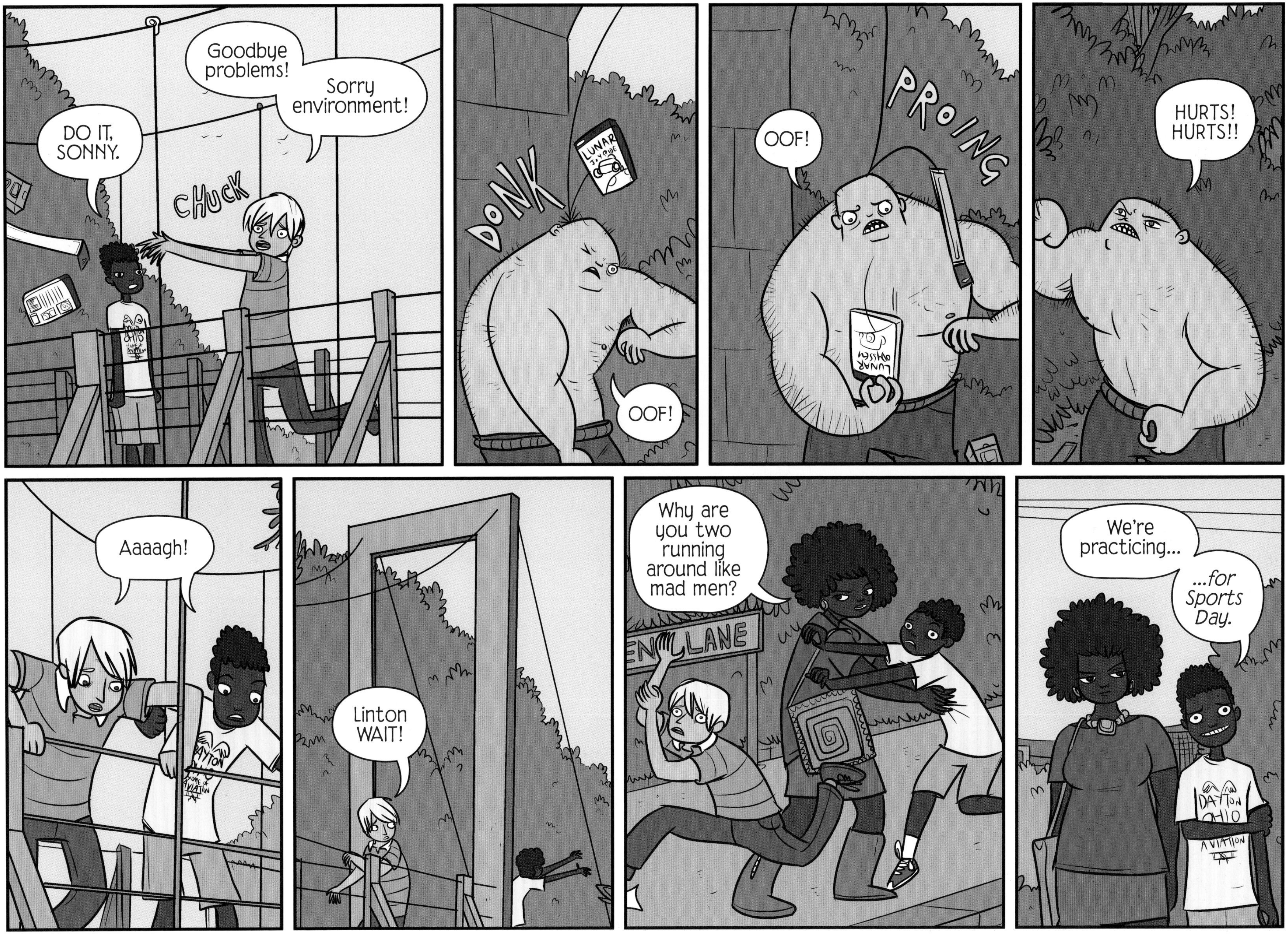
Goodbye problems!
Sorry environment!
DO IT, SONNY.
CHUCK
DONK
LUNAR
OOF!
OOF!
PROING
HURTS! HURTS!!
Aaaagh!
Linton WAIT!
Why are you two running around like mad men?
LANE
We're practicing...
...for Sports Day.

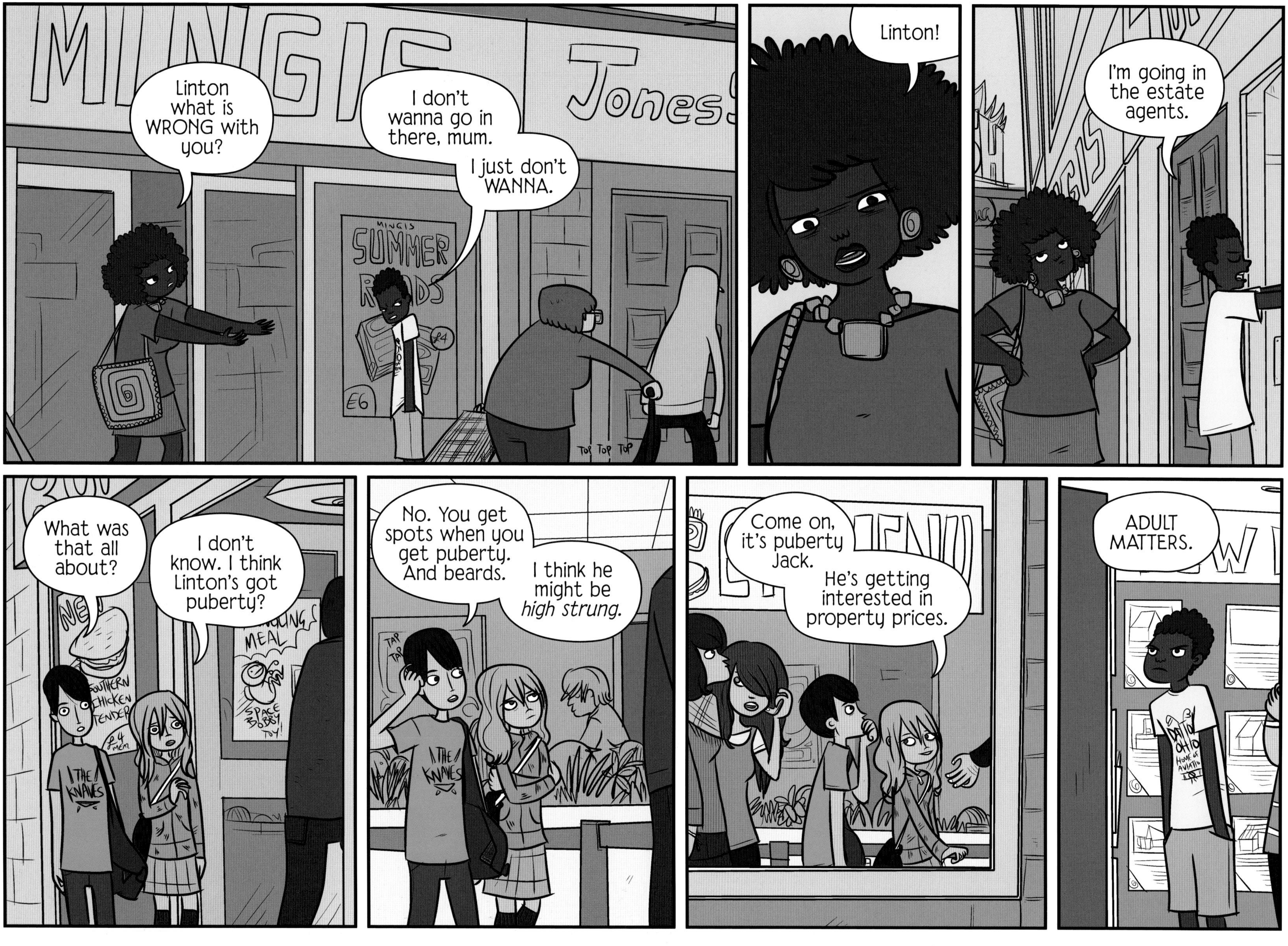
MINGIS
Jones
Linton what is WRONG with you?
I don't wanna go in there, mum.
I just don't WANNA.
MINGIS SUMMER ROADS
£4
£6
TOP TOP TOP
Linton!
I'm going in the estate agents.
What was that all about?
I don't know. I think Linton's got puberty?
SOUTHERN CHICKEN TENDER
MEAL
SPACE BOBBY TOY!
THE KNAVES
No. You get spots when you get puberty. And beards.
I think he might be *high strung*.
TAP TAP
THE KNAVES
Come on, it's puberty Jack.
He's getting interested in property prices.
ADULT MATTERS.
DAYTON OHIO HOME OF AVIATION

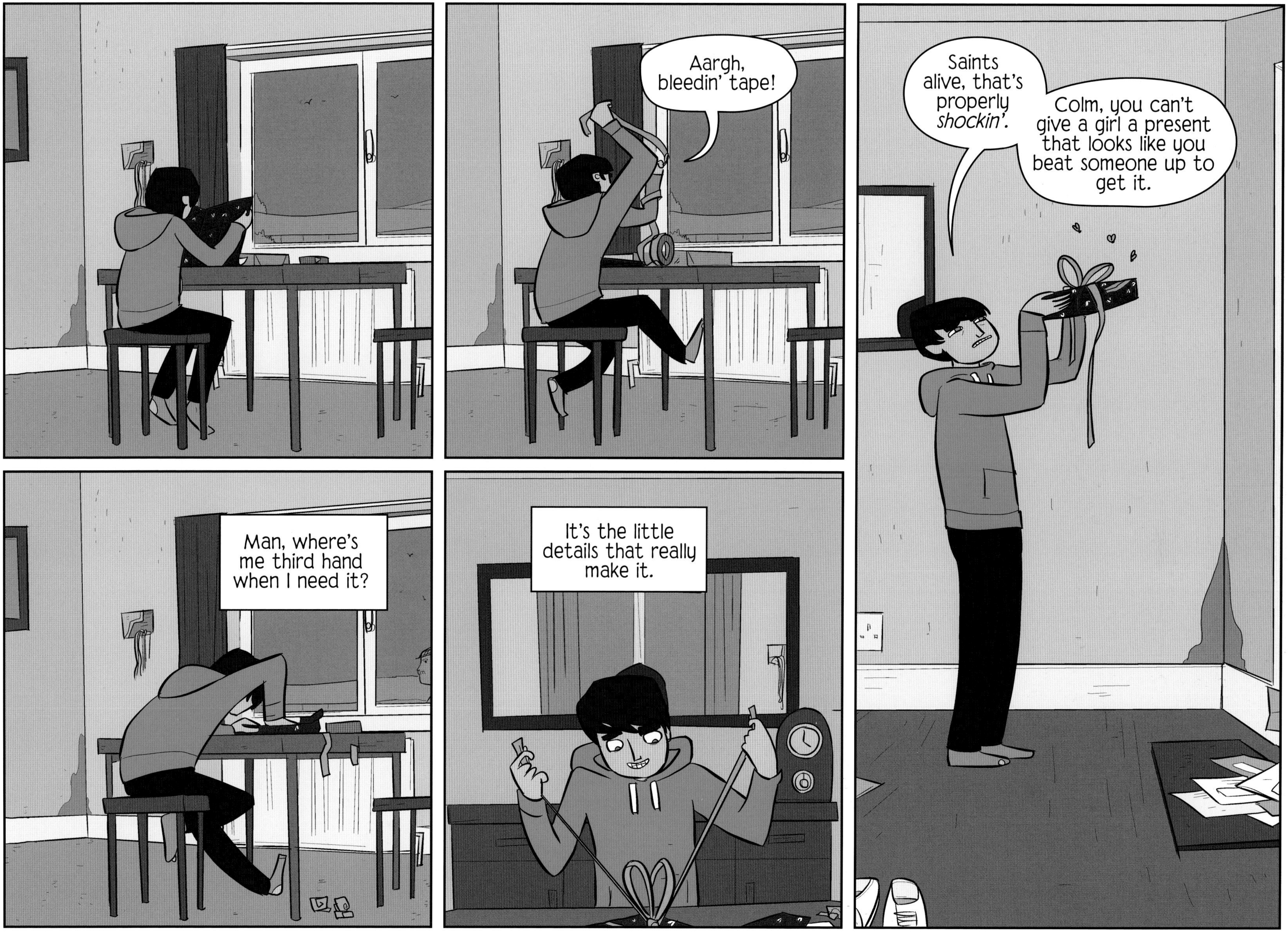
Aargh, bleedin' tape!
Saints alive, that's properly *shockin'*.
Colm, you can't give a girl a present that looks like you beat someone up to get it.
Man, where's me third hand when I need it?
It's the little details that really make it.

Bad Machinery, Volume Three

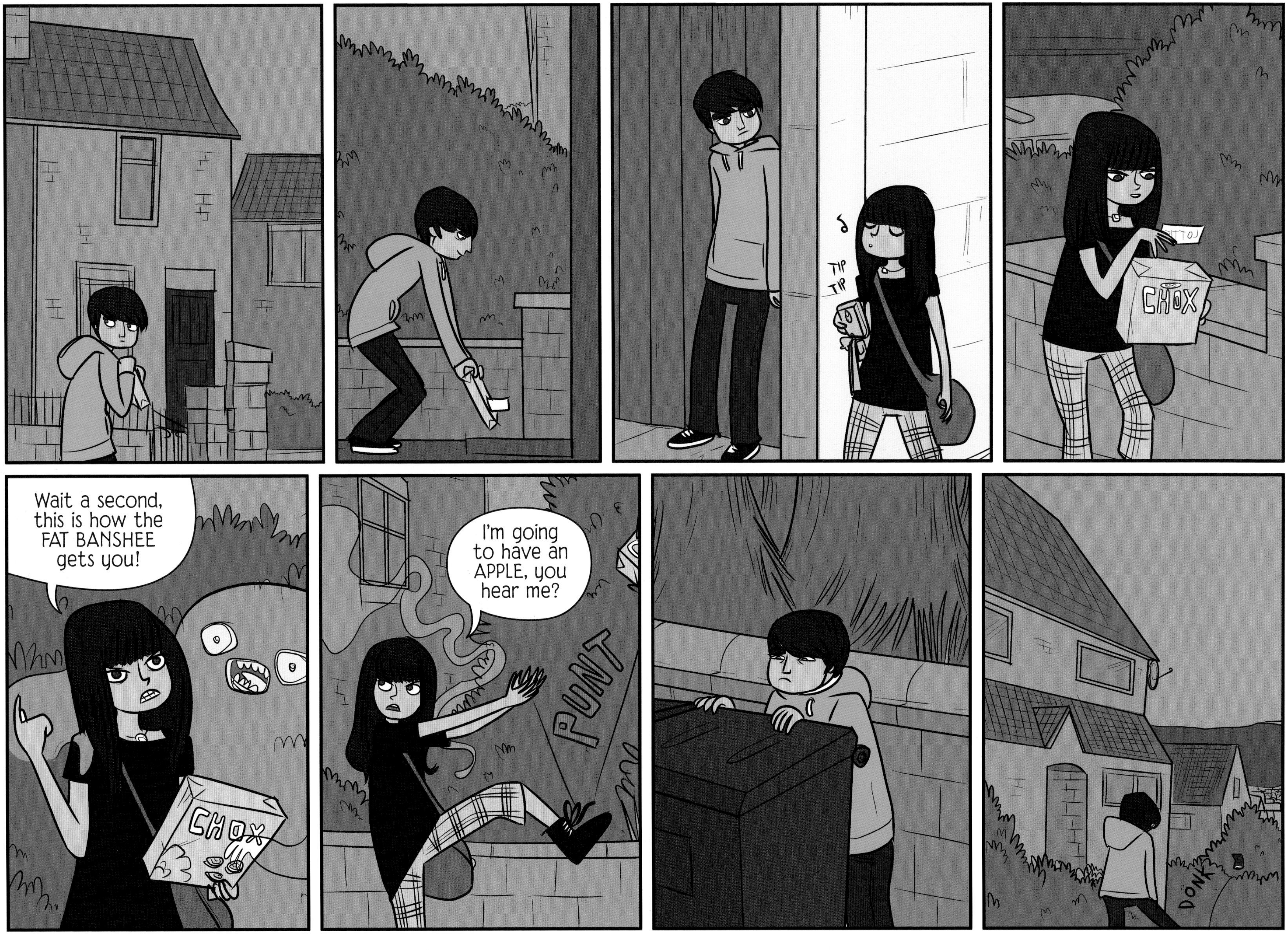
TIP
TIP
CHOX
Wait a second, this is how the FAT BANSHEE gets you!
CHOX
I'm going to have an APPLE, you hear me?
PUNT
DÖNK

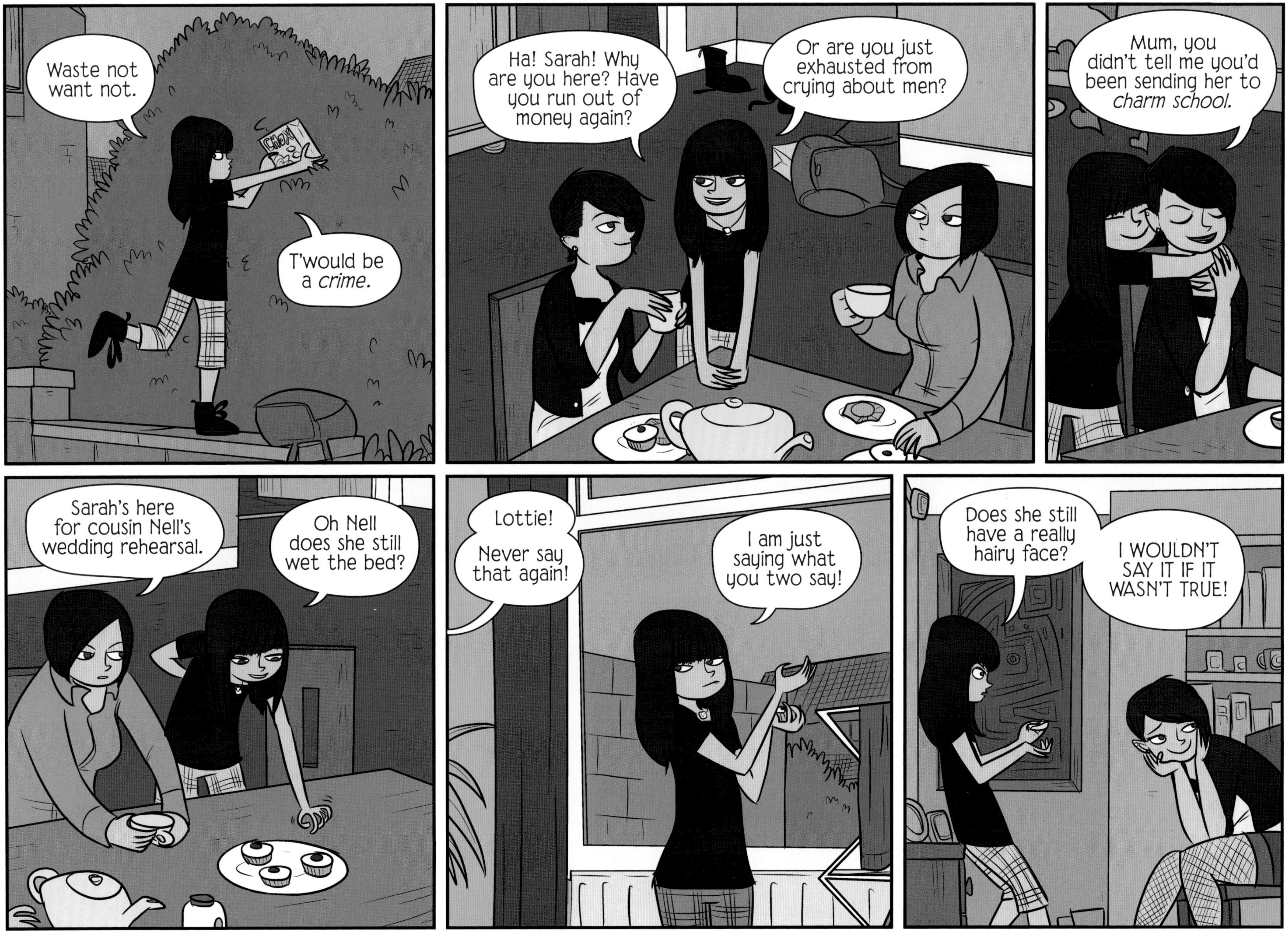
Waste not want not.
T'would be a *crime*.
Ha! Sarah! Why are you here? Have you run out of money again?
Or are you just exhausted from crying about men?
Mum, you didn't tell me you'd been sending her to *charm school*.
Sarah's here for cousin Nell's wedding rehearsal.
Oh Nell does she still wet the bed?
Lottie!
Never say that again!
I am just saying what you two say!
Does she still have a really hairy face?
I WOULDN'T SAY IT IF IT WASN'T TRUE!

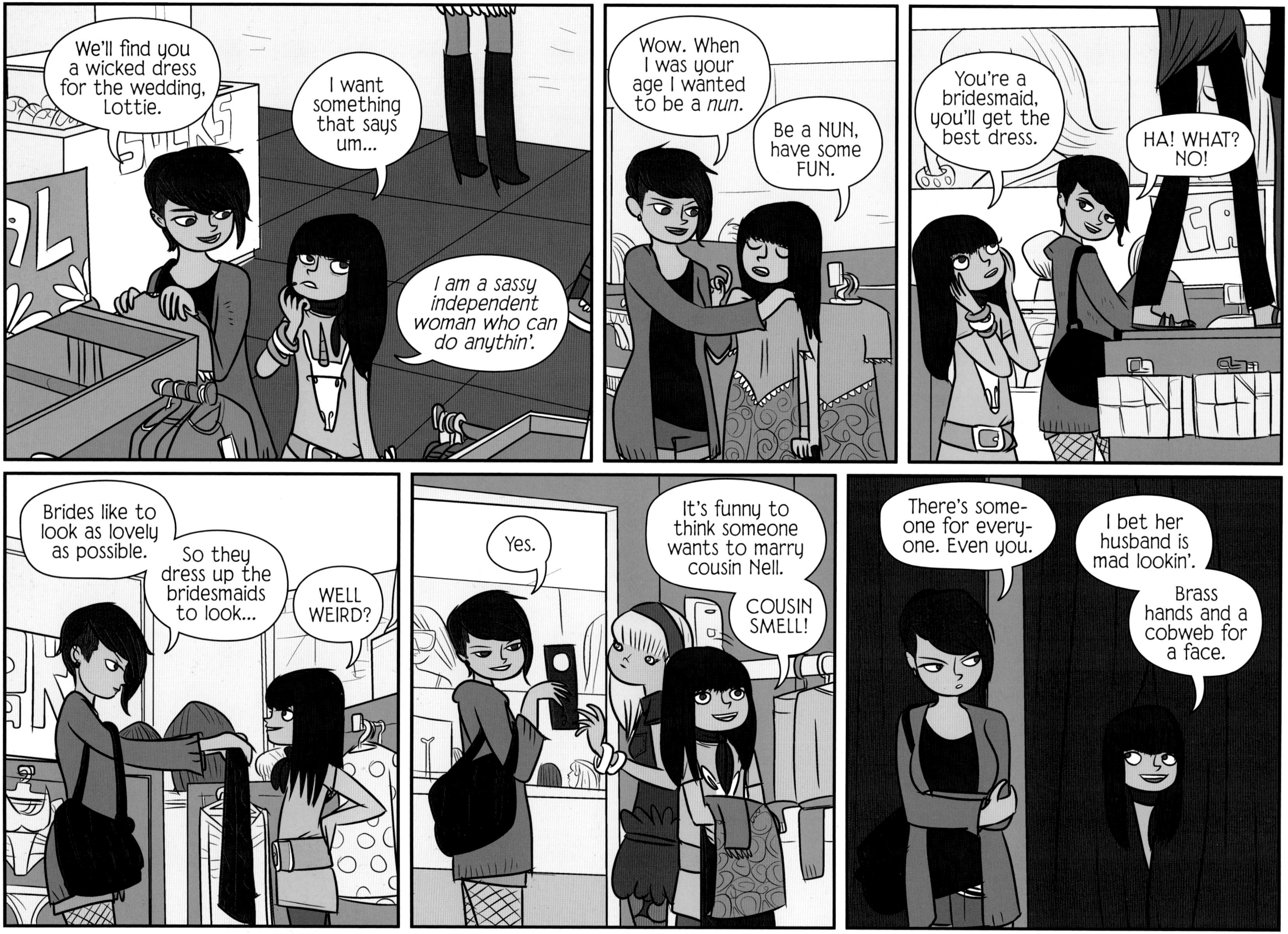
We'll find you a wicked dress for the wedding, Lottie.
I want something that says um...
I am a sassy independent woman who can do anythin'.
Wow. When I was your age I wanted to be a *nun*.
Be a NUN, have some FUN.
You're a bridesmaid, you'll get the best dress.
HA! WHAT? NO!
Brides like to look as lovely as possible.
So they dress up the bridesmaids to look...
WELL WEIRD?
Yes.
It's funny to think someone wants to marry cousin Nell.
COUSIN SMELL!
There's some-one for every-one. Even you.
I bet her husband is mad lookin'.
Brass hands and a cobweb for a face.

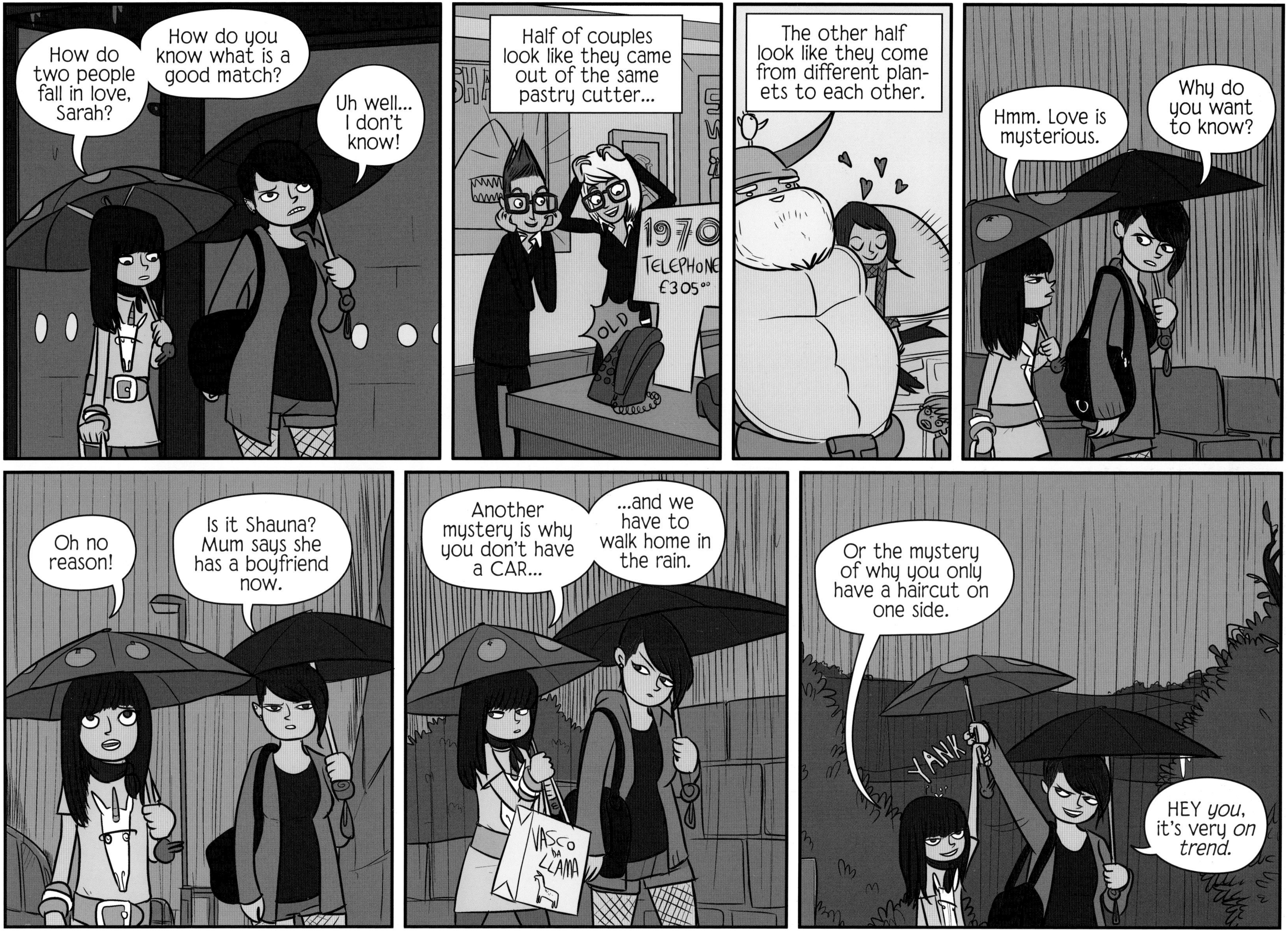
How do two people fall in love, Sarah?
How do you know what is a good match?
Uh well... I don't know!
Half of couples look like they came out of the same pastry cutter...
1970 TELEPHONE £305.00
OLD
The other half look like they come from different planets to each other.
Hmm. Love is mysterious.
Why do you want to know?
Oh no reason!
Is it Shauna? Mum says she has a boyfriend now.
Another mystery is why you don't have a CAR...
...and we have to walk home in the rain.
VASCO DA LLAMA
Or the mystery of why you only have a haircut on one side.
YANK
HEY *you*, it's very *on trend.*

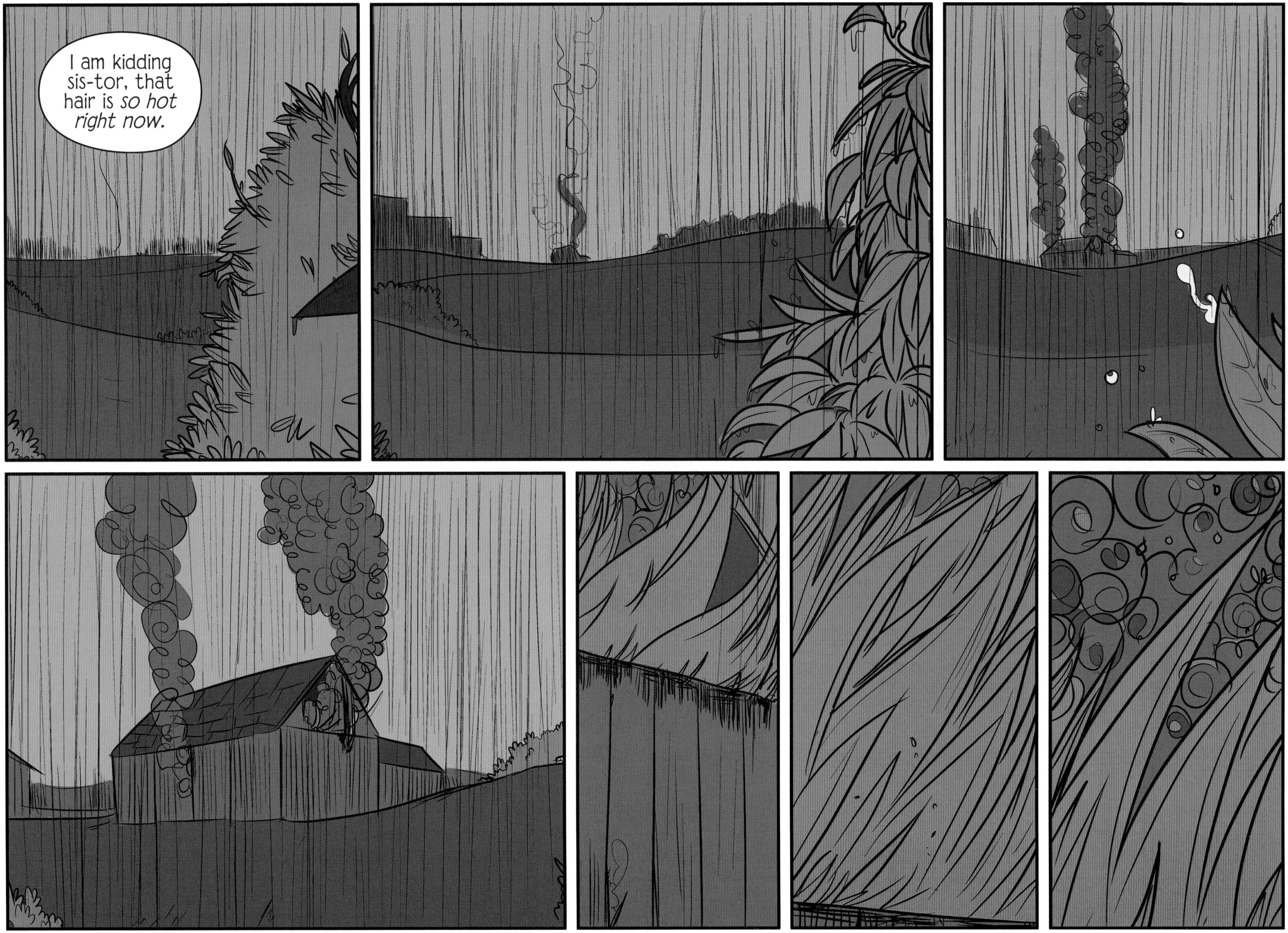
I am kidding sis-tor, that hair is *so hot right now.*

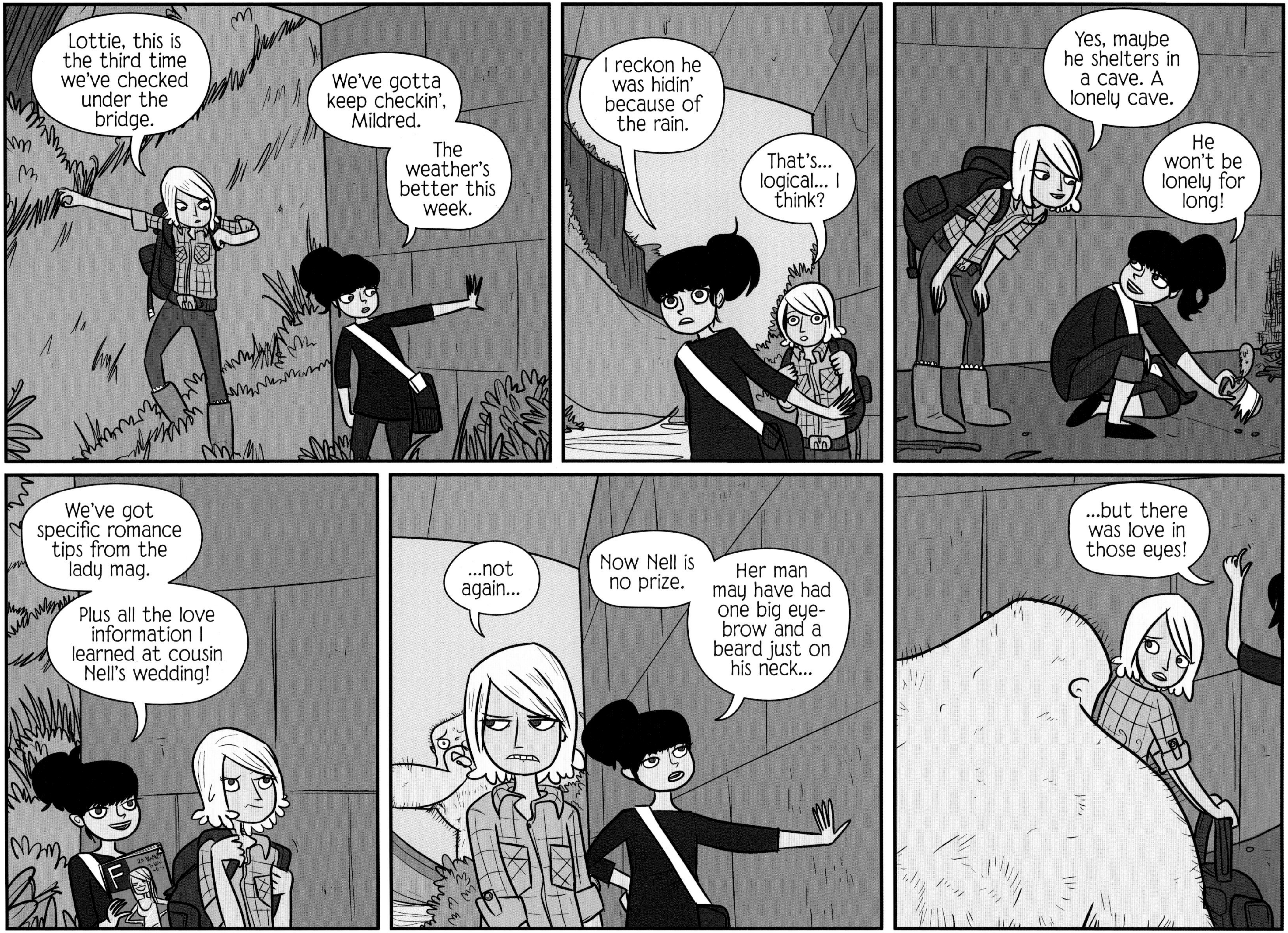
Lottie, this is the third time we've checked under the bridge.
We've gotta keep checkin', Mildred.
The weather's better this week.
I reckon he was hidin' because of the rain.
That's... logical... I think?
Yes, maybe he shelters in a cave. A lonely cave.
He won't be lonely for long!
We've got specific romance tips from the lady mag.
Plus all the love information I learned at cousin Nell's wedding!
...not again...
Now Nell is no prize.
Her man may have had one big eye-brow and a beard just on his neck...
...but there was love in those eyes!

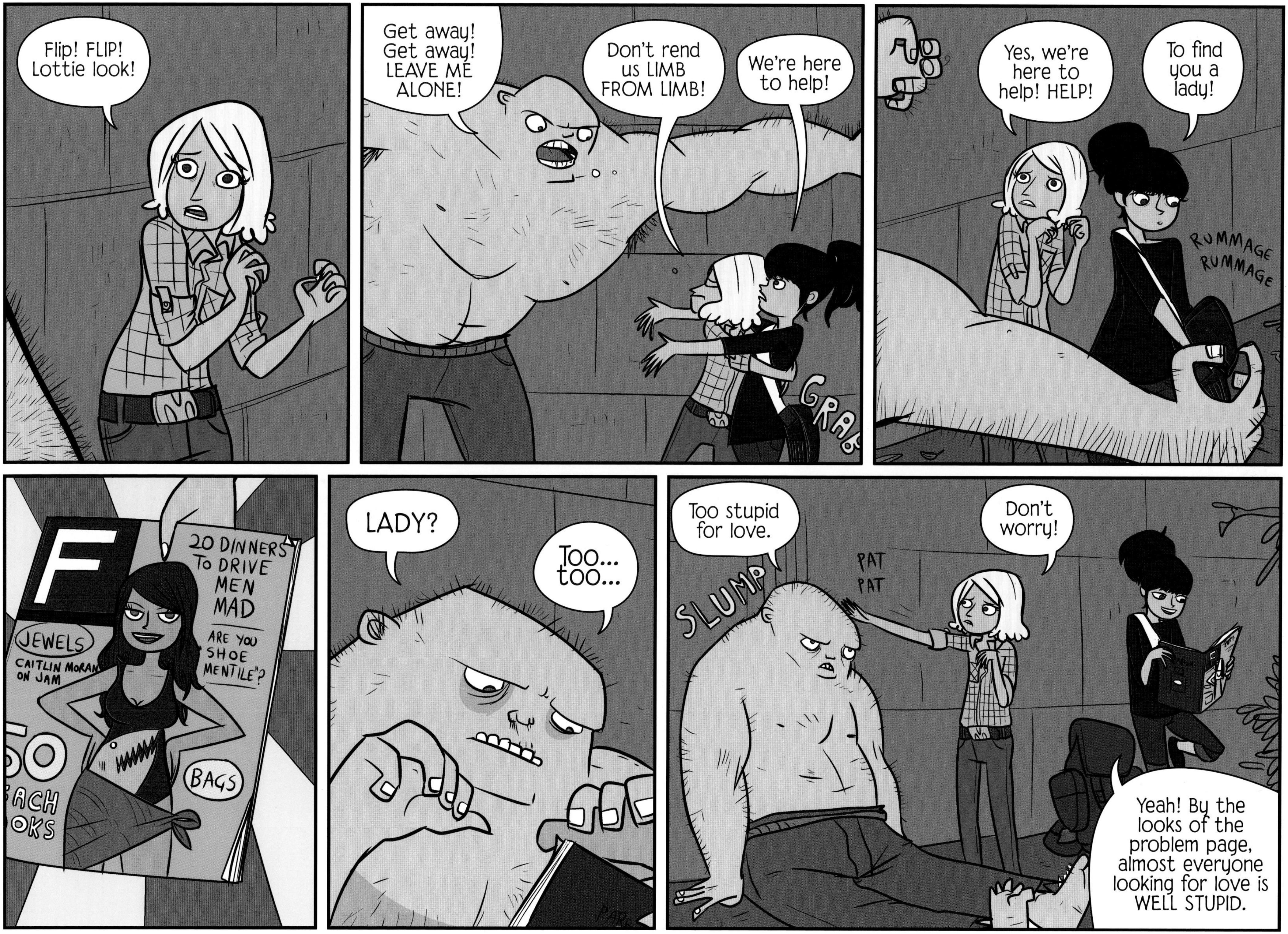
Flip! FLIP! Lottie look!
Get away! Get away! LEAVE ME ALONE!
Don't rend us LIMB FROM LIMB!
We're here to help!
GRAB
Yes, we're here to help! HELP!
To find you a lady!
RUMMAGE RUMMAGE
F
20 DINNERS TO DRIVE MEN MAD
JEWELS
CAITLIN MORAN ON JAM
ARE YOU SHOE MENTILE"?
BAGS
LADY?
Too... too...
Too stupid for love.
SLUMP
PAT PAT
Don't worry!
Yeah! By the looks of the problem page, almost everyone looking for love is WELL STUPID.

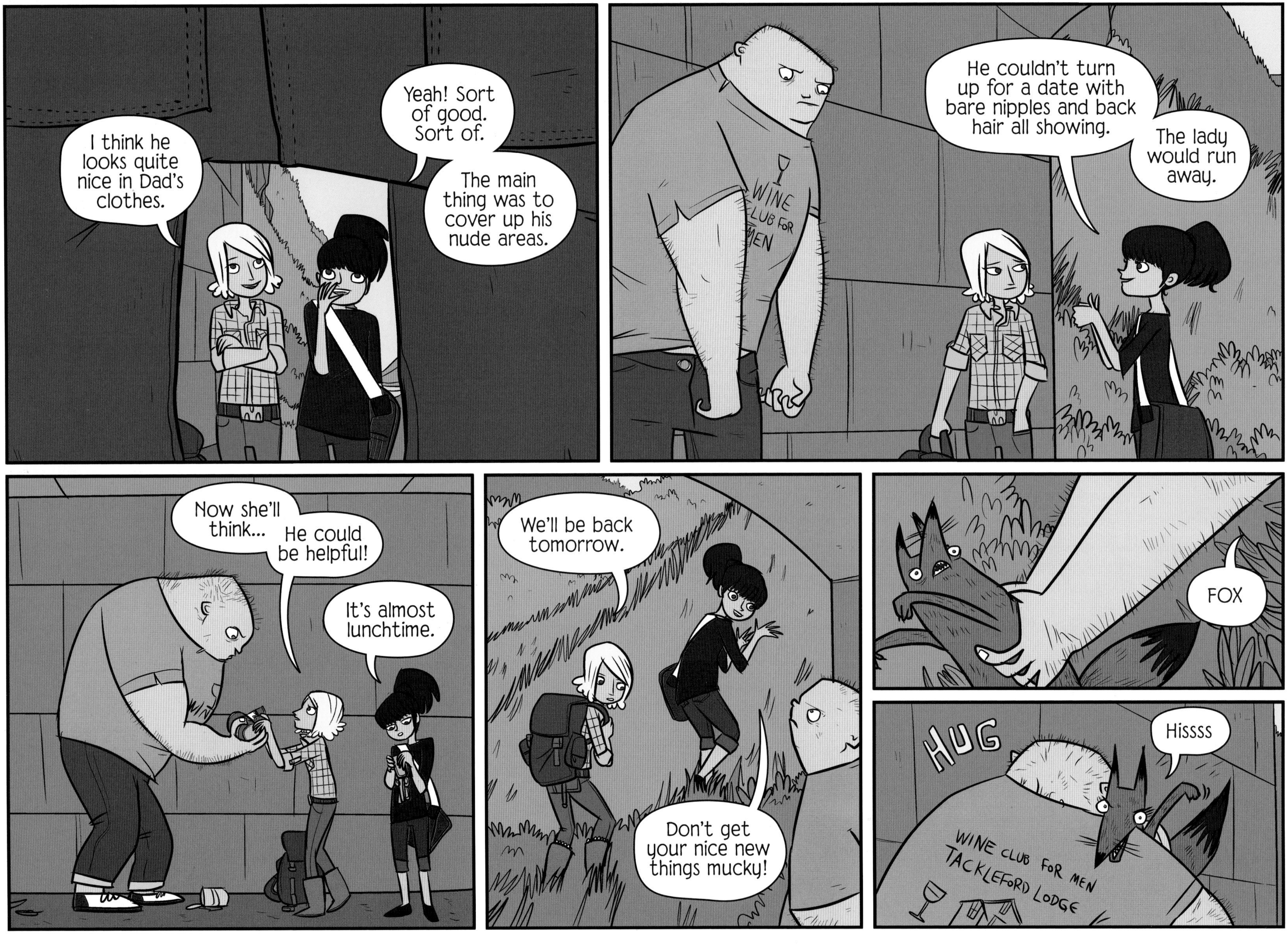
I think he looks quite nice in Dad's clothes.
Yeah! Sort of good. Sort of.
The main thing was to cover up his nude areas.
WINE CLUB FOR MEN
He couldn't turn up for a date with bare nipples and back hair all showing.
The lady would run away.
Now she'll think...
He could be helpful!
It's almost lunchtime.
We'll be back tomorrow.
Don't get your nice new things mucky!
FOX
HUG
Hissss
WINE CLUB FOR MEN
TACKLEFORD LODGE

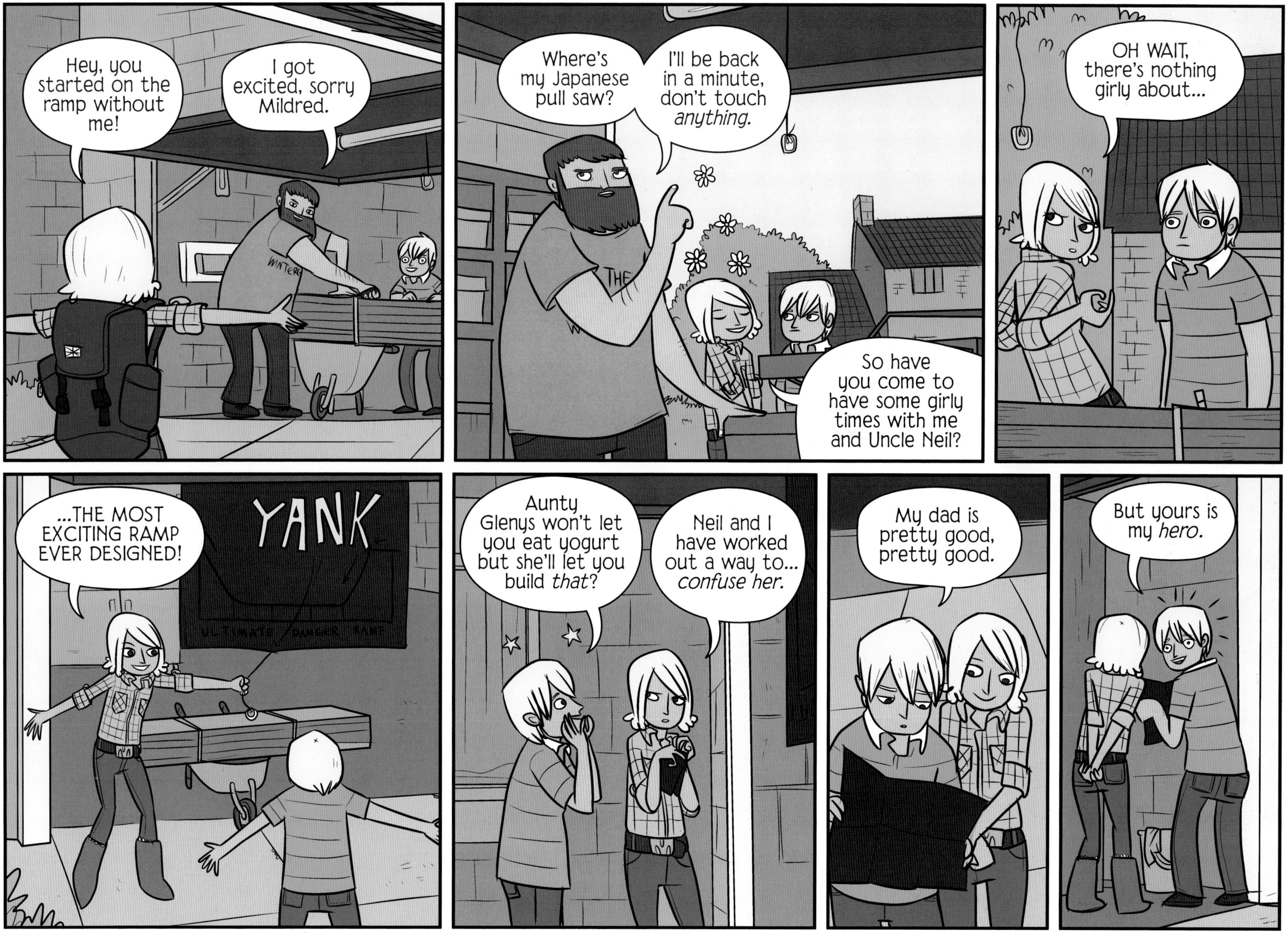
Hey, you started on the ramp without me!
I got excited, sorry Mildred.
Where's my Japanese pull saw?
I'll be back in a minute, don't touch *anything*.
So have you come to have some girly times with me and Uncle Neil?
OH WAIT, there's nothing girly about...
...THE MOST EXCITING RAMP EVER DESIGNED!
YANK
ULTIMATE DANGER RAMP
Aunty Glenys won't let you eat yogurt but she'll let you build *that*?
Neil and I have worked out a way to... *confuse her.*
My dad is pretty good, pretty good.
But yours is my *hero*.

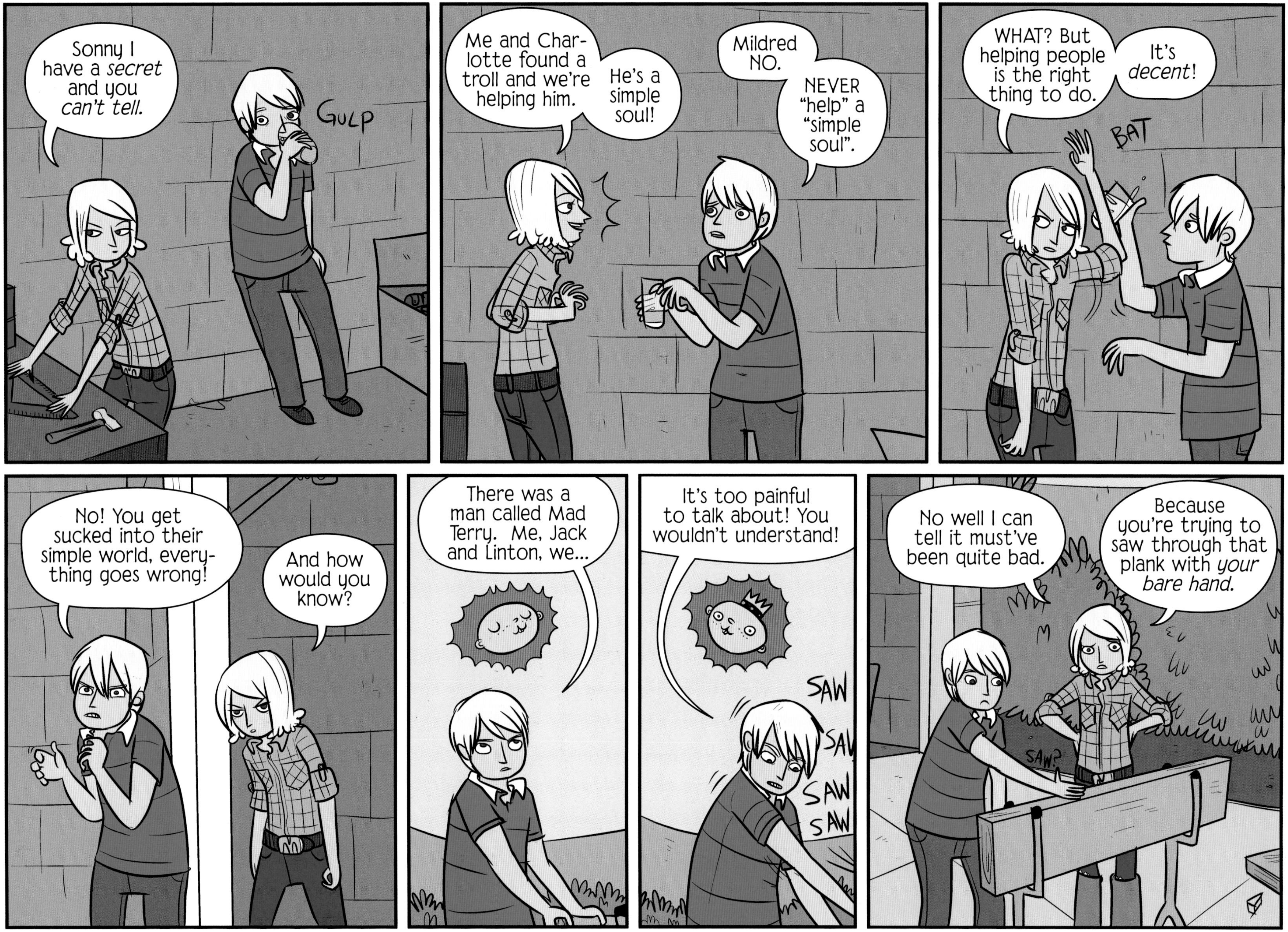
Sonny I have a *secret* and you *can't tell.*
GULP
Me and Charlotte found a troll and we're helping him.
He's a simple soul!
Mildred NO.
NEVER "help" a "simple soul".
WHAT? But helping people is the right thing to do.
It's *decent*!
BAT
No! You get sucked into their simple world, everything goes wrong!
And how would you know?
There was a man called Mad Terry. Me, Jack and Linton, we...
It's too painful to talk about! You wouldn't understand!
SAW
SAW
SAW
SAW
No well I can tell it must've been quite bad.
Because you're trying to saw through that plank with *your bare hand.*
SAW?

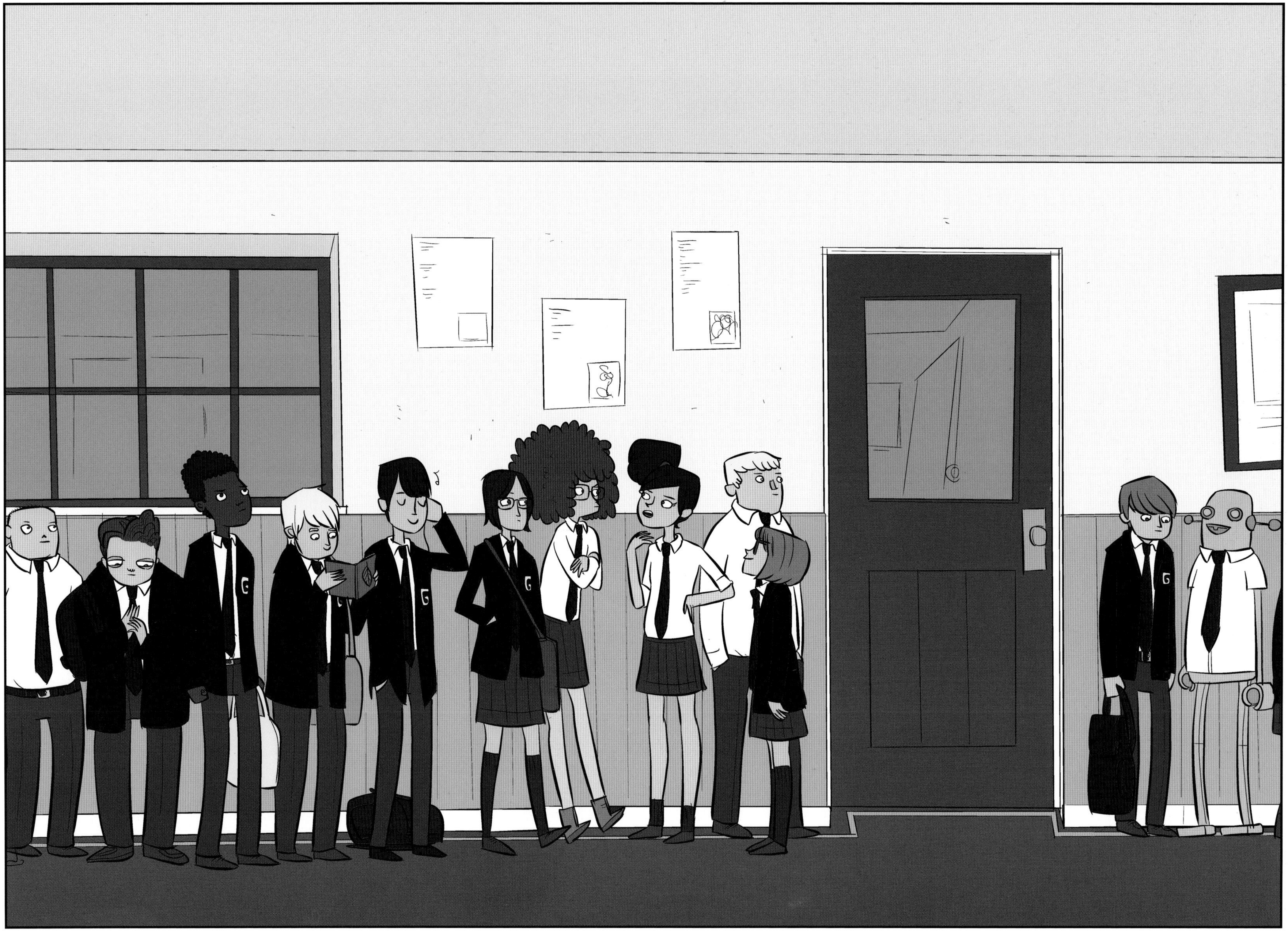

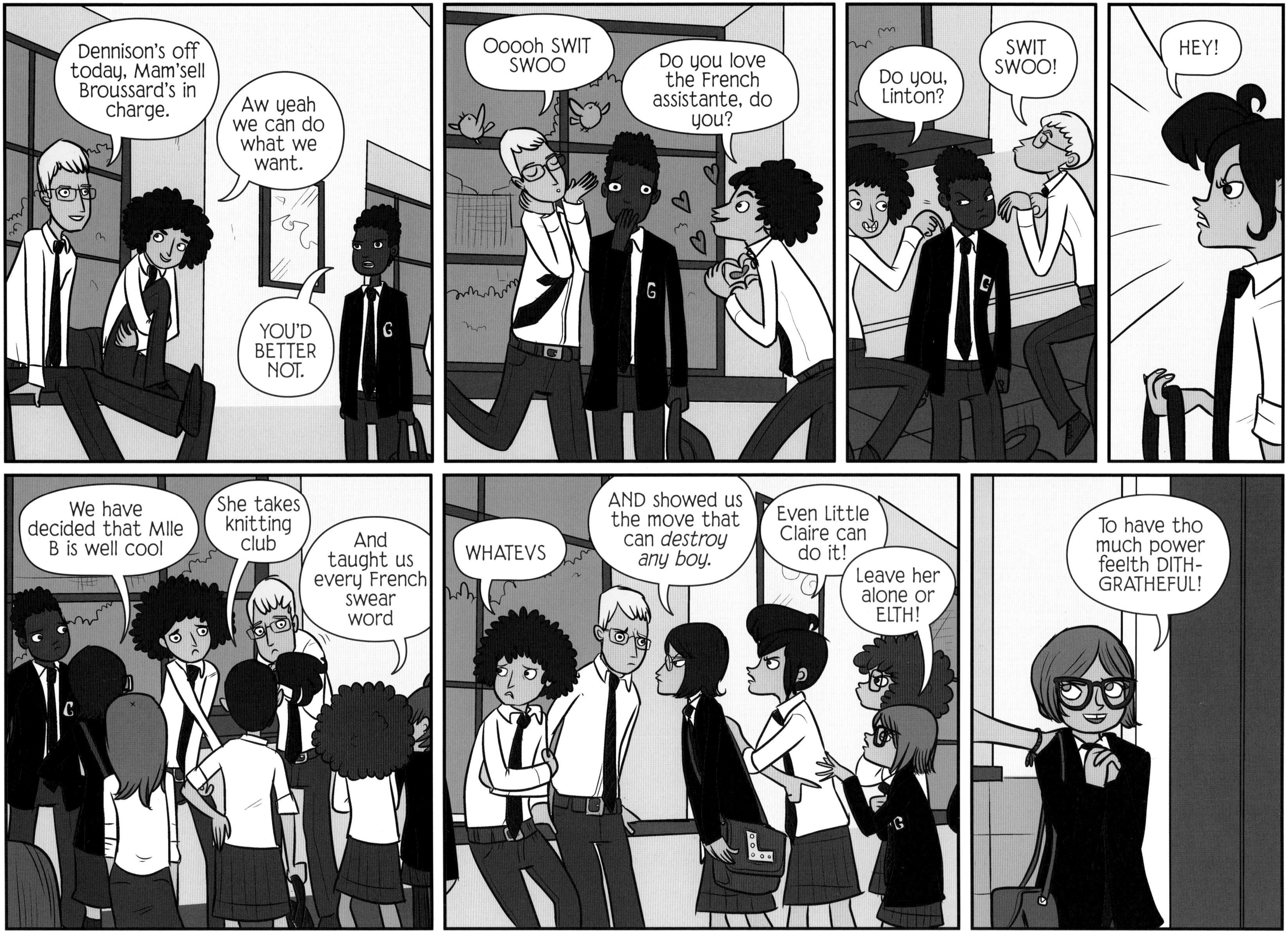
Dennison's off today, Mam'sell Broussard's in charge.
Aw yeah we can do what we want.
YOU'D BETTER NOT.
Ooooh SWIT SWOO
Do you love the French assistante, do you?
Do you, Linton?
SWIT SWOO!
HEY!
We have decided that Mlle B is well cool
She takes knitting club
And taught us every French swear word
WHATEVS
AND showed us the move that can *destroy any boy.*
Even Little Claire can do it!
Leave her alone or ELTH!
To have tho much power feelth DITH-GRATHEFUL!

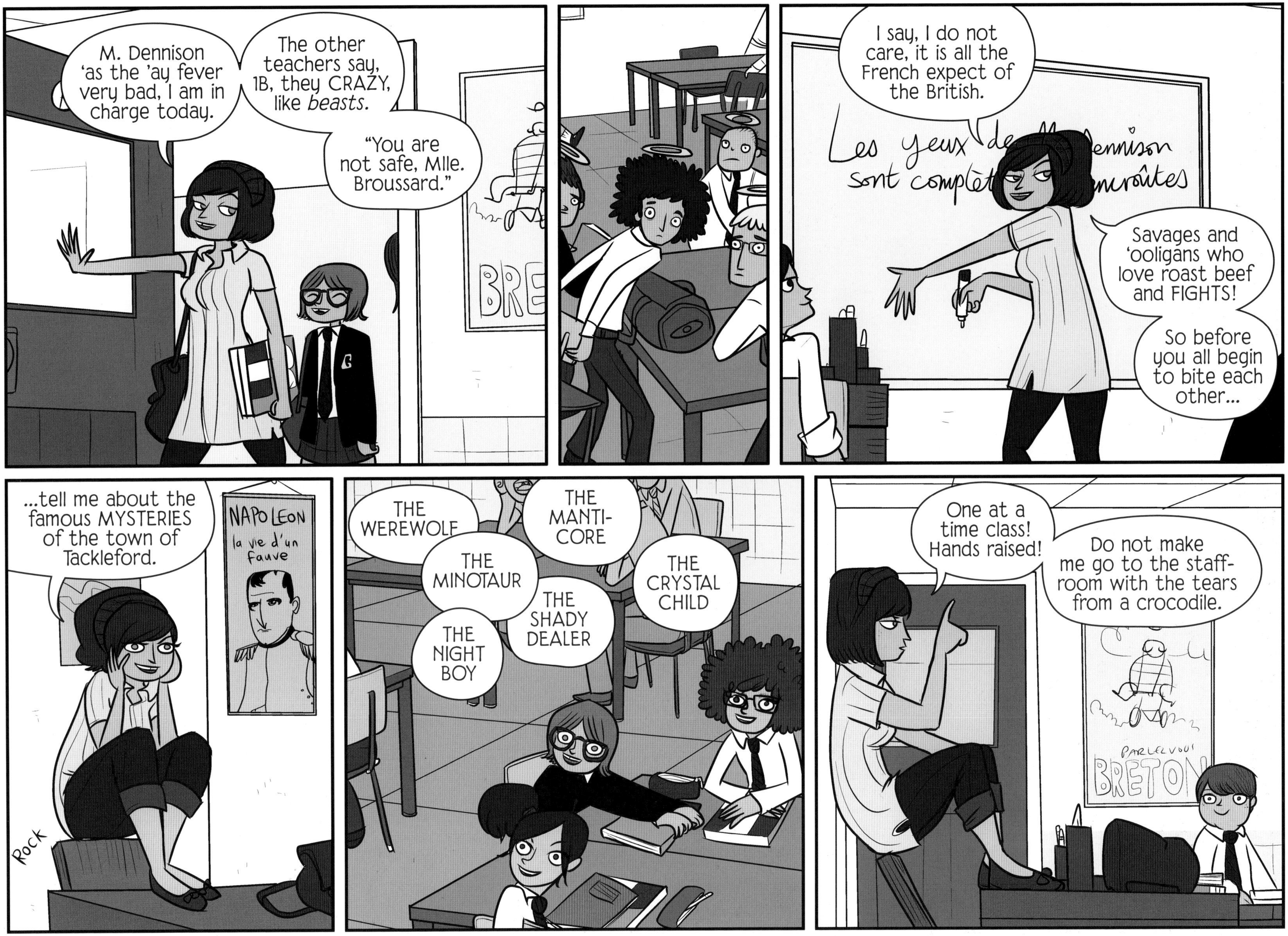
M. Dennison 'as the 'ay fever very bad, I am in charge today.
The other teachers say, 1B, they CRAZY, like *beasts*.
"You are not safe, Mlle. Broussard."
BRE
I say, I do not care, it is all the French expect of the British.
Savages and 'ooligans who love roast beef and FIGHTS!
So before you all begin to bite each other...
...tell me about the famous MYSTERIES of the town of Tackleford.
NAPOLEON
la vie d'un fauve
ROCK
THE WEREWOLF
THE MANTICORE
THE MINOTAUR
THE SHADY DEALER
THE CRYSTAL CHILD
THE NIGHT BOY
One at a time class! Hands raised!
Do not make me go to the staff-room with the tears from a crocodile.
PARLEZ VOUS
BRETON

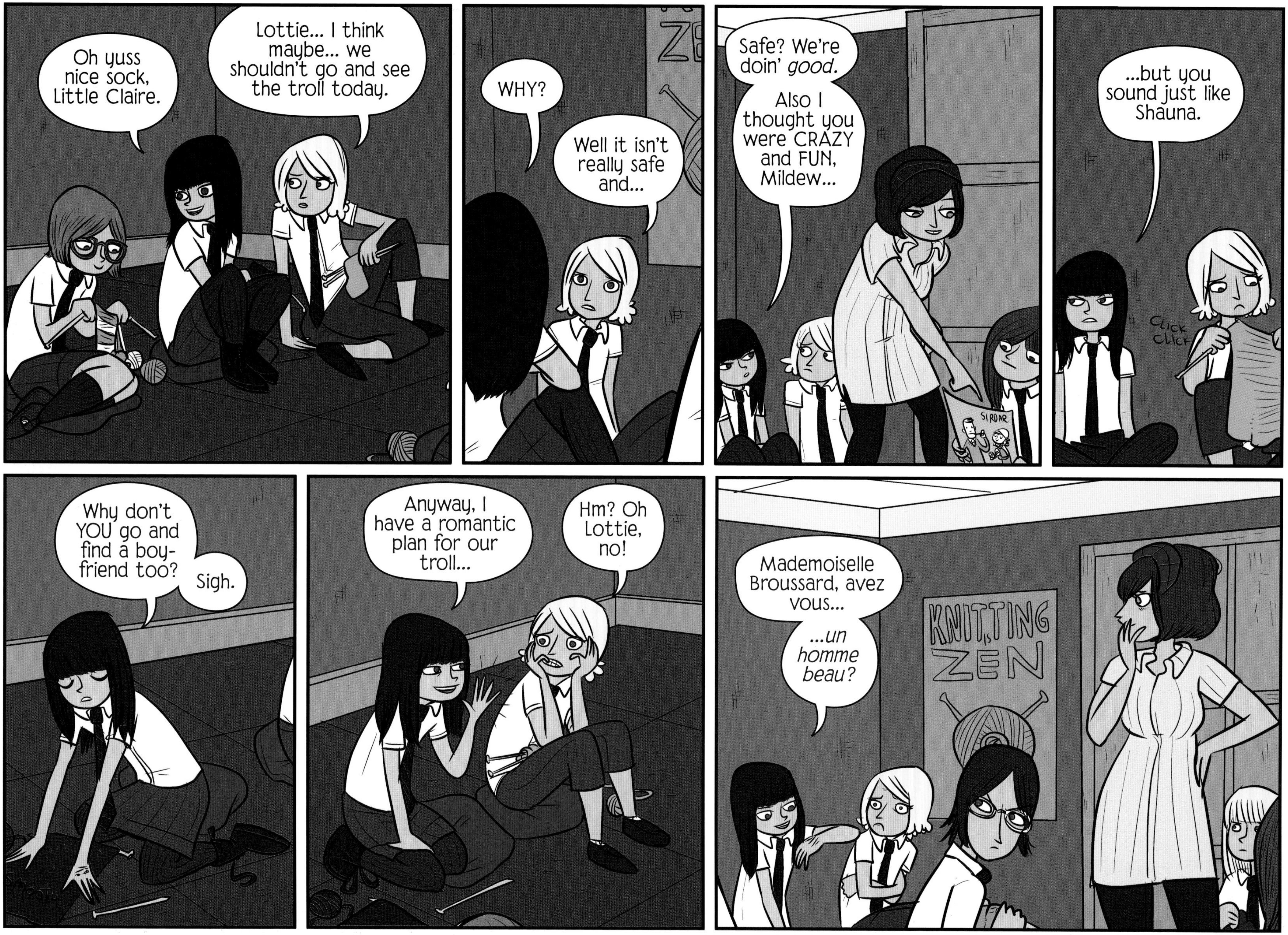
Oh yuss nice sock, Little Claire.
Lottie... I think maybe... we shouldn't go and see the troll today.
WHY?
Well it isn't really safe and...
Safe? We're doin' *good.*
Also I thought you were CRAZY and FUN, Mildew...
SIRDAR
...but you sound just like Shauna.
CLICK CLICK
Why don't YOU go and find a boy-friend too?
Sigh.
Anyway, I have a romantic plan for our troll...
Hm? Oh Lottie, no!
Mademoiselle Broussard, avez vous...
...un homme beau?
KNITTING IS ZEN

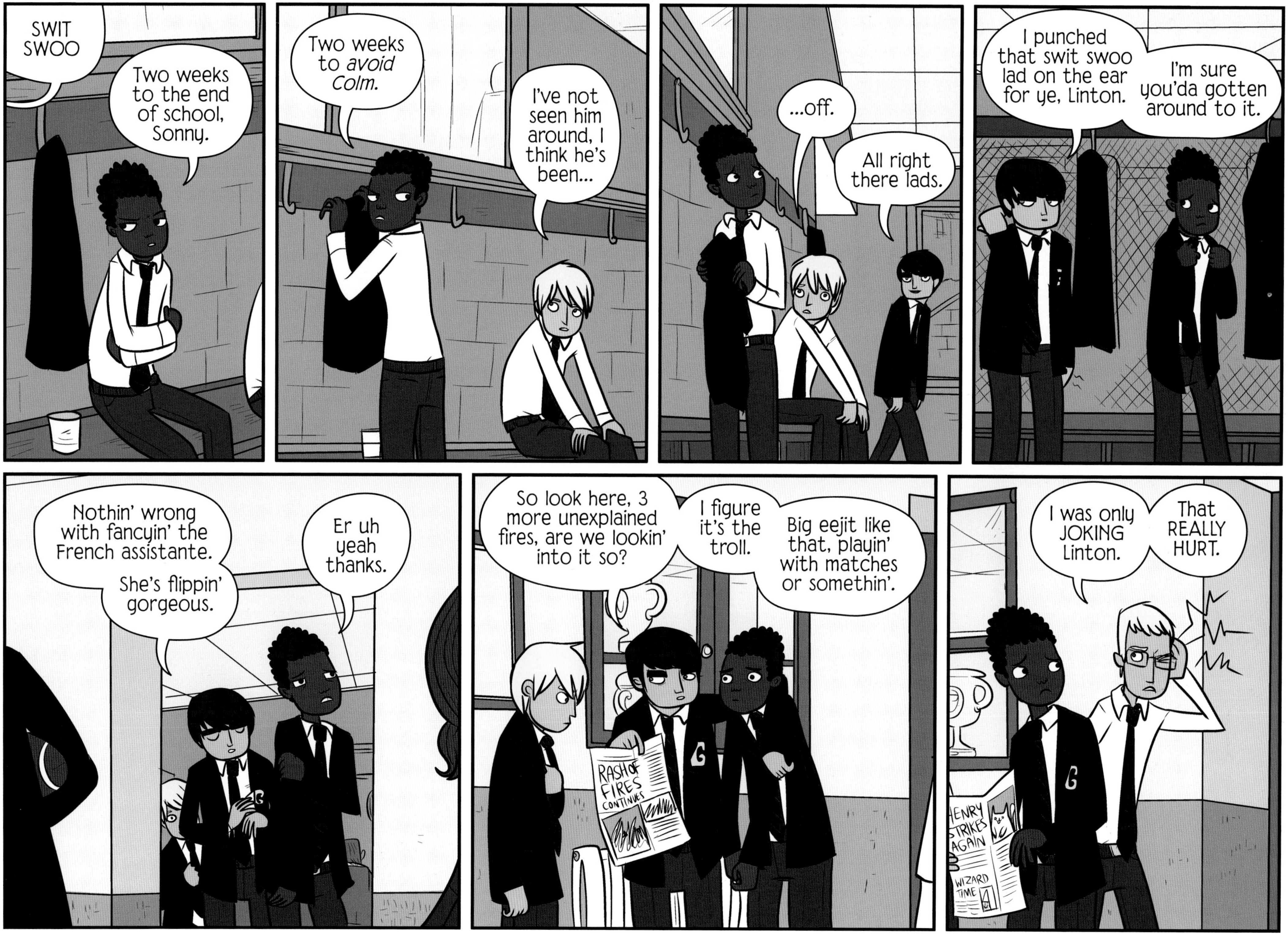
SWIT SWOO
Two weeks to the end of school, Sonny.
Two weeks to *avoid Colm.*
I've not seen him around, I think he's been...
...off.
All right there lads.
I punched that swit swoo lad on the ear for ye, Linton.
I'm sure you'da gotten around to it.
Nothin' wrong with fancyin' the French assistante.
She's flippin' gorgeous.
Er uh yeah thanks.
So look here, 3 more unexplained fires, are we lookin' into it so?
RASH OF FIRES CONTINUES
I figure it's the troll.
Big eejit like that, playin' with matches or somethin'.
I was only JOKING Linton.
That REALLY HURT.
HENRY STRIKES AGAIN
WIZARD TIME

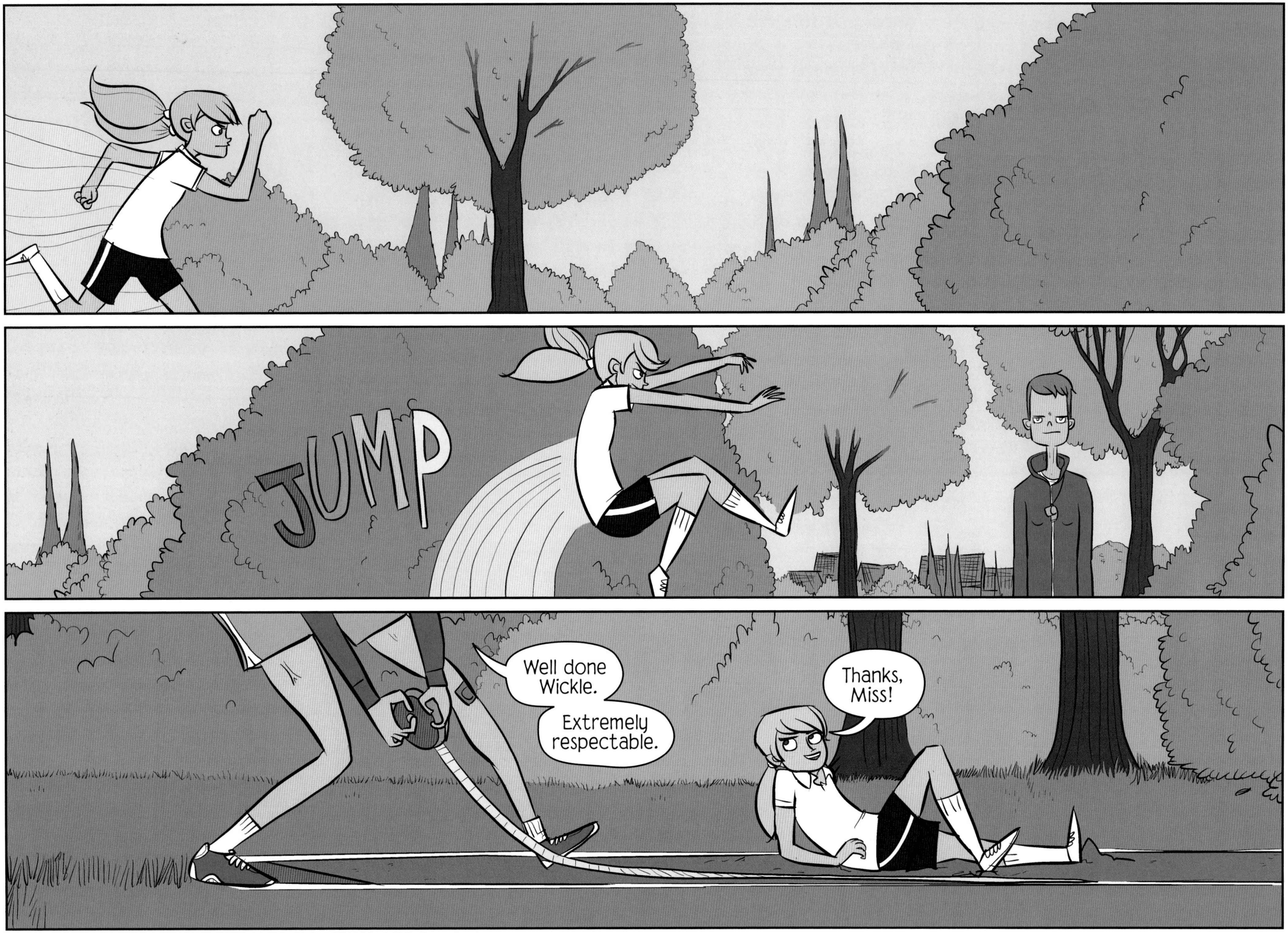
JUMP
Well done Wickle.
Extremely respectable.
Thanks, Miss!

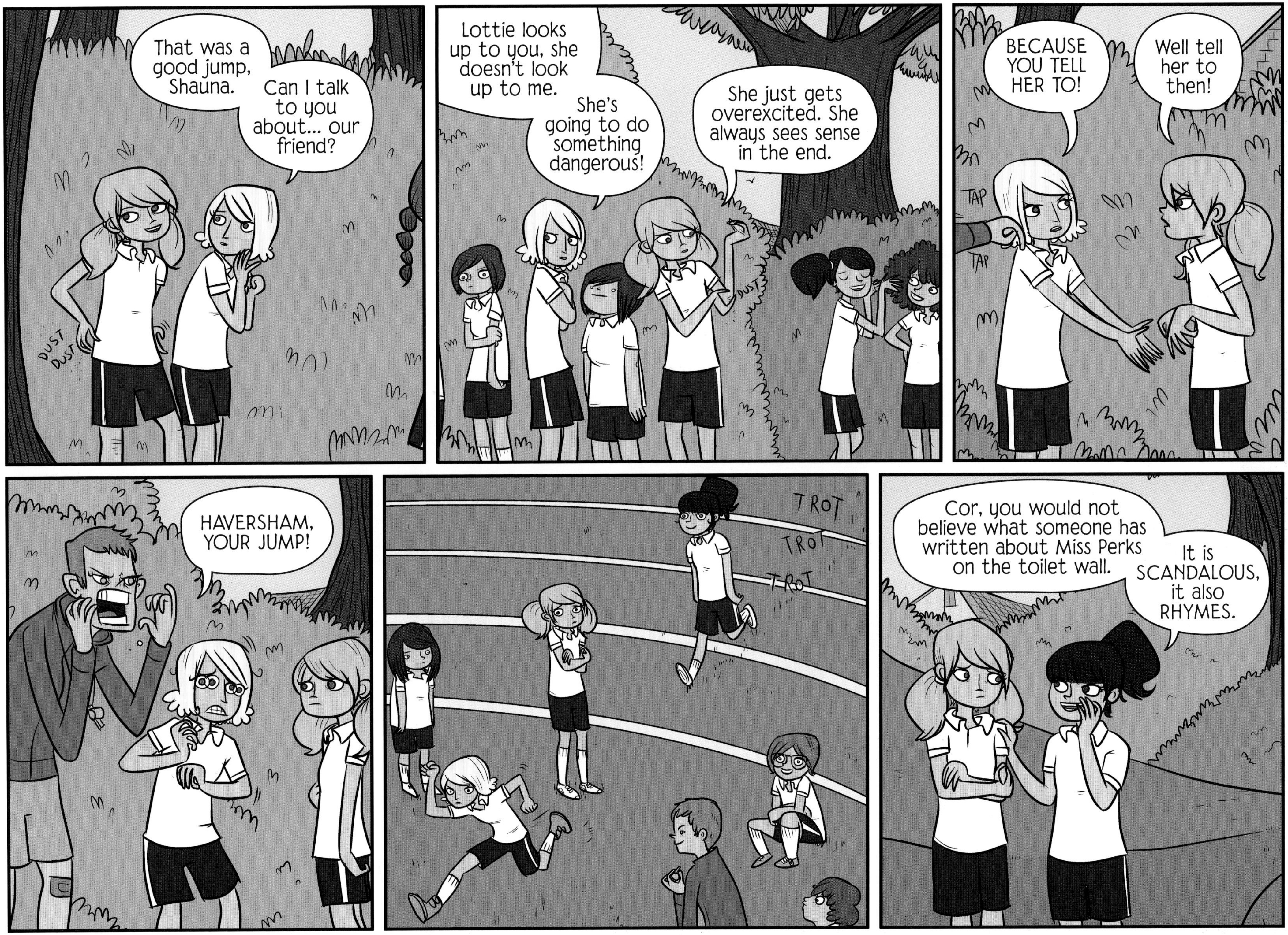

That was a good jump, Shauna.
Can I talk to you about... our friend?
DUST DUST
Lottie looks up to you, she doesn't look up to me.
She's going to do something dangerous!
She just gets overexcited. She always sees sense in the end.
DUST
BECAUSE YOU TELL HER TO!
Well tell her to then!
TAP
TAP
HAVERSHAM, YOUR JUMP!
TROT
TROT
TROT
Cor, you would not believe what someone has written about Miss Perks on the toilet wall.
It is SCANDALOUS, it also RHYMES.

Bad Machinery, Volume Three

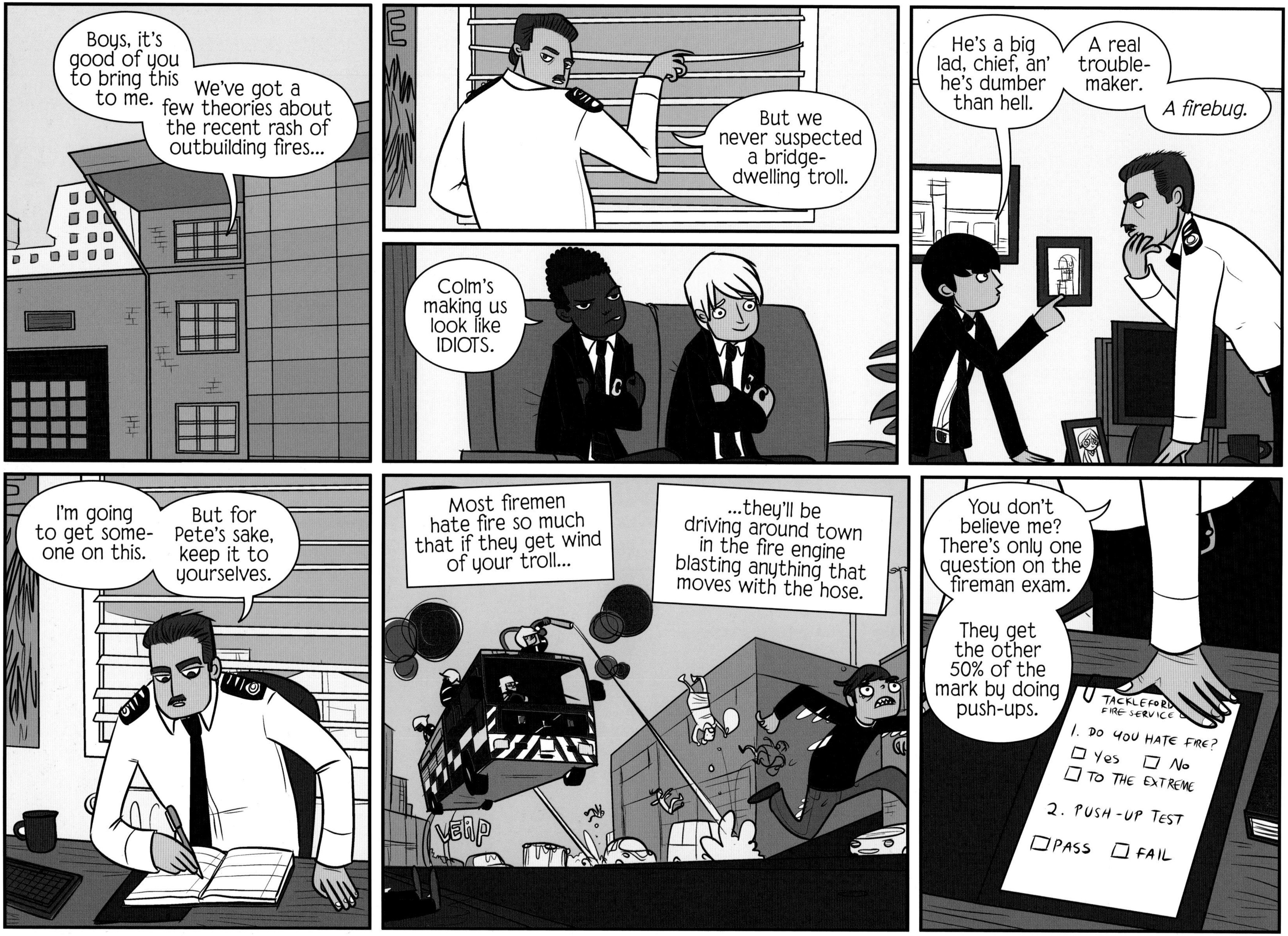
Boys, it's good of you to bring this to me.
We've got a few theories about the recent rash of outbuilding fires...
But we never suspected a bridge-dwelling troll.
Colm's making us look like IDIOTS.
He's a big lad, chief, an' he's dumber than hell.
A real trouble-maker.
A firebug.
I'm going to get some-one on this.
But for Pete's sake, keep it to yourselves.
Most firemen hate fire so much that if they get wind of your troll...
...they'll be driving around town in the fire engine blasting anything that moves with the hose.
You don't believe me? There's only one question on the fireman exam.
They get the other 50% of the mark by doing push-ups.
TACKLEFORD FIRE SERVICE
1. DO YOU HATE FIRE?
Yes No
TO THE EXTREME
2. PUSH-UP TEST
PASS FAIL

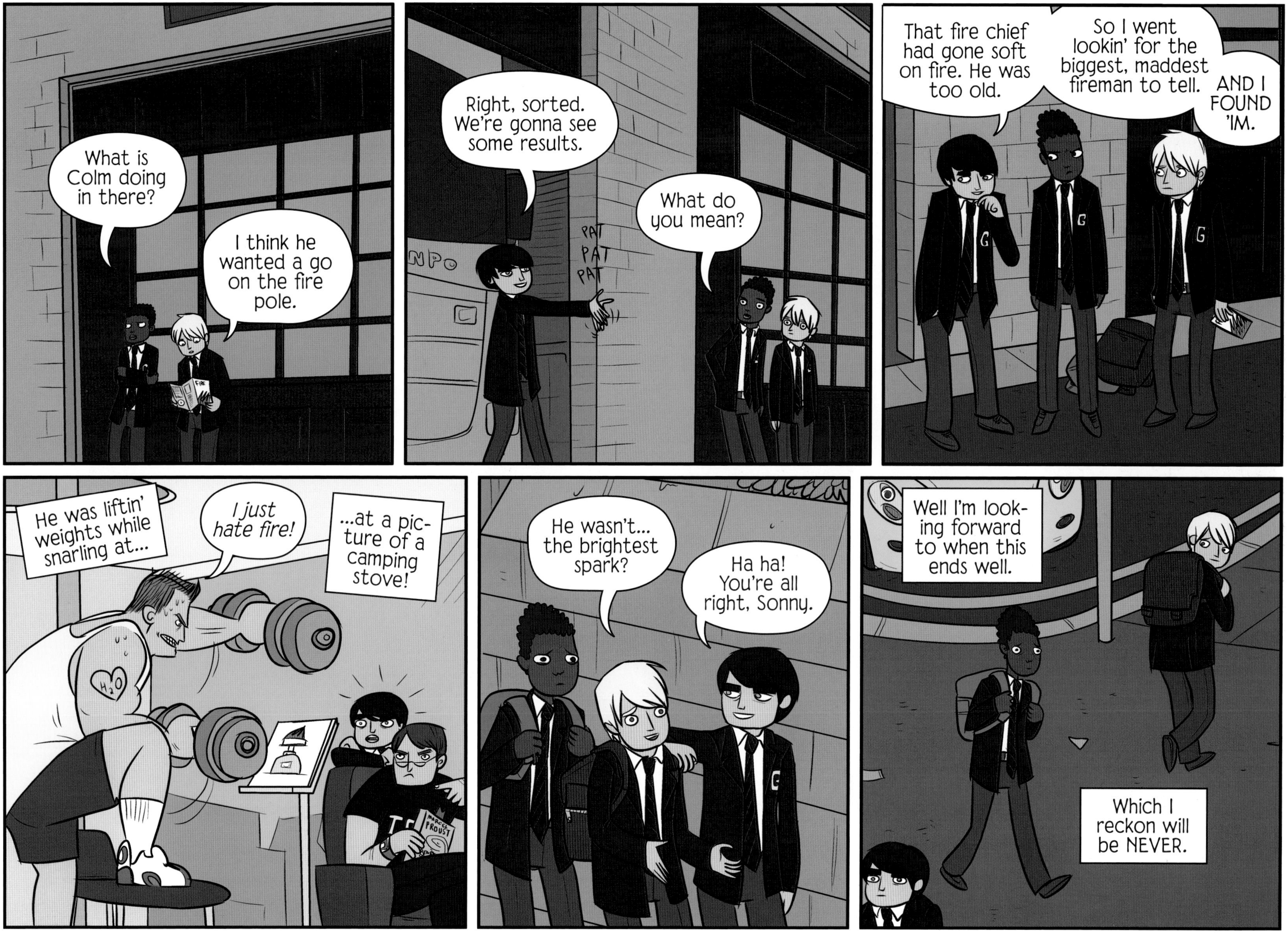
What is Colm doing in there?
I think he wanted a go on the fire pole.
Right, sorted. We're gonna see some results.
PAT PAT PAT
What do you mean?
That fire chief had gone soft on fire. He was too old.
So I went lookin' for the biggest, maddest fireman to tell.
AND I FOUND 'IM.
He was liftin' weights while snarling at...
I just hate fire!
...at a picture of a camping stove!
He wasn't... the brightest spark?
Ha ha! You're all right, Sonny.
Well I'm looking forward to when this ends well.
Which I reckon will be NEVER.

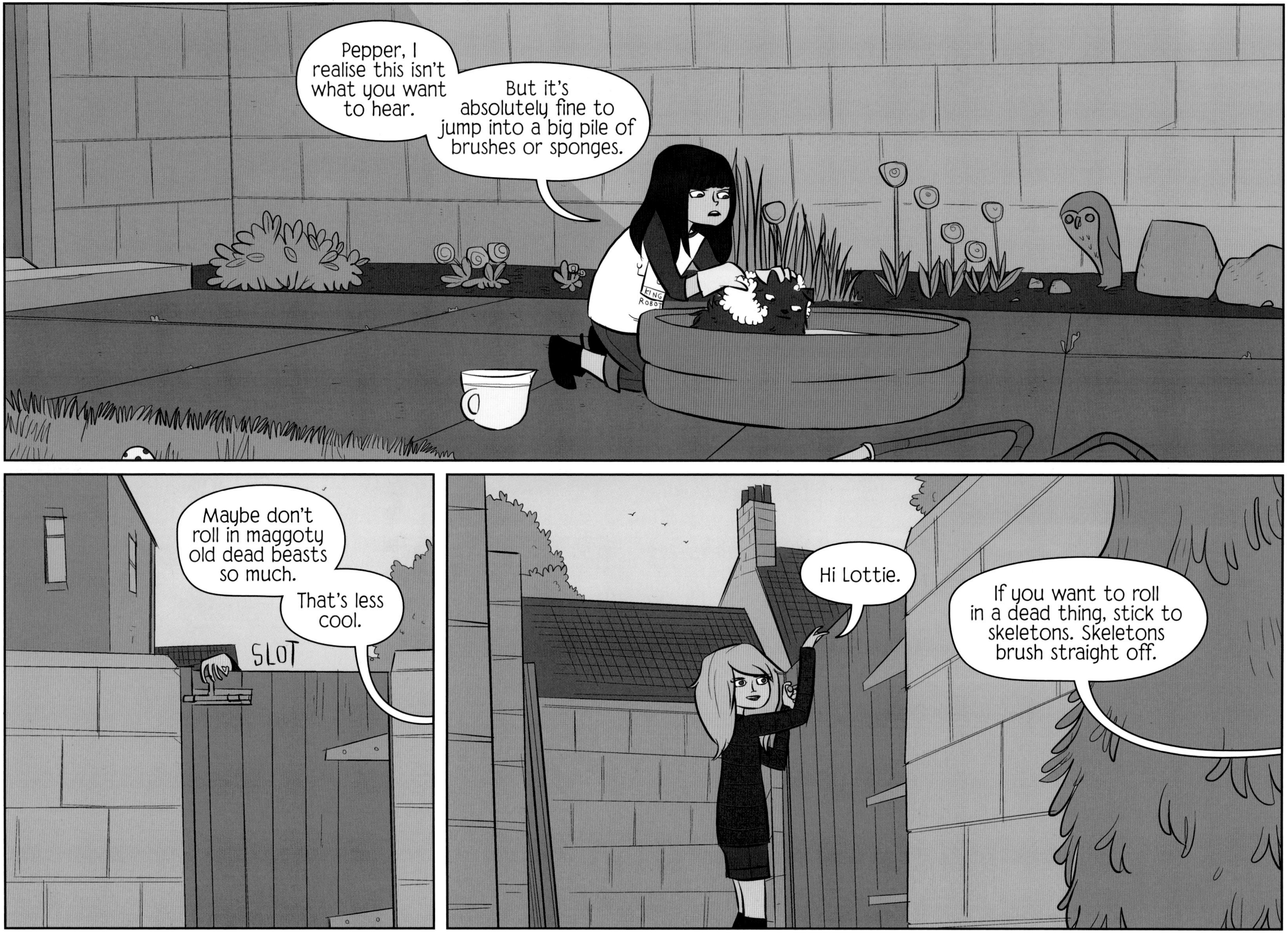
Pepper, I realise this isn't what you want to hear.
But it's absolutely fine to jump into a big pile of brushes or sponges.
Maybe don't roll in maggoty old dead beasts so much.
That's less cool.
SLOT
Hi Lottie.
If you want to roll in a dead thing, stick to skeletons. Skeletons brush straight off.

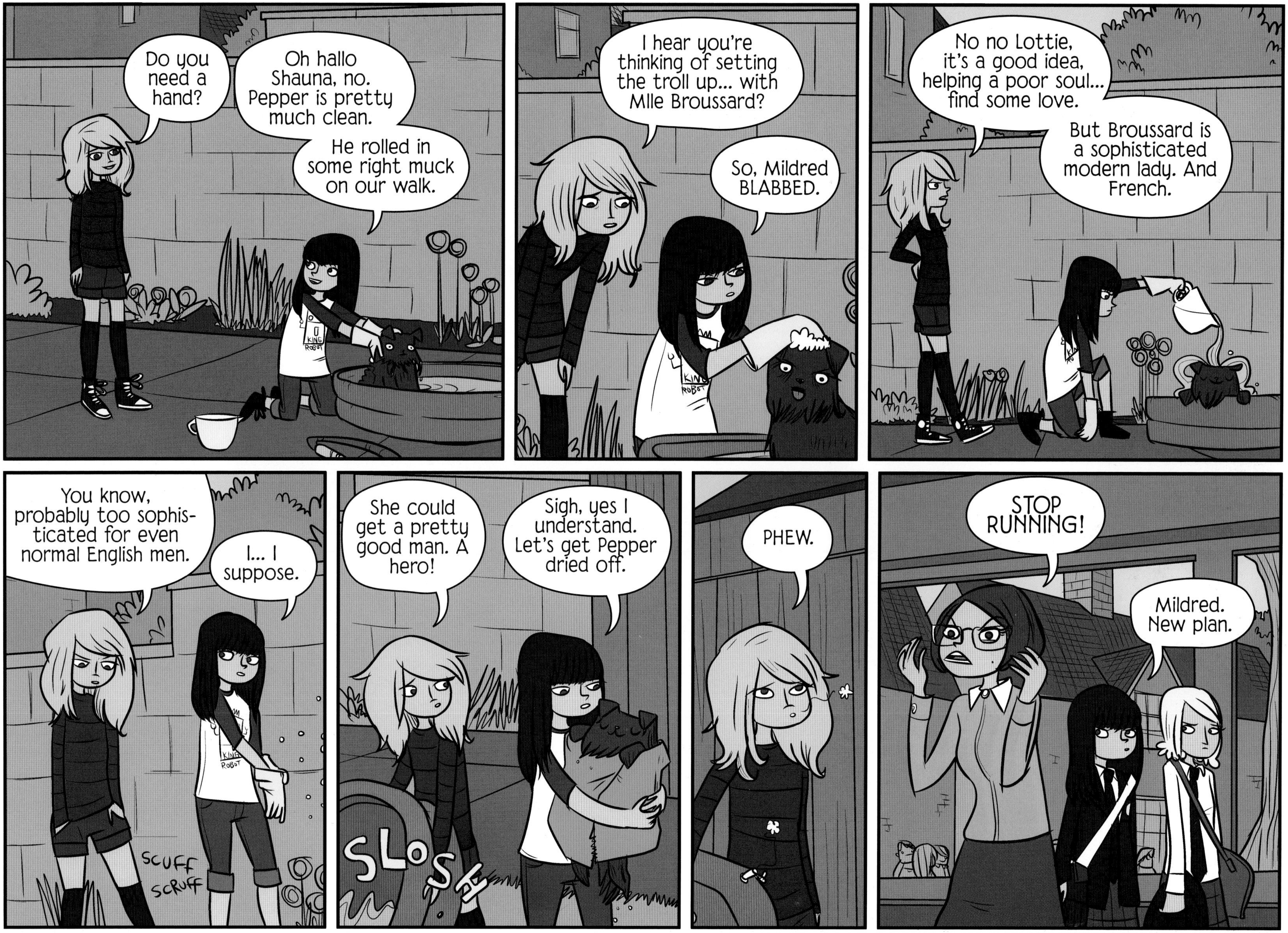
Do you need a hand?
Oh hallo Shauna, no. Pepper is pretty much clean.
He rolled in some right muck on our walk.
I hear you're thinking of setting the troll up... with Mlle Broussard?
So, Mildred BLABBED.
No no Lottie, it's a good idea, helping a poor soul... find some love.
But Broussard is a sophisticated modern lady. And French.
You know, probably too sophisticated for even normal English men.
I... I suppose.
SCUFF
SCRUFF
She could get a pretty good man. A hero!
Sigh, yes I understand. Let's get Pepper dried off.
SLOSH
PHEW.
STOP RUNNING!
Mildred. New plan.

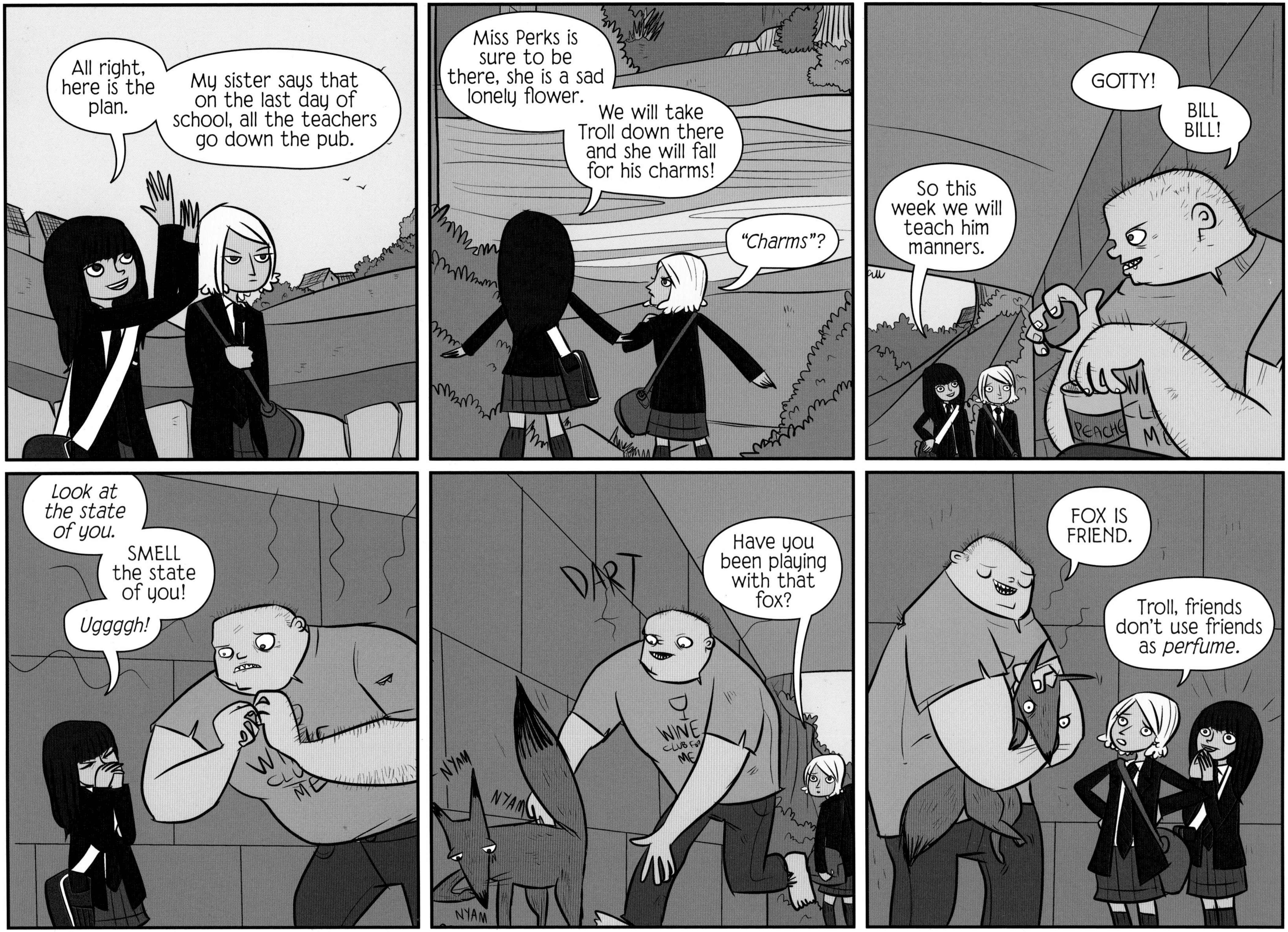
All right, here is the plan.
My sister says that on the last day of school, all the teachers go down the pub.
Miss Perks is sure to be there, she is a sad lonely flower.
We will take Troll down there and she will fall for his charms!
"Charms"?
GOTTY!
BILL BILL!
So this week we will teach him manners.
PEACHE
Look at the state of you.
SMELL the state of you!
Uggggh!
DART
Have you been playing with that fox?
NYAM
NYAM
NYAM
WINE CLUB FOR ME
FOX IS FRIEND.
Troll, friends don't use friends as *perfume*.

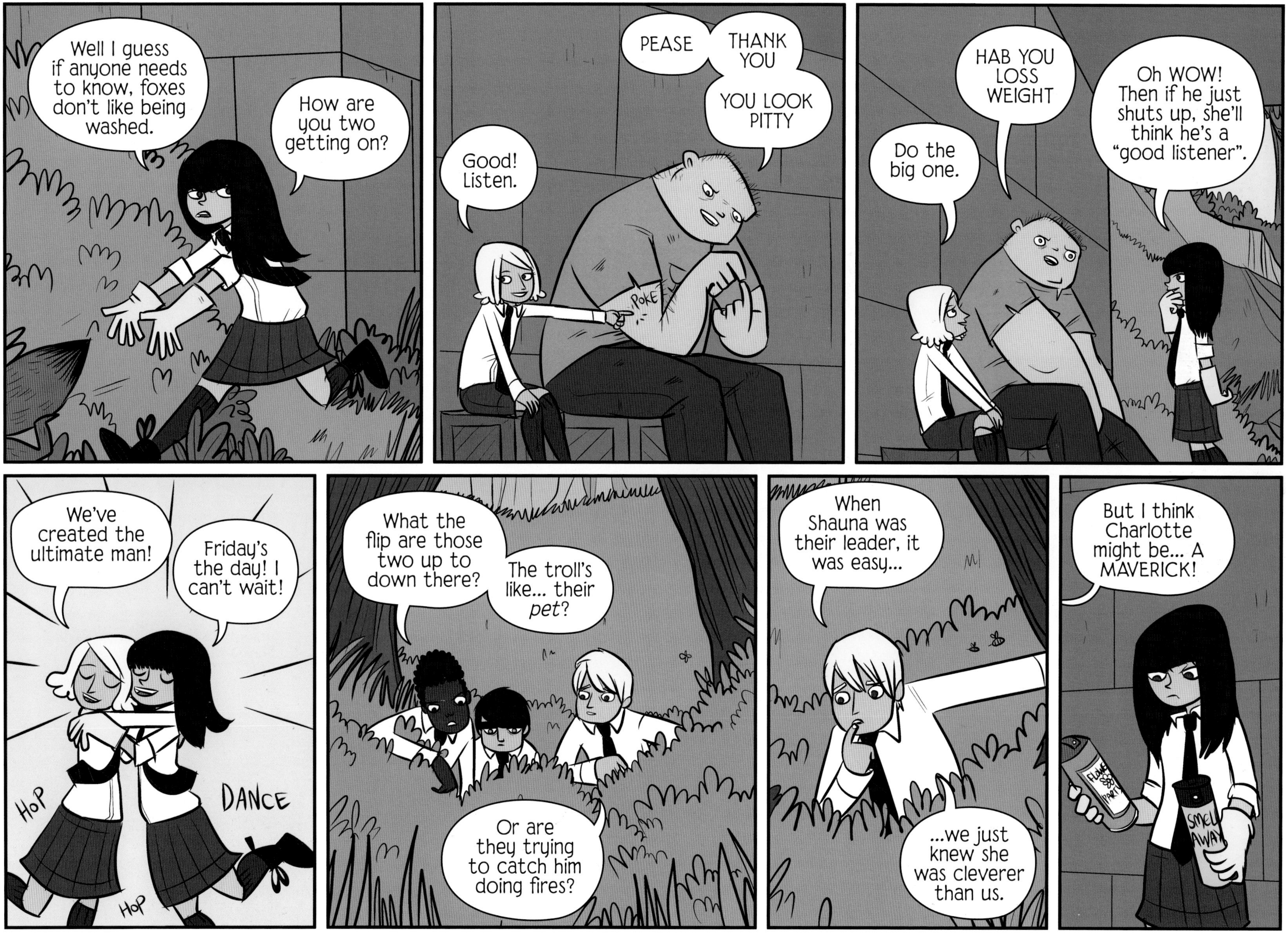
Well I guess if anyone needs to know, foxes don't like being washed.
How are you two getting on?
Good! Listen.
POKE
PEASE
THANK YOU
YOU LOOK PITTY
Do the big one.
HAB YOU LOSS WEIGHT
Oh WOW! Then if he just shuts up, she'll think he's a "good listener".
We've created the ultimate man!
Friday's the day! I can't wait!
HoP
DANCE
HoP
What the flip are those two up to down there?
The troll's like... their *pet*?
Or are they trying to catch him doing fires?
When Shauna was their leader, it was easy...
...we just knew she was cleverer than us.
But I think Charlotte might be... A MAVERICK!

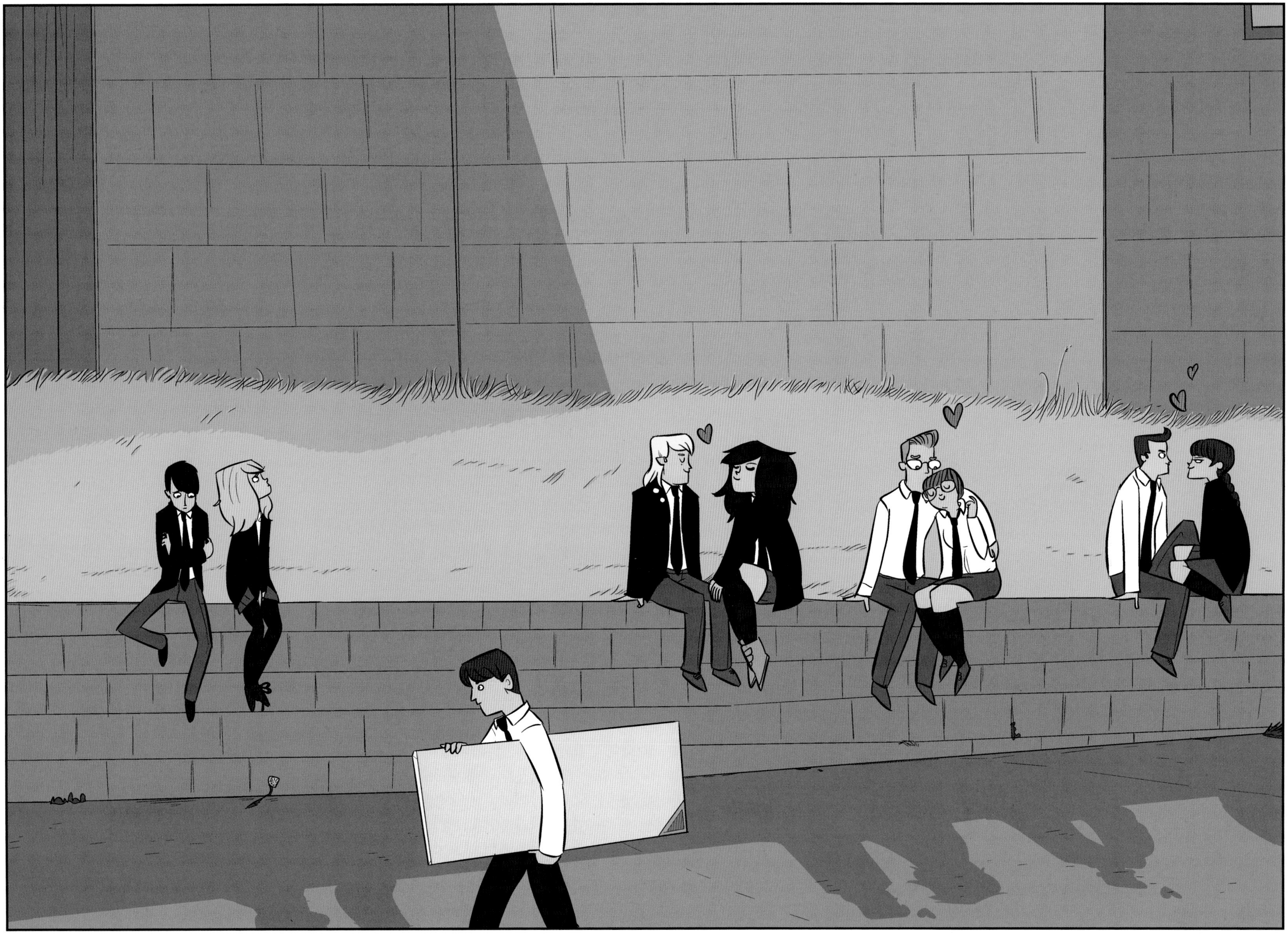

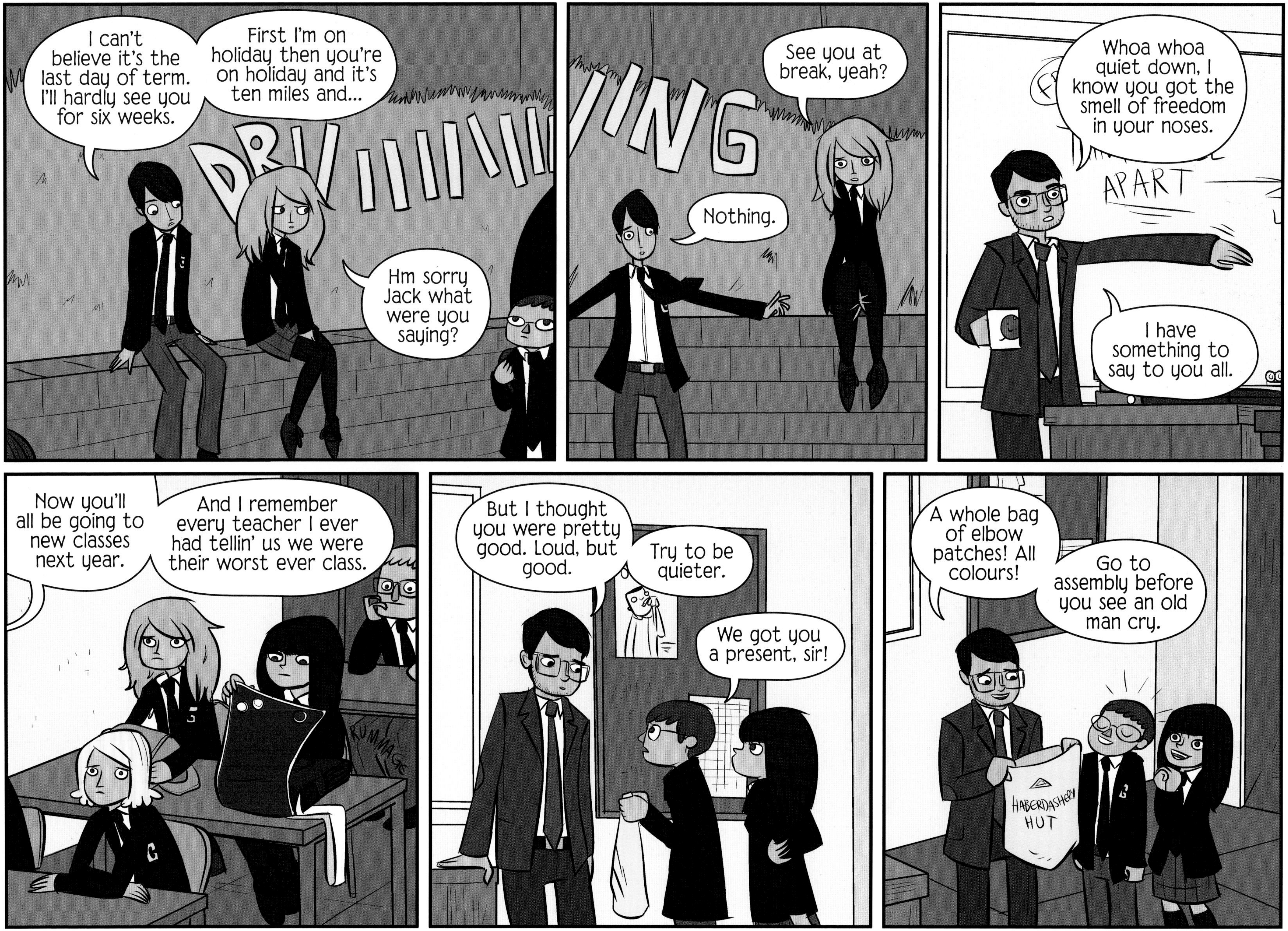
I can't believe it's the last day of term. I'll hardly see you for six weeks.
First I'm on holiday then you're on holiday and it's ten miles and...
DRIIIIIIIIIIING
Hm sorry Jack what were you saying?
See you at break, yeah?
Nothing.
Whoa whoa quiet down, I know you got the smell of freedom in your noses.
APART
I have something to say to you all.
Now you'll all be going to new classes next year.
And I remember every teacher I ever had tellin' us we were their worst ever class.
RUMMAGE
But I thought you were pretty good. Loud, but good.
Try to be quieter.
We got you a present, sir!
A whole bag of elbow patches! All colours!
Go to assembly before you see an old man cry.
HABERDASHERY HUT

The firemen are doin' nothing.

I think we should tell the local paper about the troll.

AUGH, ERIN WINTERS?

HENRY IN MORE TROUBLE

CARAVAN WORLD

To be honest witcher, lads, I wanna meet her.

She looks real pretty on her little photo.

Bins

Reporter-at-la ERIN WINTERS

Refuse all over Tackleford remains collected as council cuts continue to bite.

Council Ronald claims unless it is lit

What happens is we discover something...

...then she gets our names wrong and takes all the credit.

Aw well, I don't want my name gettin' out anyway.

YORKSHIRE CRUSH BY CHERCHESTERSHIRE

Could create issues, you know.

Wouldn't want to lose my five finger discount in town.

What's going to happen then, she'll see you and decide to marry you?

Well I could spend the rest of my life lookin' at my shoes like you, Linton.

Prayin' nothin' bad ever happens.

TACKLEFORD CORMORANT

But that's not me.

Set your sights high, you might just get there, you know?

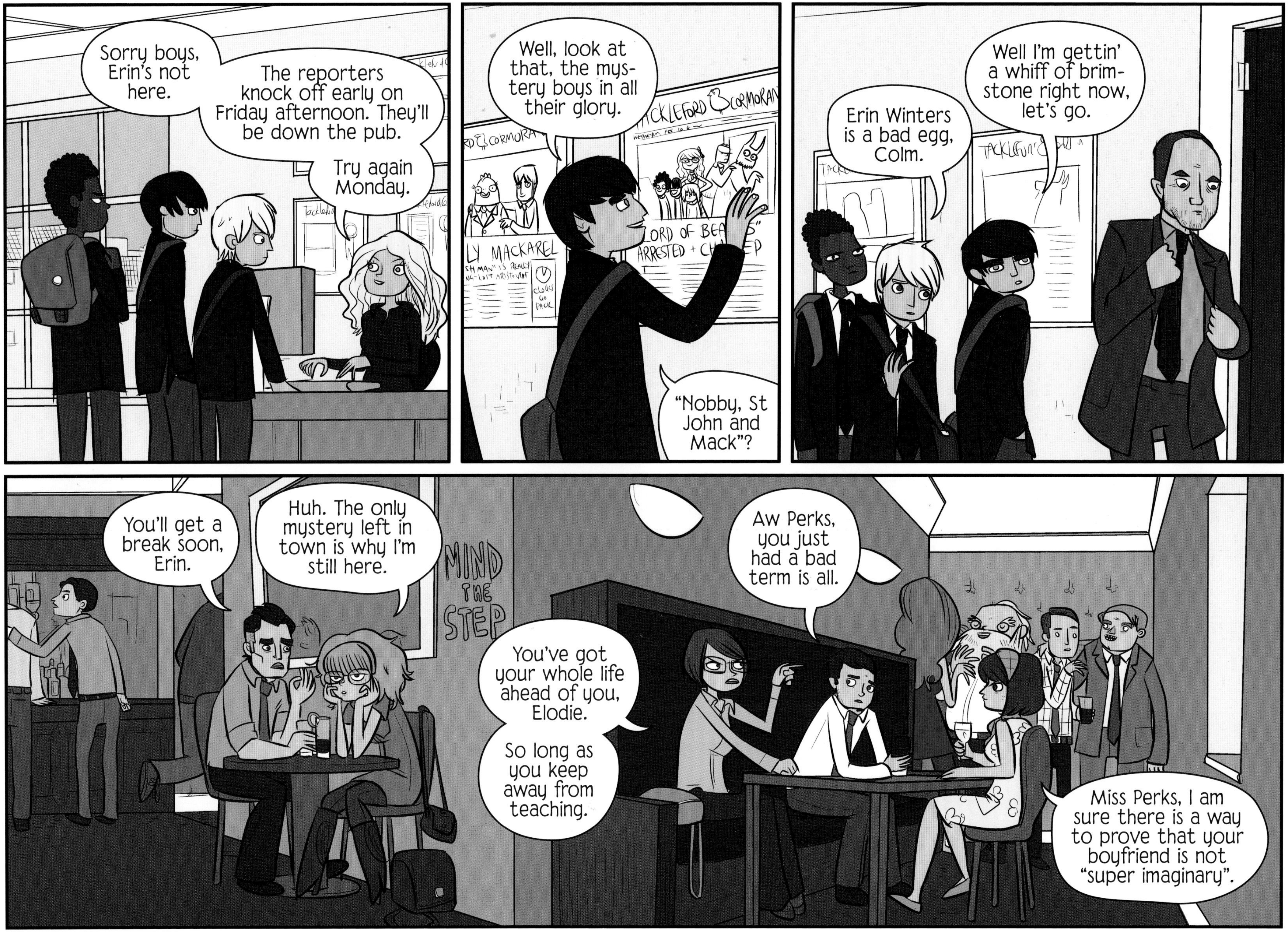
Sorry boys, Erin's not here.
The reporters knock off early on Friday afternoon. They'll be down the pub.
Try again Monday.
Well, look at that, the mystery boys in all their glory.
TACKLEFORD CORMORANT
LORD OF BEASTS ARRESTED + CHARGED
"Nobby, St John and Mack"?
Erin Winters is a bad egg, Colm.
Well I'm gettin' a whiff of brimstone right now, let's go.
You'll get a break soon, Erin.
Huh. The only mystery left in town is why I'm still here.
MIND THE STEP
You've got your whole life ahead of you, Elodie.
So long as you keep away from teaching.
Aw Perks, you just had a bad term is all.
Miss Perks, I am sure there is a way to prove that your boyfriend is not "super imaginary".

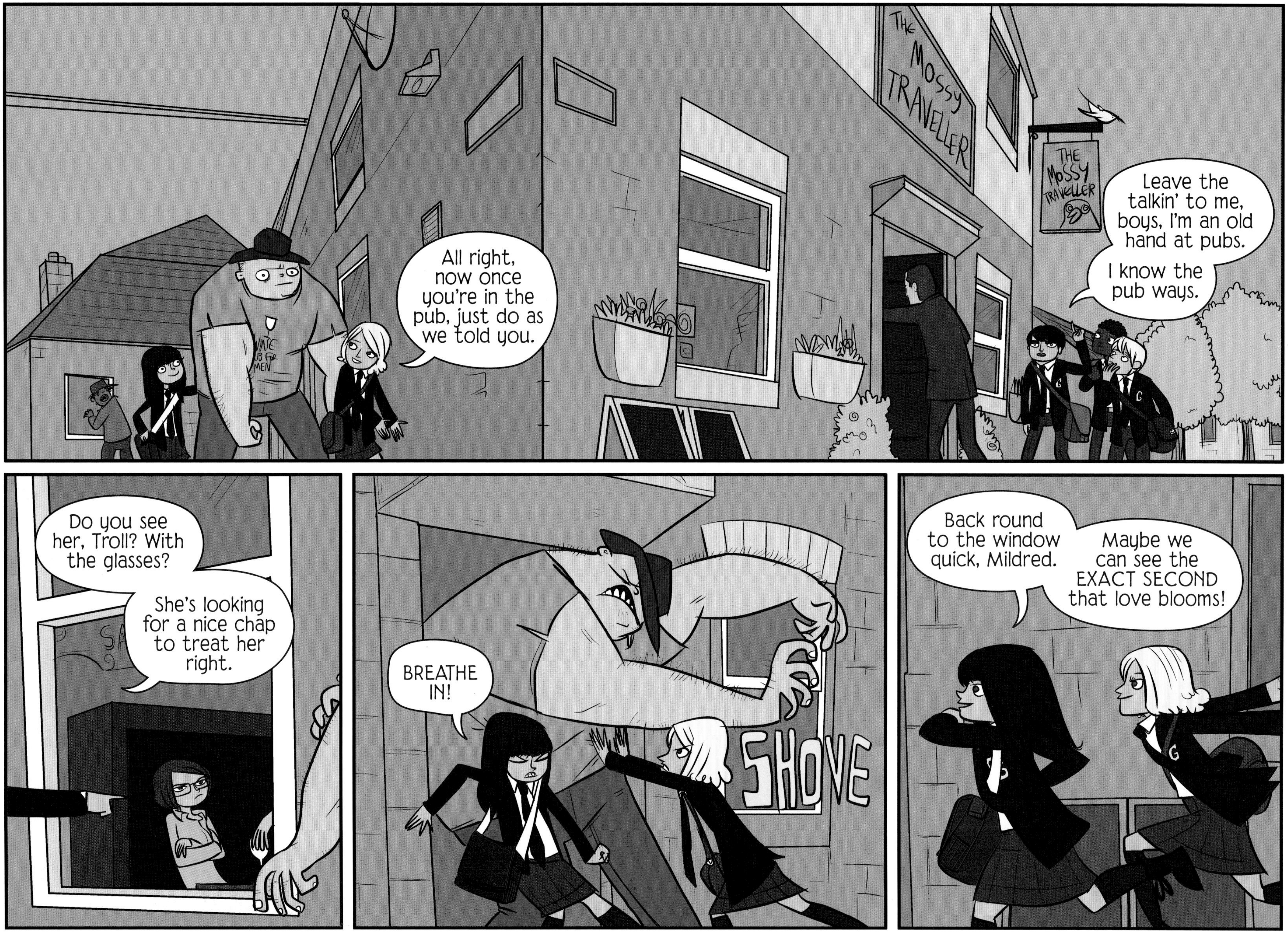
All right, now once you're in the pub, just do as we told you.
THE MOSSY TRAVELLER
THE MOSSY TRAVELLER
Leave the talkin' to me, boys, I'm an old hand at pubs.
I know the pub ways.
Do you see her, Troll? With the glasses?
She's looking for a nice chap to treat her right.
BREATHE IN!
SHOVE
Back round to the window quick, Mildred.
Maybe we can see the EXACT SECOND that love blooms!

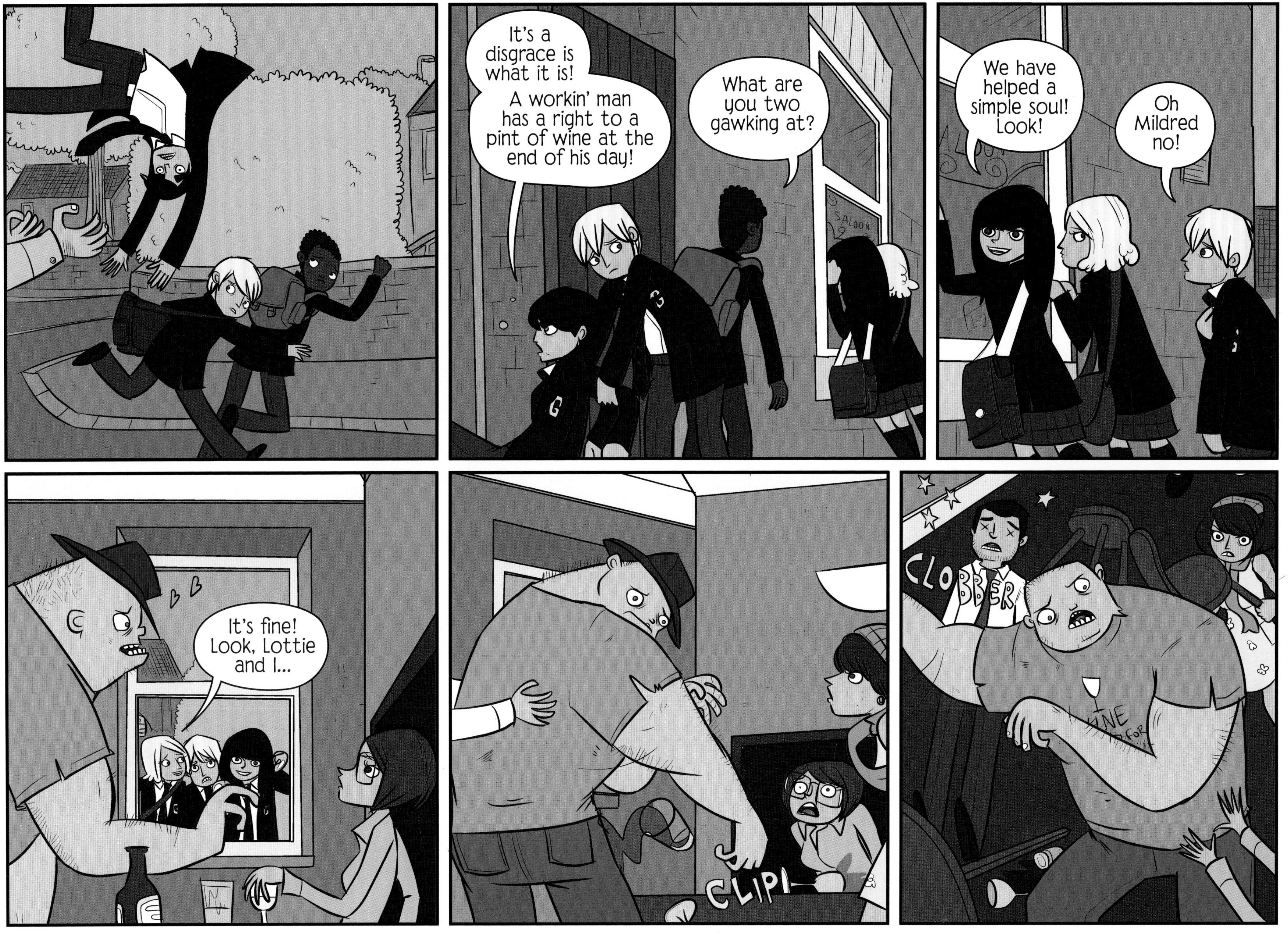

It's a disgrace is what it is!
A workin' man has a right to a pint of wine at the end of his day!
What are you two gawking at?
SALOON
We have helped a simple soul! Look!
Oh Mildred no!
It's fine! Look, Lottie and I...
CLIP!
CLOBBER

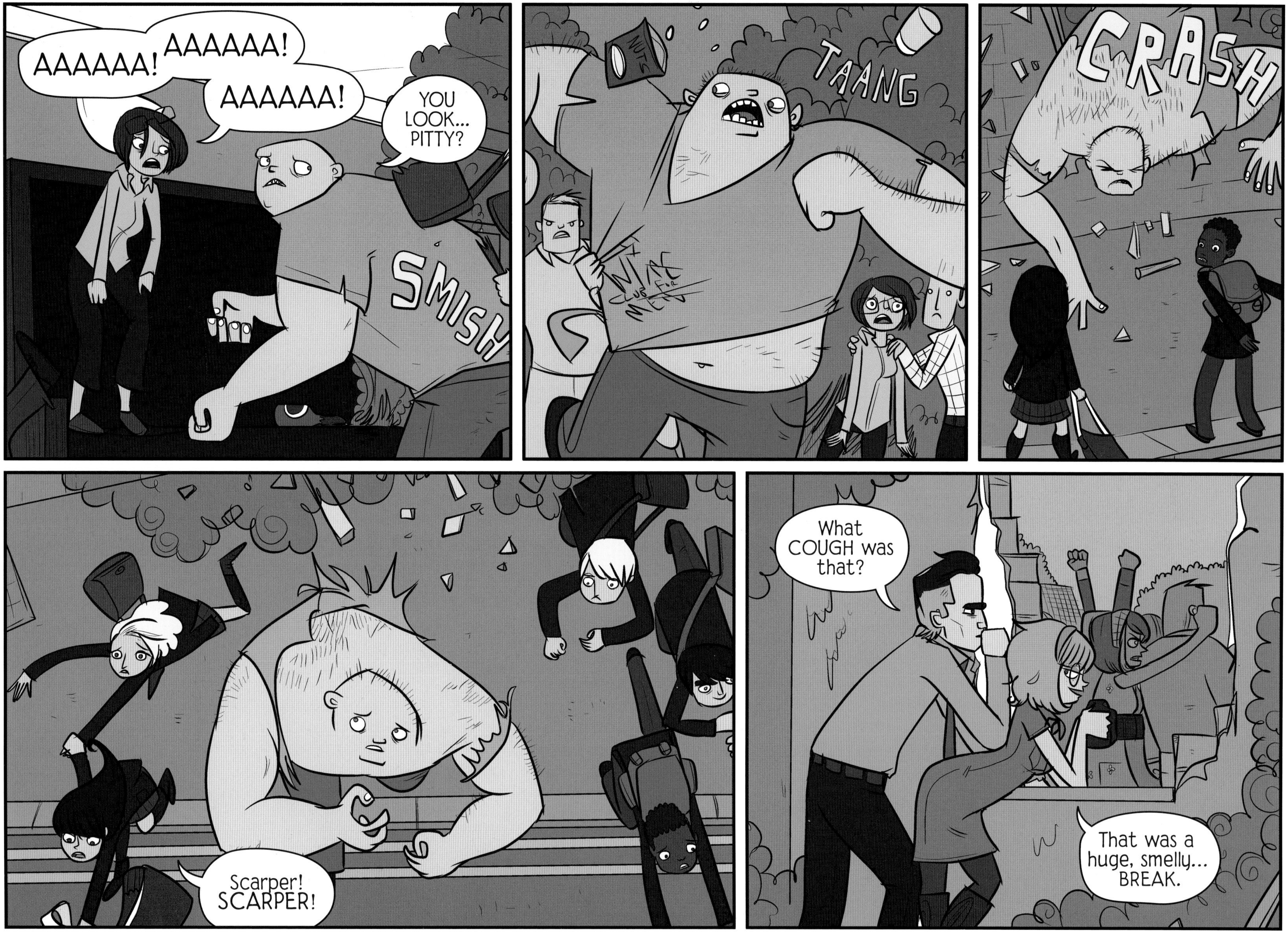
AAAAAA!
AAAAAA!
AAAAAA!
YOU LOOK... PITTY?
SMISH
TAANG
NUTS
CRASH
Scarper! SCARPER!
What COUGH was that?
That was a huge, smelly... BREAK.

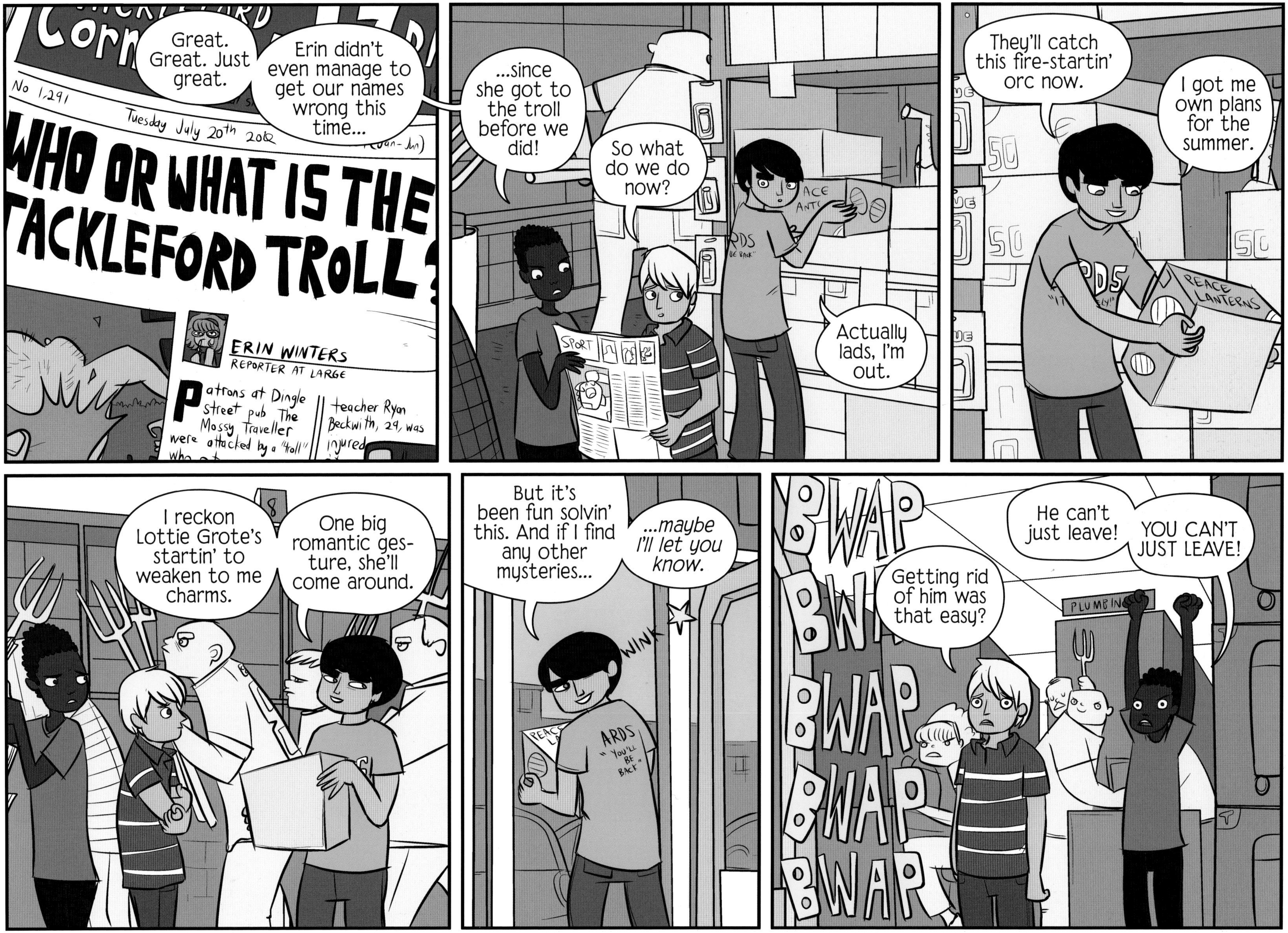
Great. Great. Just great.
Erin didn't even manage to get our names wrong this time...
No 1,291
Tuesday July 20th 2012
WHO OR WHAT IS THE TACKLEFORD TROLL?
ERIN WINTERS
REPORTER AT LARGE
Patrons at Dingle street pub The Mossy Traveller were attacked by a "troll"
teacher Ryan Beckwith, 29, was injured
...since she got to the troll before we did!
So what do we do now?
SPORT
Actually lads, I'm out.
They'll catch this fire-startin' orc now.
I got me own plans for the summer.
PEACE LANTERNS
I reckon Lottie Grote's startin' to weaken to me charms.
One big romantic gesture, she'll come around.
But it's been fun solvin' this. And if I find any other mysteries...
...maybe I'll let you know.
WINK
"YOU'LL BE BACK"
BWAP
BWAP
BWAP
BWAP
BWAP
BWAP
Getting rid of him was that easy?
He can't just leave!
YOU CAN'T JUST LEAVE!
PLUMBING

Bad Machinery, Volume Three

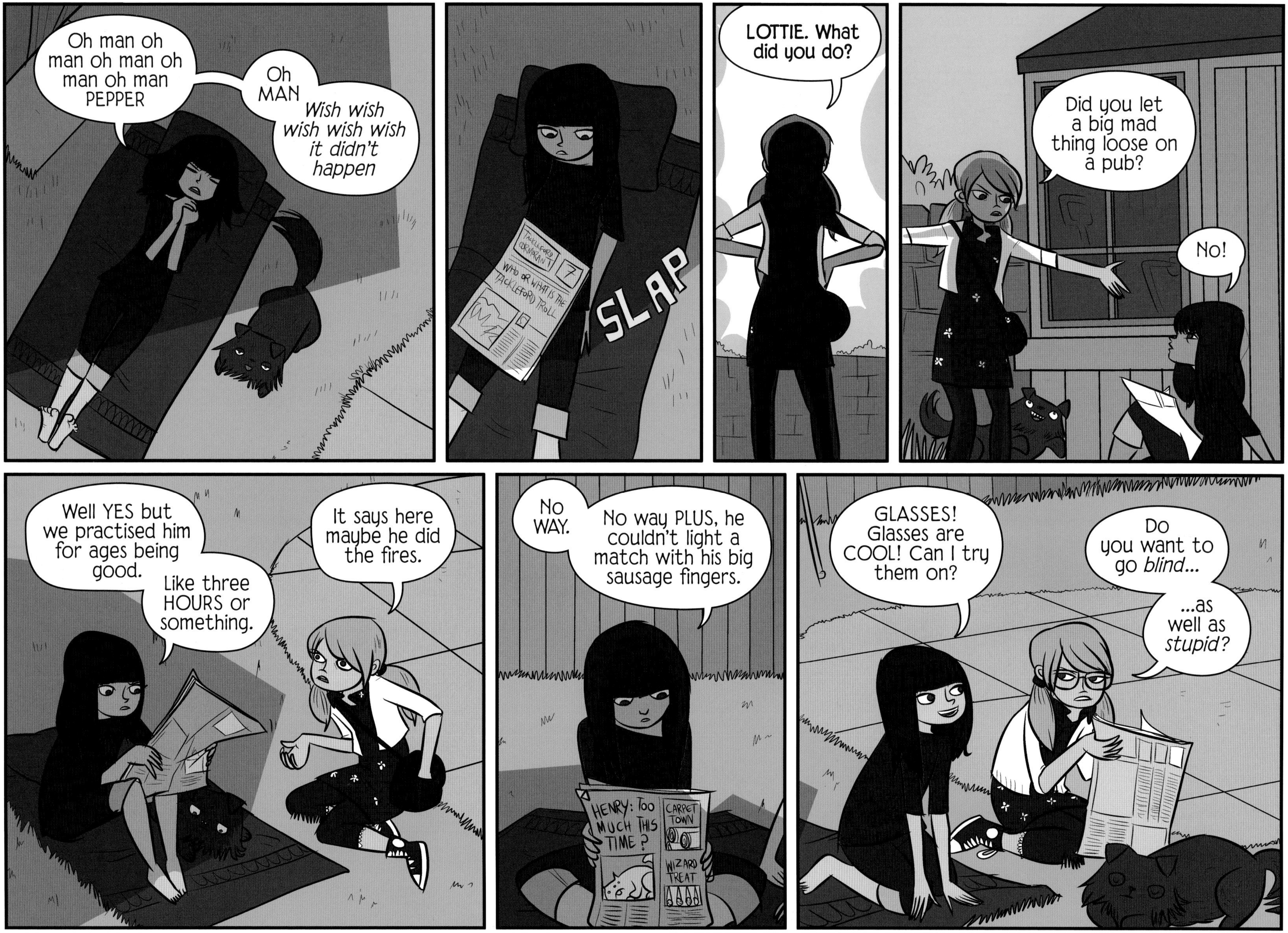
Oh man oh man oh man oh man oh man PEPPER
Oh MAN
Wish wish wish wish wish wish wish it didn't happen
TACKLEFORD CORMORANT 7
WHO OR WHAT IS THE TACKLEFORD TROLL
SLAP
LOTTIE. What did you do?
Did you let a big mad thing loose on a pub?
No!
Well YES but we practised him for ages being good.
Like three HOURS or something.
It says here maybe he did the fires.
No WAY.
No way PLUS, he couldn't light a match with his big sausage fingers.
HENRY: TOO MUCH THIS TIME?
CARPET TOWN
WIZARD TREAT
GLASSES! Glasses are COOL! Can I try them on?
Do you want to go *blind*...
...as well as *stupid*?

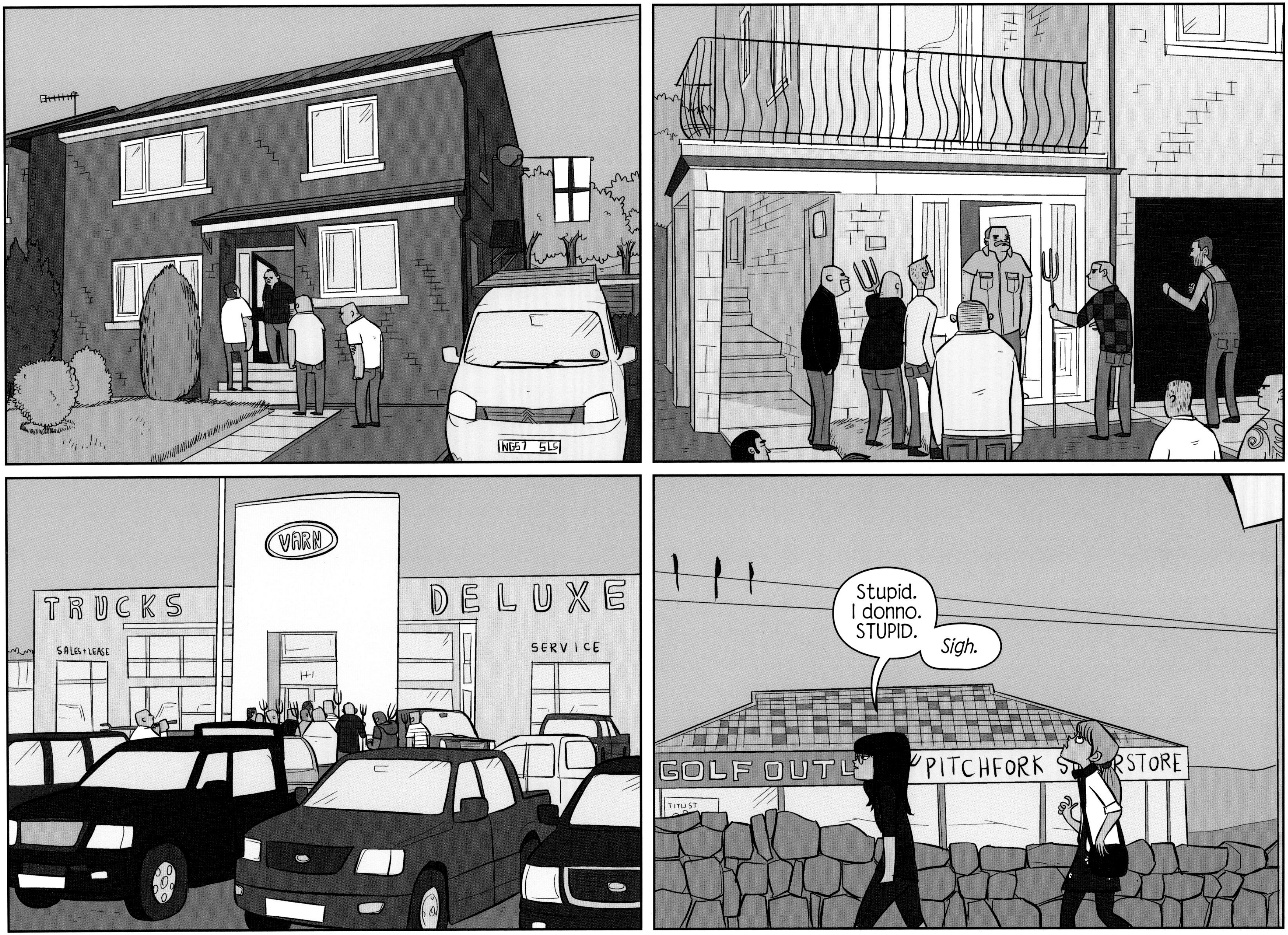
VARN
TRUCKS
DELUXE
SALES+LEASE
SERVICE
Stupid. I donno. STUPID.
Sigh.

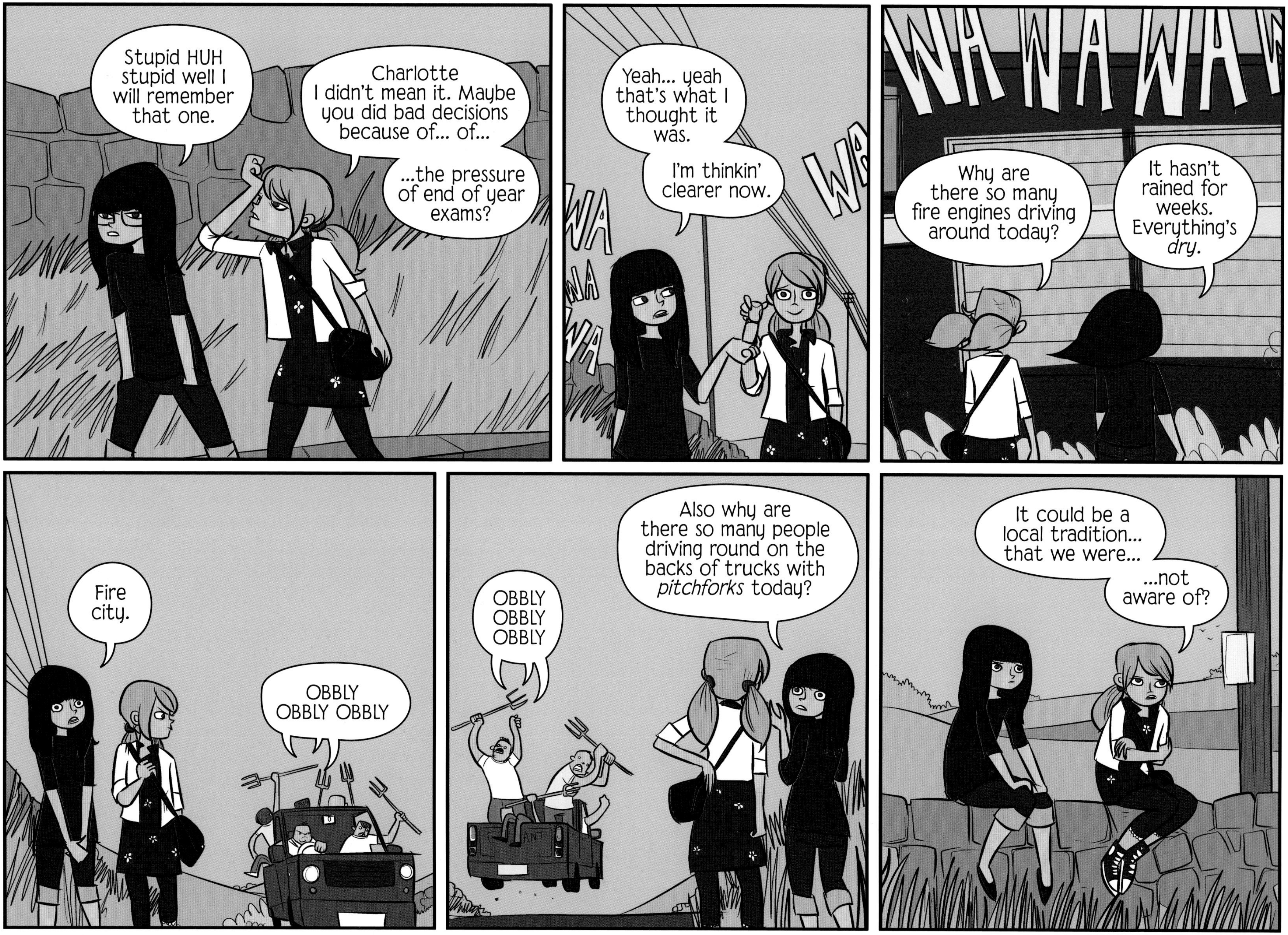

Stupid HUH stupid well I will remember that one.
Charlotte I didn't mean it. Maybe you did bad decisions because of... of...
...the pressure of end of year exams?
Yeah... yeah that's what I thought it was.
I'm thinkin' clearer now.
WA
WA
WA
WA
WA WA WA
Why are there so many fire engines driving around today?
It hasn't rained for weeks. Everything's *dry*.
Fire city.
OBBLY OBBLY OBBLY
OBBLY OBBLY OBBLY
Also why are there so many people driving round on the backs of trucks with *pitchforks* today?
It could be a local tradition... that we were...
...not aware of?

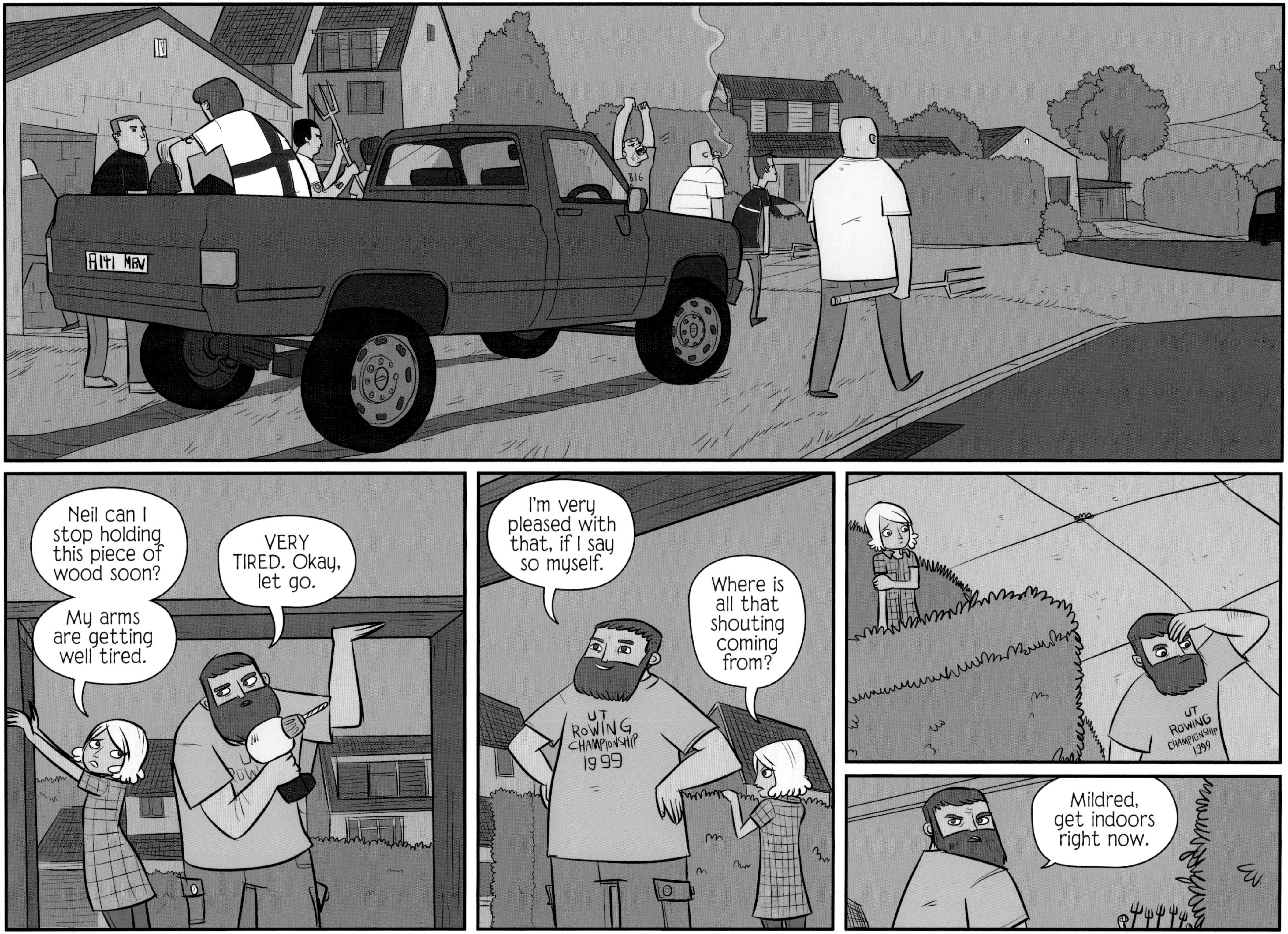
Neil can I stop holding this piece of wood soon?
My arms are getting well tired.
VERY TIRED. Okay, let go.
I'm very pleased with that, if I say so myself.
Where is all that shouting coming from?
Mildred, get indoors right now.

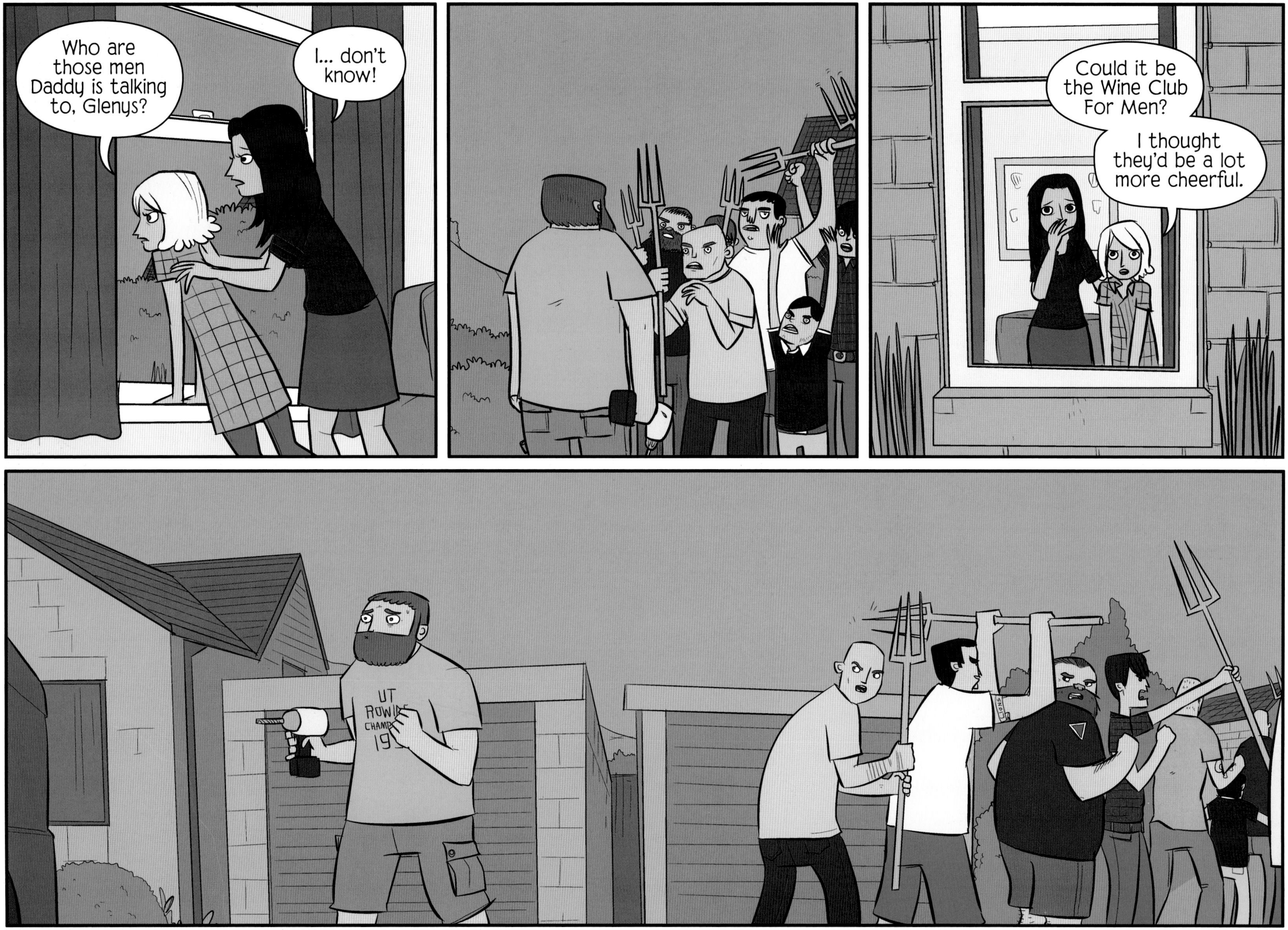
Who are those men Daddy is talking to, Glenys?
I... don't know!
Could it be the Wine Club For Men?
I thought they'd be a lot more cheerful.

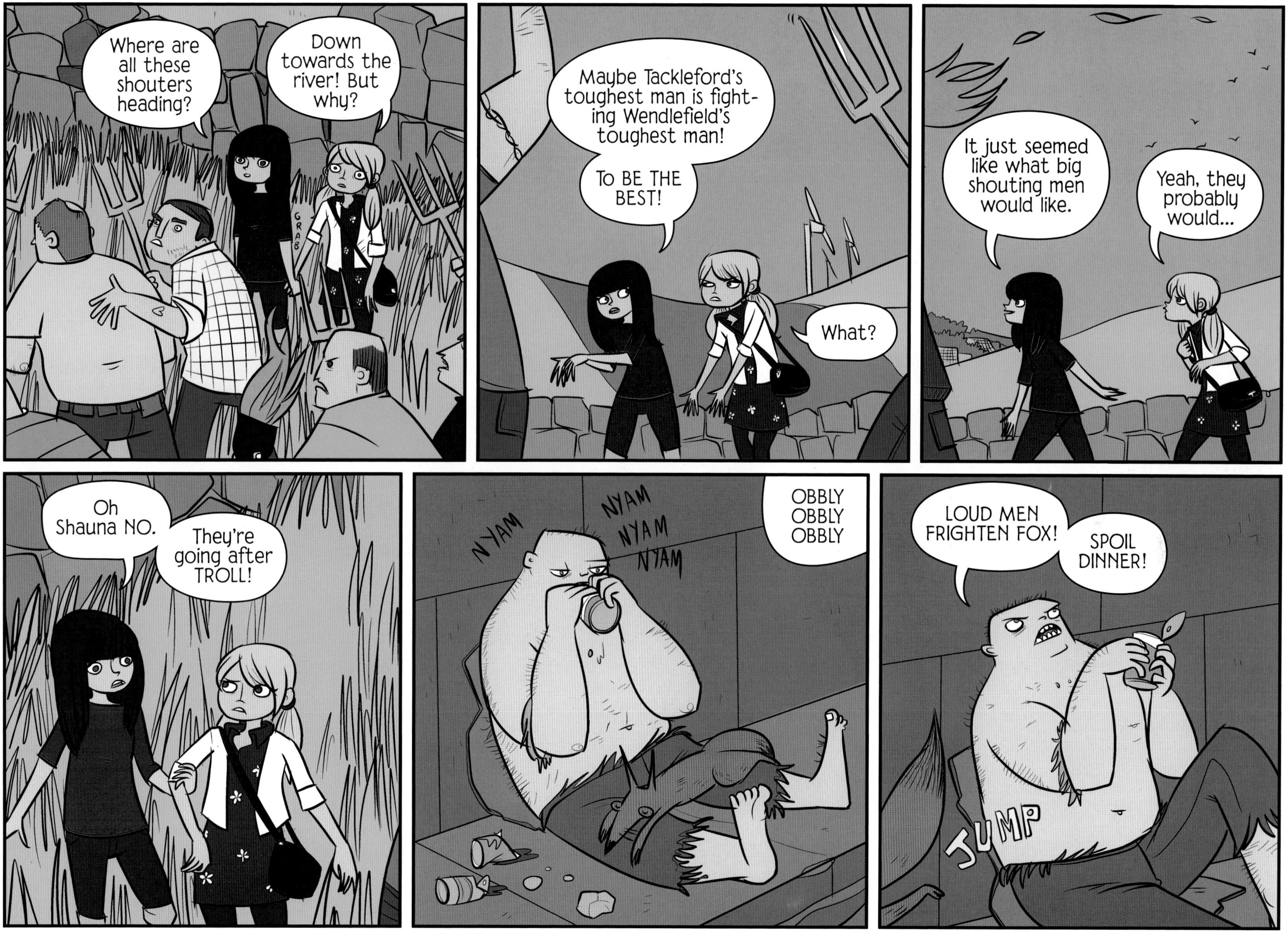
Where are all these shouters heading?
Down towards the river! But why?
GRAB
Maybe Tackleford's toughest man is fighting Wendlefield's toughest man!
To BE THE BEST!
What?
It just seemed like what big shouting men would like.
Yeah, they probably would...
Oh Shauna NO.
They're going after TROLL!
NYAM
NYAM NYAM NYAM
OBBLY OBBLY OBBLY
LOUD MEN FRIGHTEN FOX!
SPOIL DINNER!
JUMP

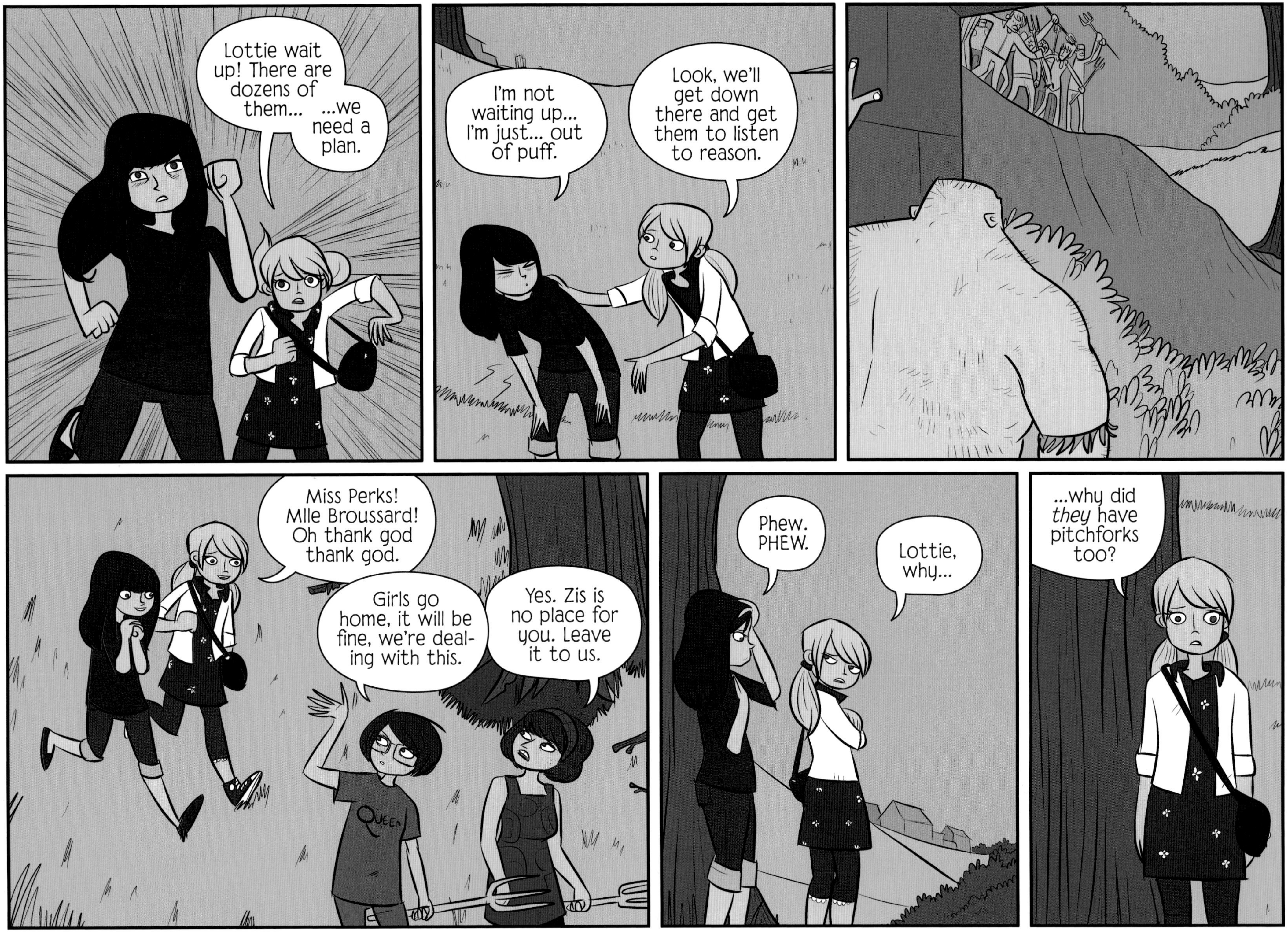
Lottie wait up! There are dozens of them... ...we need a plan.
I'm not waiting up... I'm just... out of puff.
Look, we'll get down there and get them to listen to reason.
Miss Perks! Mlle Broussard! Oh thank god thank god.
Girls go home, it will be fine, we're dealing with this.
Yes. Zis is no place for you. Leave it to us.
QUEEN
Phew. PHEW.
Lottie, why...
...why did *they* have pitchforks too?

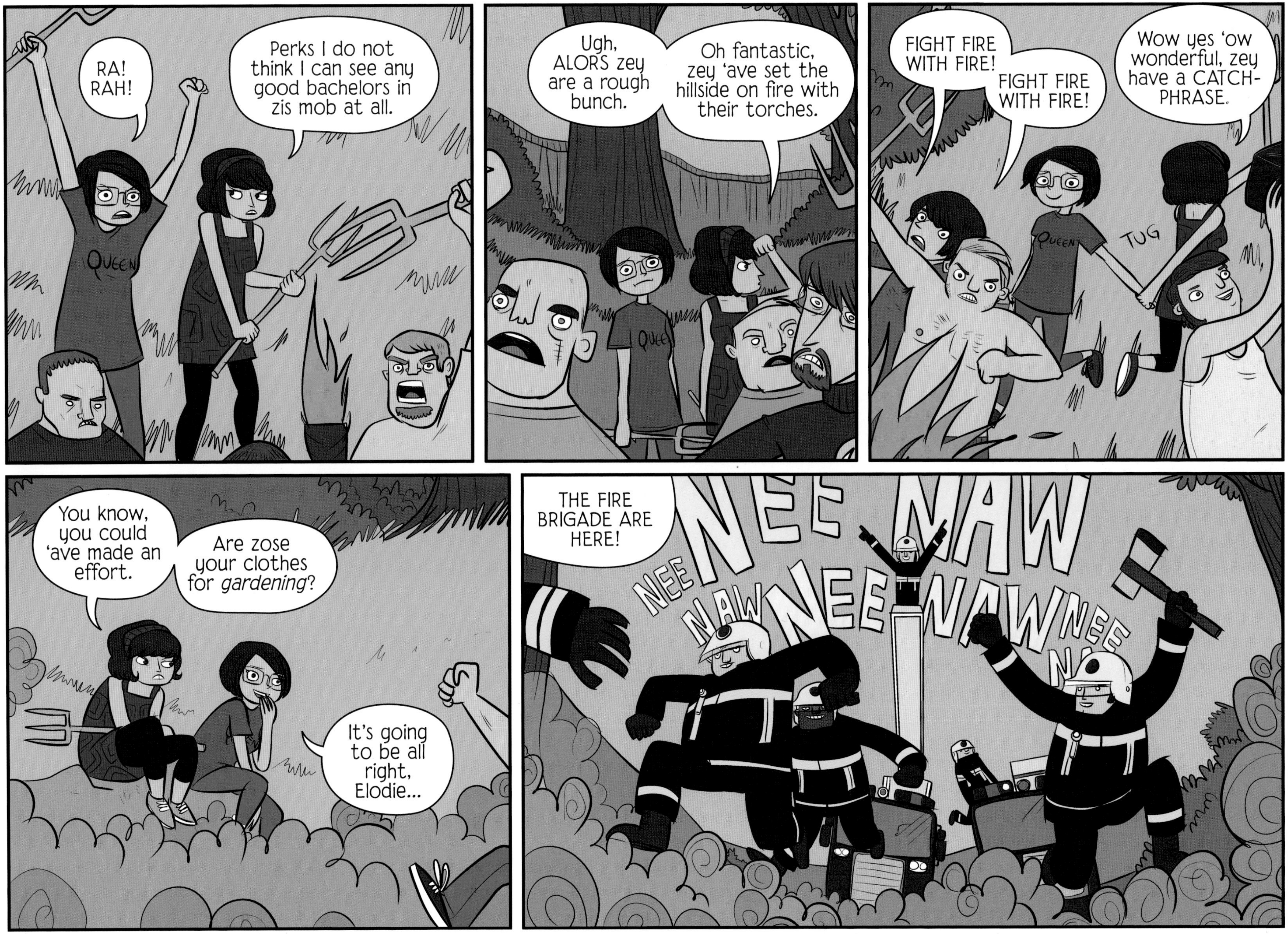
RA! RAH!
Perks I do not think I can see any good bachelors in zis mob at all.
Ugh, ALORS zey are a rough bunch.
Oh fantastic, zey 'ave set the hillside on fire with their torches.
FIGHT FIRE WITH FIRE!
FIGHT FIRE WITH FIRE!
Wow yes 'ow wonderful, zey have a CATCH-PHRASE.
TUG
You know, you could 'ave made an effort.
Are zose your clothes for *gardening*?
It's going to be all right, Elodie...
THE FIRE BRIGADE ARE HERE!
NEE NAW
NEE
NAW NEE NAW NEE

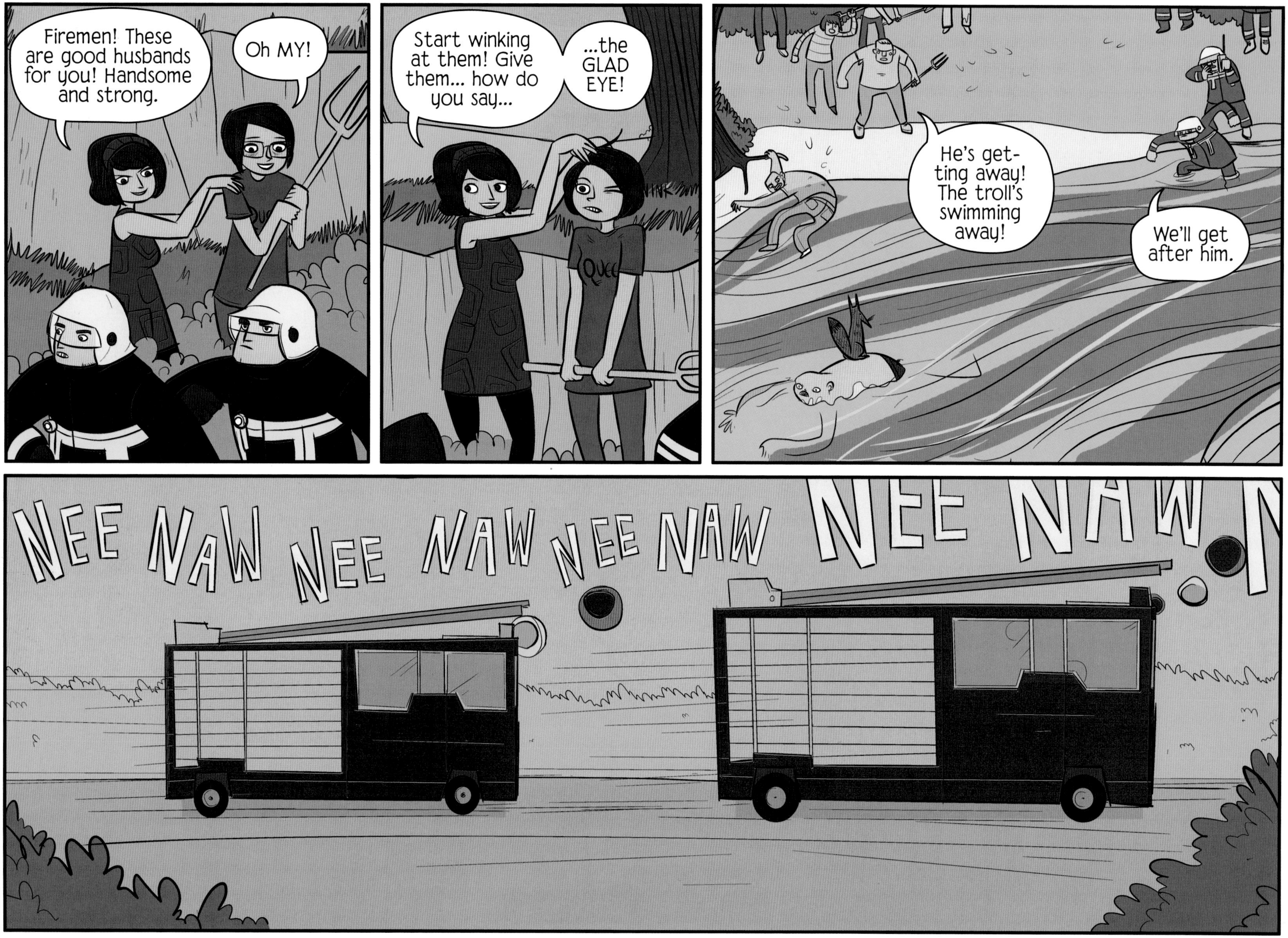

Firemen! These are good husbands for you! Handsome and strong.
Oh MY!
Start winking at them! Give them... how do you say...
...the GLAD EYE!
He's get-ting away! The troll's swimming away!
We'll get after him.
NEE NAW NEE NAW NEE NAW NEE NAW

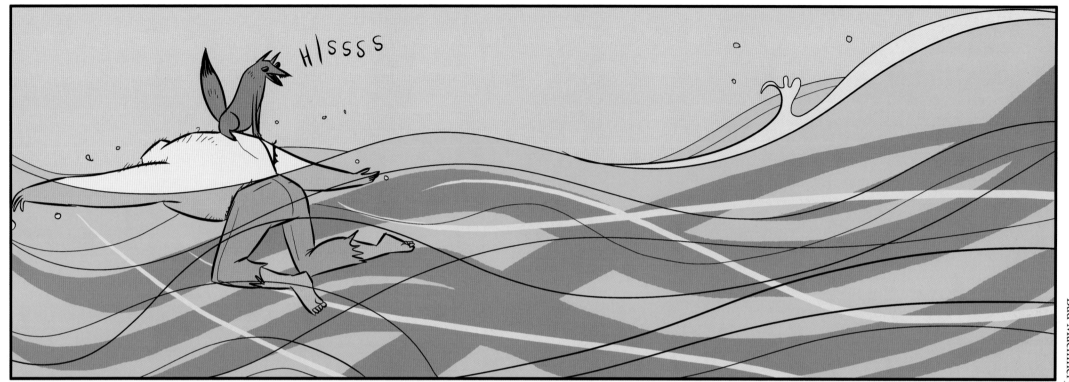

HISSSS

NEE NAW NEE NAW NEE NAW NEE NAW

TWANG

A mob is a very interestin' creature, Charlotte.

An animal without a brain.

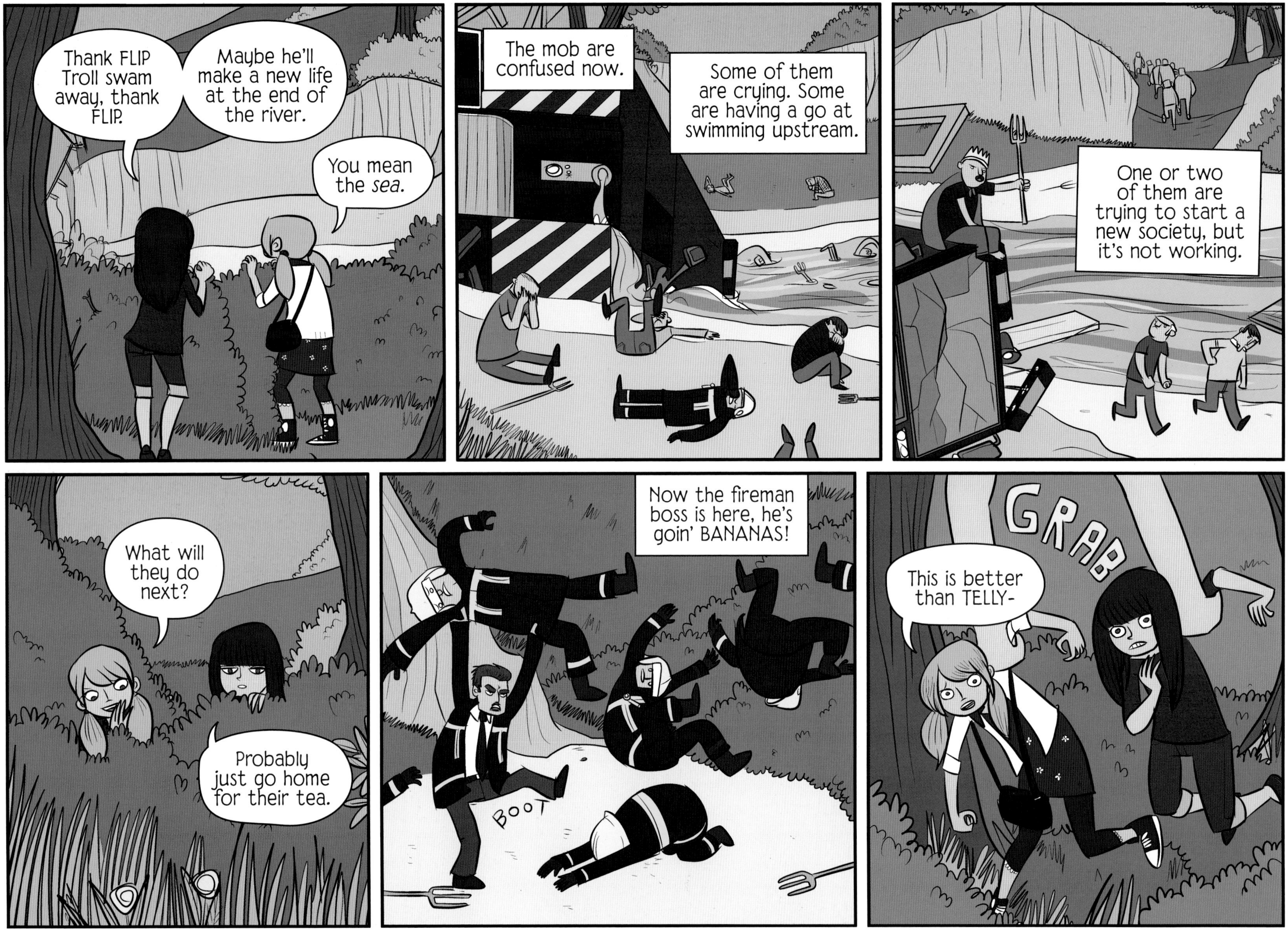
Thank FLIP Troll swam away, thank FLIP.
Maybe he'll make a new life at the end of the river.
You mean the *sea*.
The mob are confused now.
Some of them are crying. Some are having a go at swimming upstream.
One or two of them are trying to start a new society, but it's not working.
What will they do next?
Probably just go home for their tea.
Now the fireman boss is here, he's goin' BANANAS!
BOOT
GRAB
This is better than TELLY-

The Case of Simple Soul

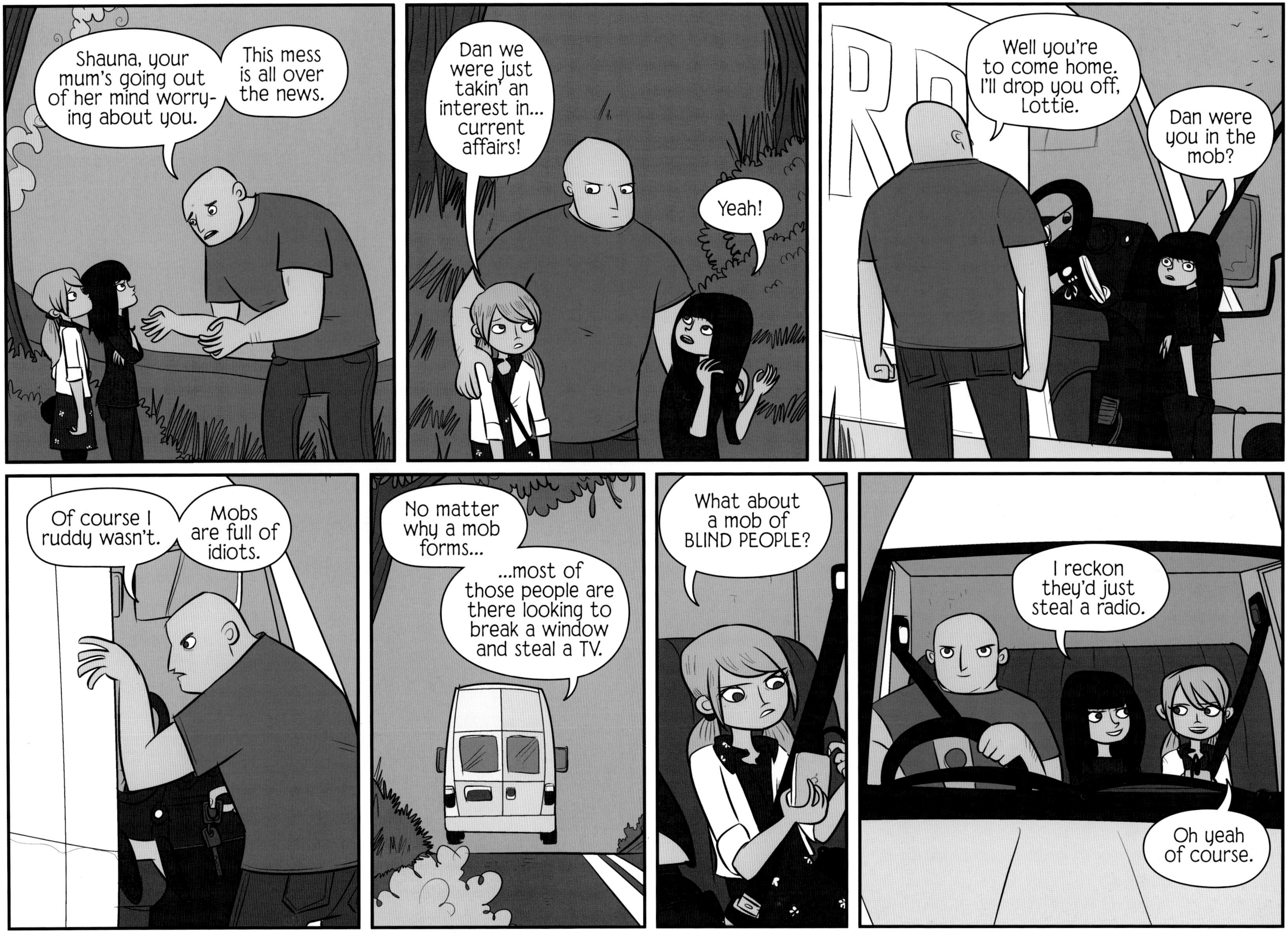
Shauna, your mum's going out of her mind worrying about you.
This mess is all over the news.
Dan we were just takin' an interest in... current affairs!
Yeah!
Well you're to come home. I'll drop you off, Lottie.
Dan were you in the mob?
Of course I ruddy wasn't.
Mobs are full of idiots.
No matter why a mob forms...
...most of those people are there looking to break a window and steal a TV.
What about a mob of BLIND PEOPLE?
I reckon they'd just steal a radio.
Oh yeah of course.

Get inside, stay inside, wait for your mum to come home.
All right Dan!
Ugh Colm what are you doing here?
Go home to whatever mad shed it is you live in.
I got some-thin' to show you round the back. Something you're gonna like.
Close your eyes and come with me.
I DON'T TRUST YOU.
You'll put the garden hose on me or something.
CAN I OPEN THEM?
Ah actually er maybe you shouldn't oughta open them. Let's go back round.
Why are you shoving-
SHRUG
COLM!
WHAT HAVE YOU DONE?

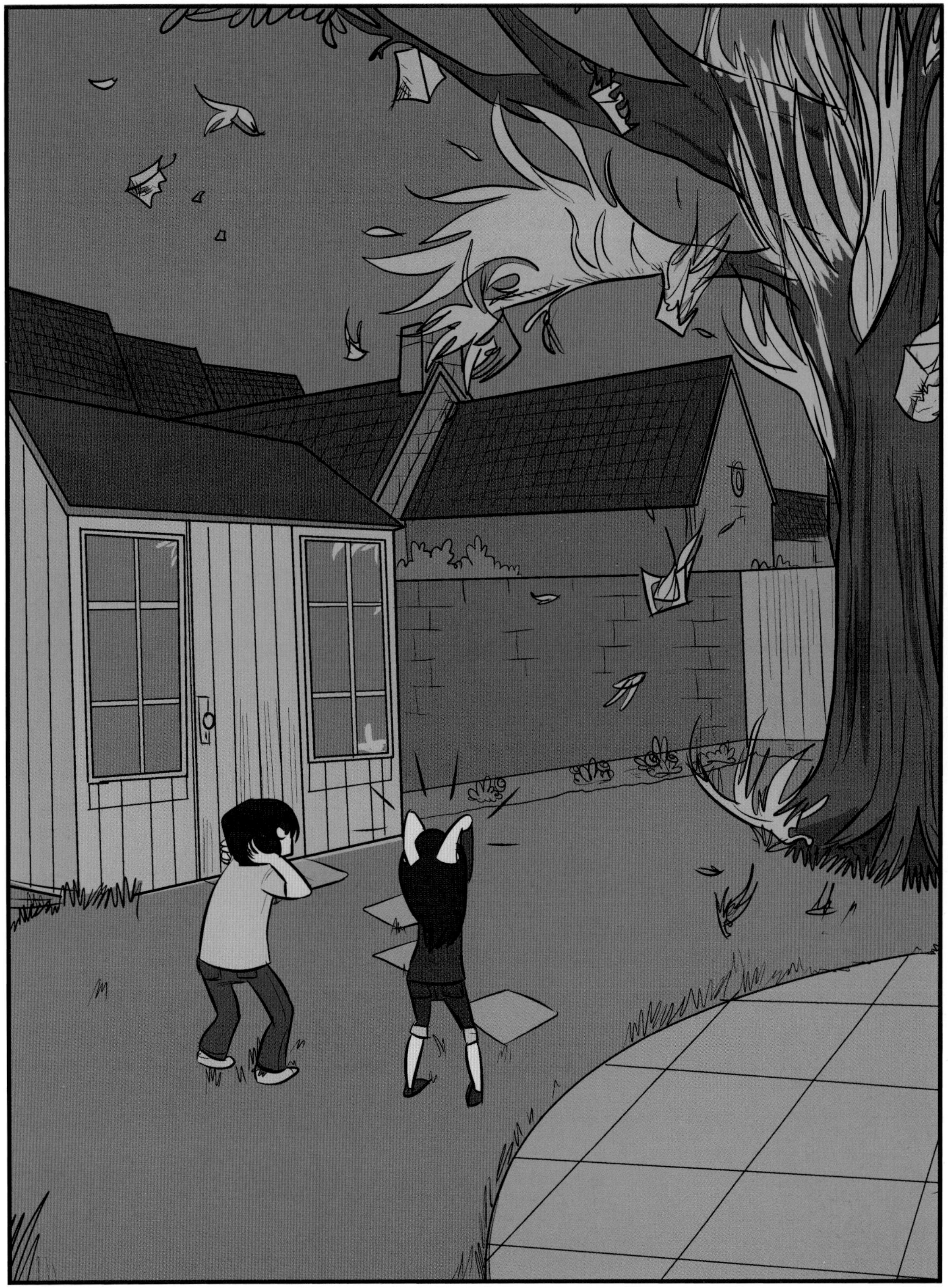

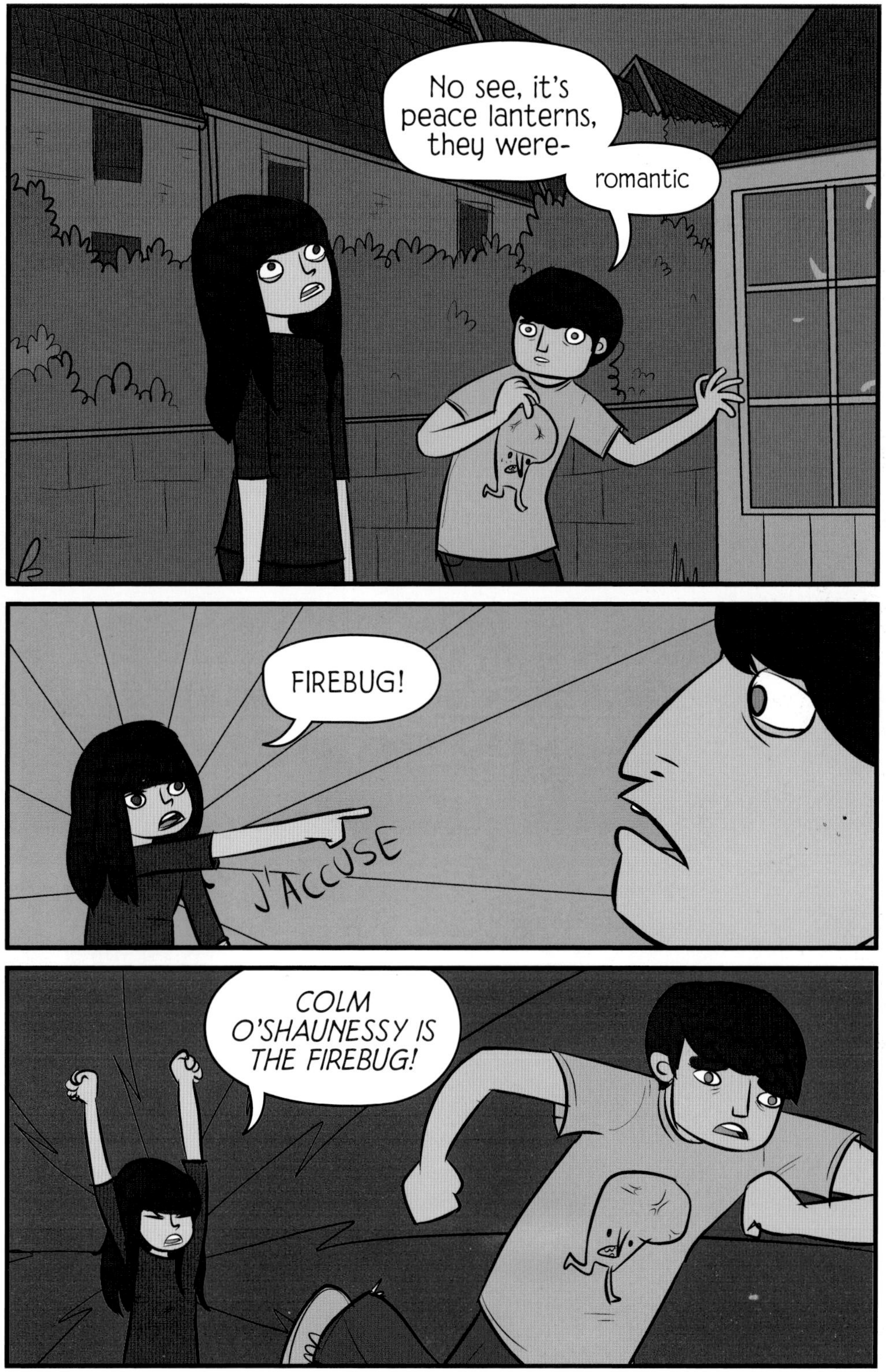
No see, it's peace lanterns, they were-
romantic
FIREBUG!
J'ACCUSE
COLM O'SHAUNESSY IS THE FIREBUG!

Bad Machinery, Volume Three

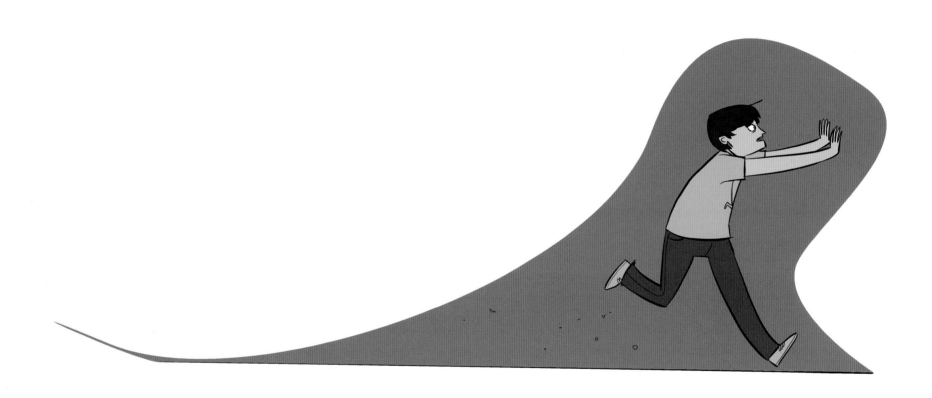

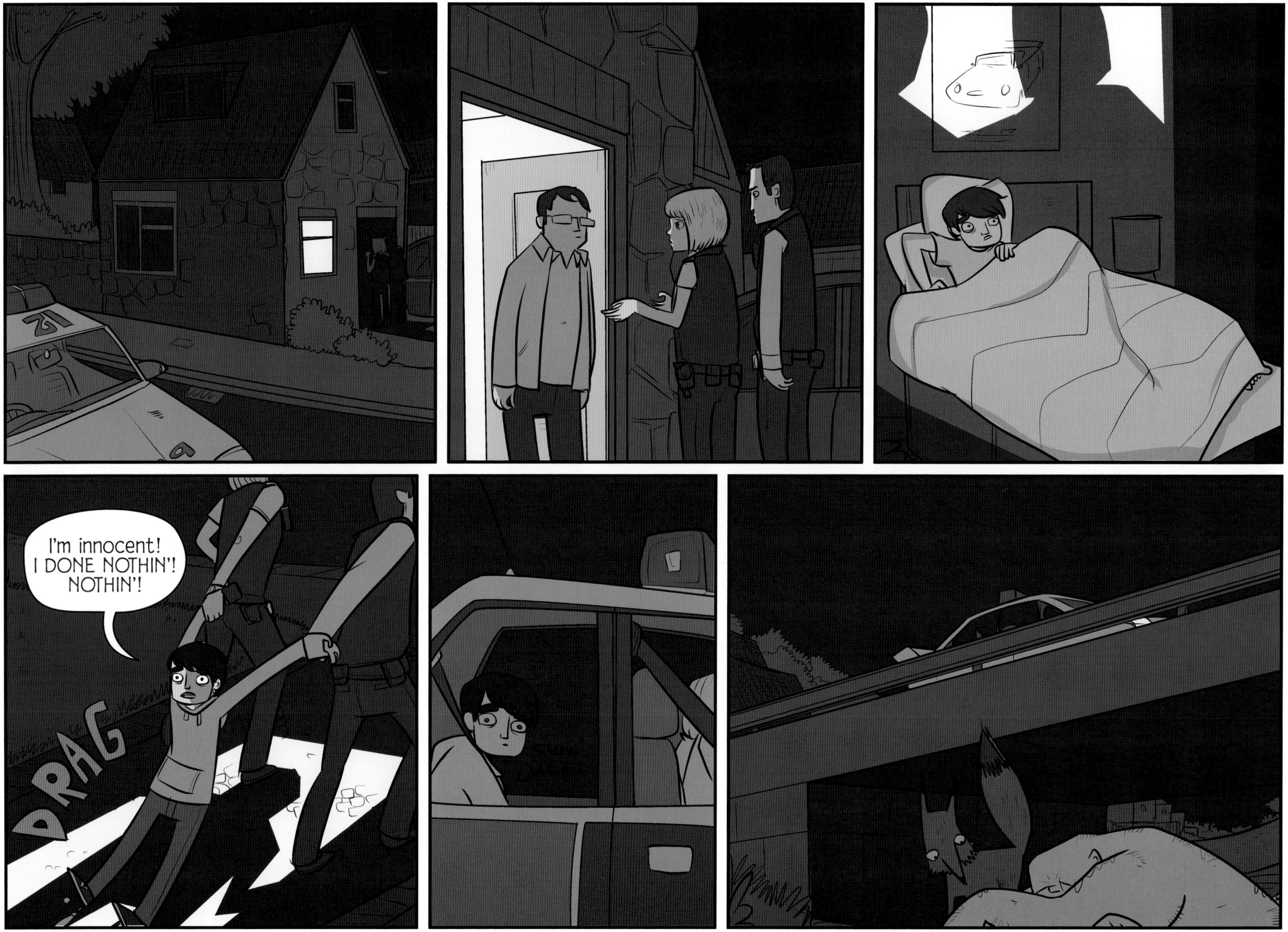
I'm innocent!
I DONE NOTHIN'!
NOTHIN'!
DRAG

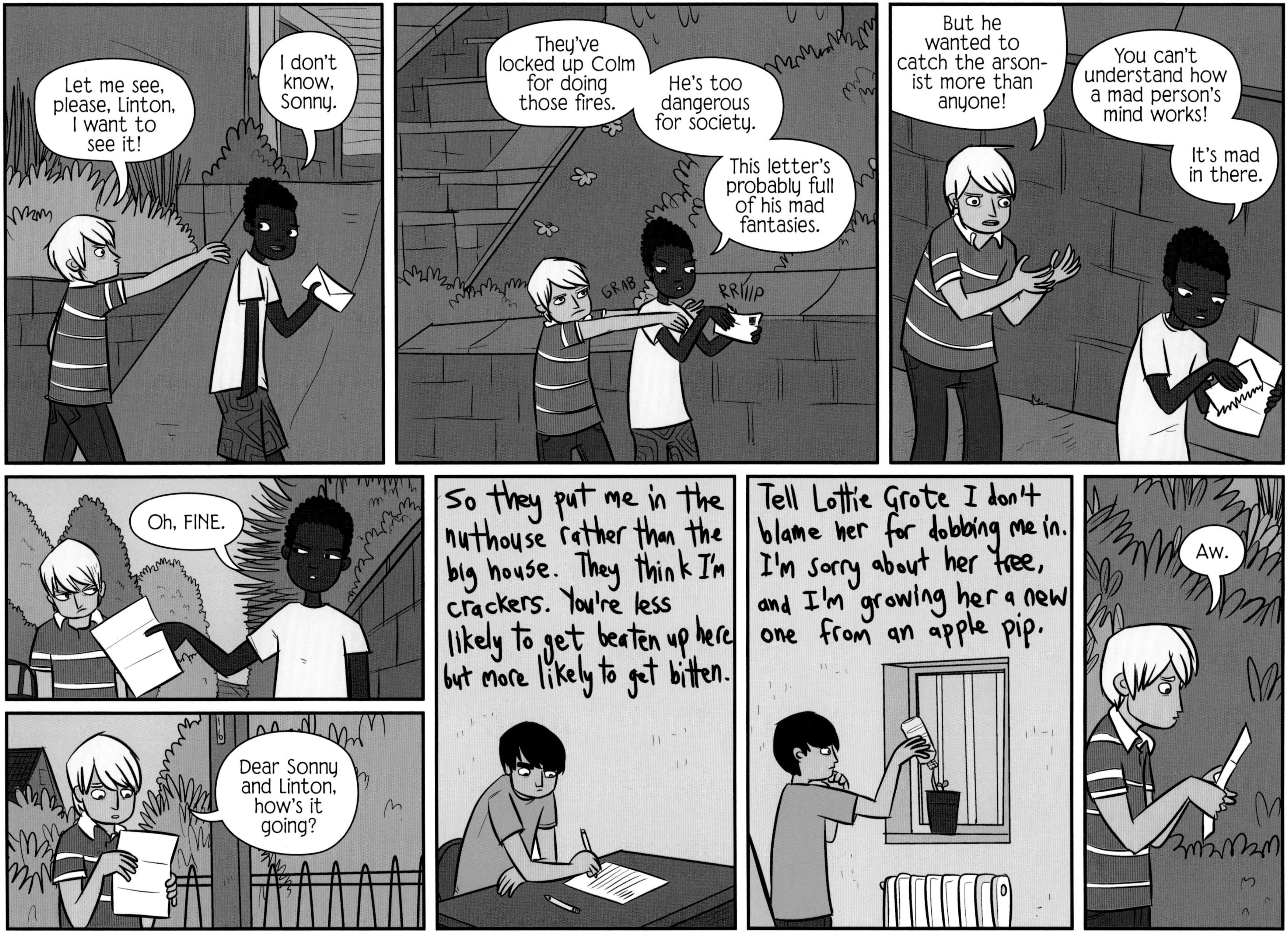
Let me see, please, Linton, I want to see it!
I don't know, Sonny.
They've locked up Colm for doing those fires.
He's too dangerous for society.
GRAB
RRIIIP
This letter's probably full of his mad fantasies.
But he wanted to catch the arson-ist more than anyone!
You can't understand how a mad person's mind works!
It's mad in there.
Oh, FINE.
Dear Sonny and Linton, how's it going?
So they put me in the nuthouse rather than the big house. They think I'm crackers. You're less likely to get beaten up here but more likely to get bitten.
Tell Lottie Grote I don't blame her for dobbing me in. I'm sorry about her tree, and I'm growing her a new one from an apple pip.
Aw.

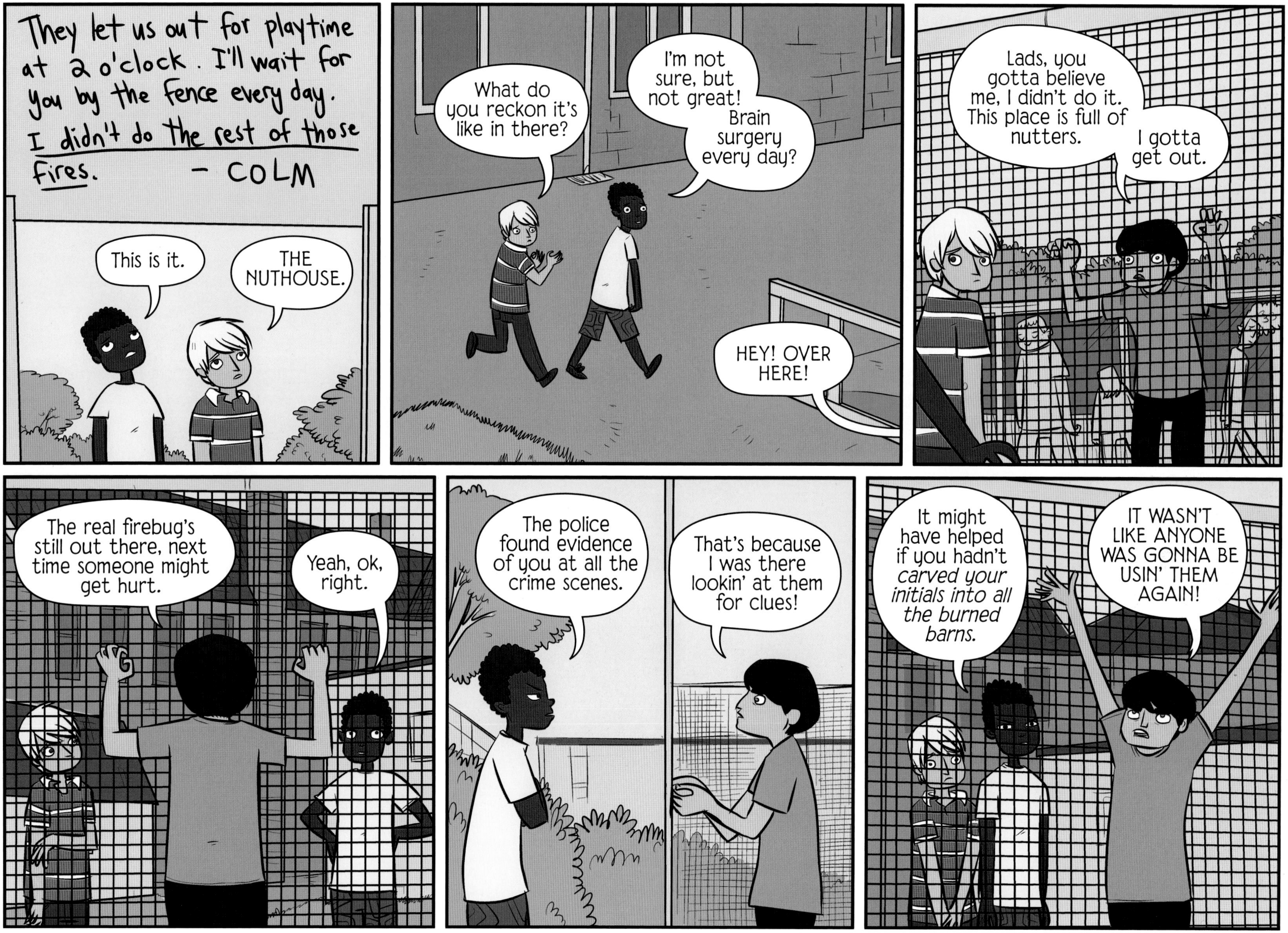
They let us out for playtime at 2 o'clock. I'll wait for you by the fence every day. I didn't do the rest of those fires. - COLM
This is it.
THE NUTHOUSE.
What do you reckon it's like in there?
I'm not sure, but not great!
Brain surgery every day?
HEY! OVER HERE!
Lads, you gotta believe me, I didn't do it. This place is full of nutters.
I gotta get out.
The real firebug's still out there, next time someone might get hurt.
Yeah, ok, right.
The police found evidence of you at all the crime scenes.
That's because I was there lookin' at them for clues!
It might have helped if you hadn't *carved your initials into all the burned barns.*
IT WASN'T LIKE ANYONE WAS GONNA BE USIN' THEM AGAIN!

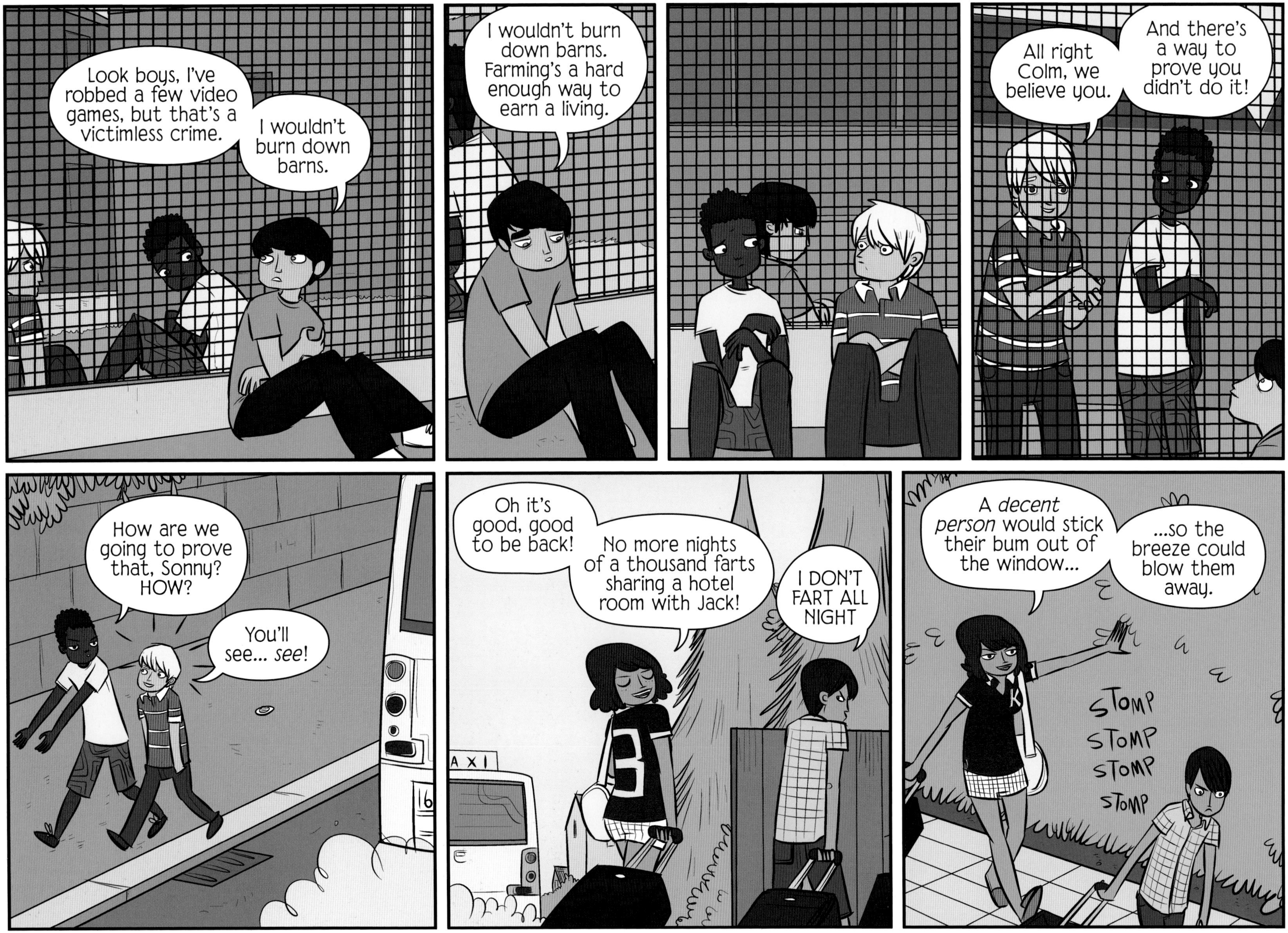
Look boys, I've robbed a few video games, but that's a victimless crime.
I wouldn't burn down barns.
I wouldn't burn down barns. Farming's a hard enough way to earn a living.
All right Colm, we believe you.
And there's a way to prove you didn't do it!
How are we going to prove that, Sonny? HOW?
You'll see... *see*!
Oh it's good, good to be back!
No more nights of a thousand farts sharing a hotel room with Jack!
I DON'T FART ALL NIGHT
A *decent person* would stick their bum out of the window...
...so the breeze could blow them away.
STOMP
STOMP
STOMP
STOMP

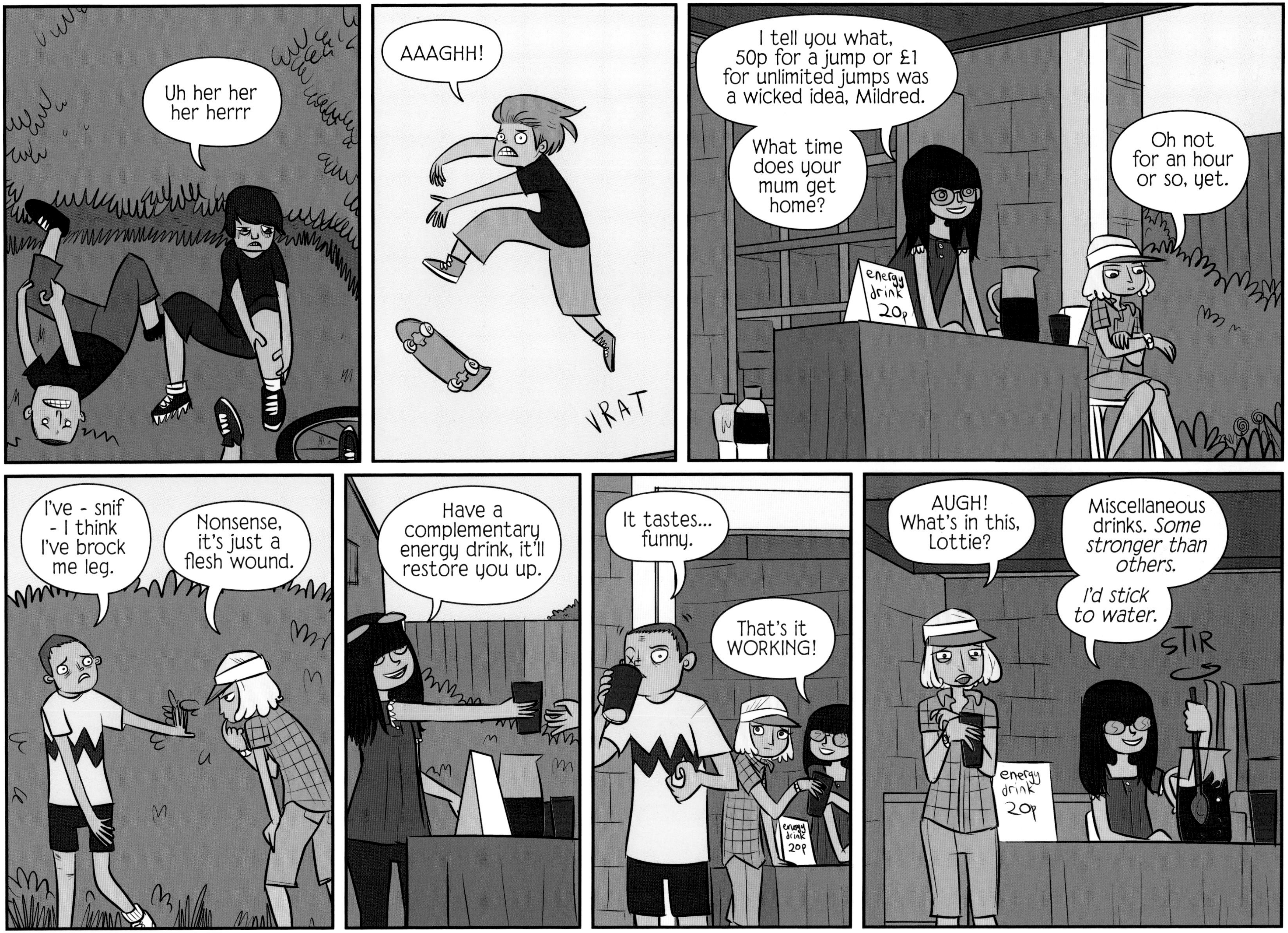
Uh her her her herrr
AAAGHH!
VRAT
I tell you what, 50p for a jump or £1 for unlimited jumps was a wicked idea, Mildred.
What time does your mum get home?
energy drink 20p
Oh not for an hour or so, yet.
I've - snif - I think I've brock me leg.
Nonsense, it's just a flesh wound.
Have a complementary energy drink, it'll restore you up.
It tastes... funny.
That's it WORKING!
energy drink 20p
AUGH! What's in this, Lottie?
Miscellaneous drinks. *Some stronger than others.*
I'd stick to water.
STIR
energy drink 20p

Pack it up, pack it up!

No more jumps today! No more "energy drink"!

SHOO

JACK IS BACK.

Oh hello *Jack.*

Fancy a ramp jump before we pack up? 50p!

Do you think...

...I'm MENTAL?

Your loss, it's well the thrill of a lifetime.

FLIP LOTTIE, IT'S MY MUM! We got greedy!

Jack! Pull that handle!

CHUNK CHONK

LEAP

DART

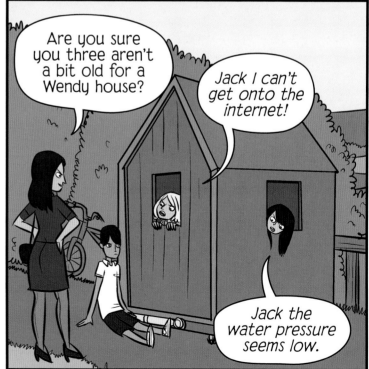

Are you sure you three aren't a bit old for a Wendy house?

Jack I can't get onto the internet!

Jack the water pressure seems low.

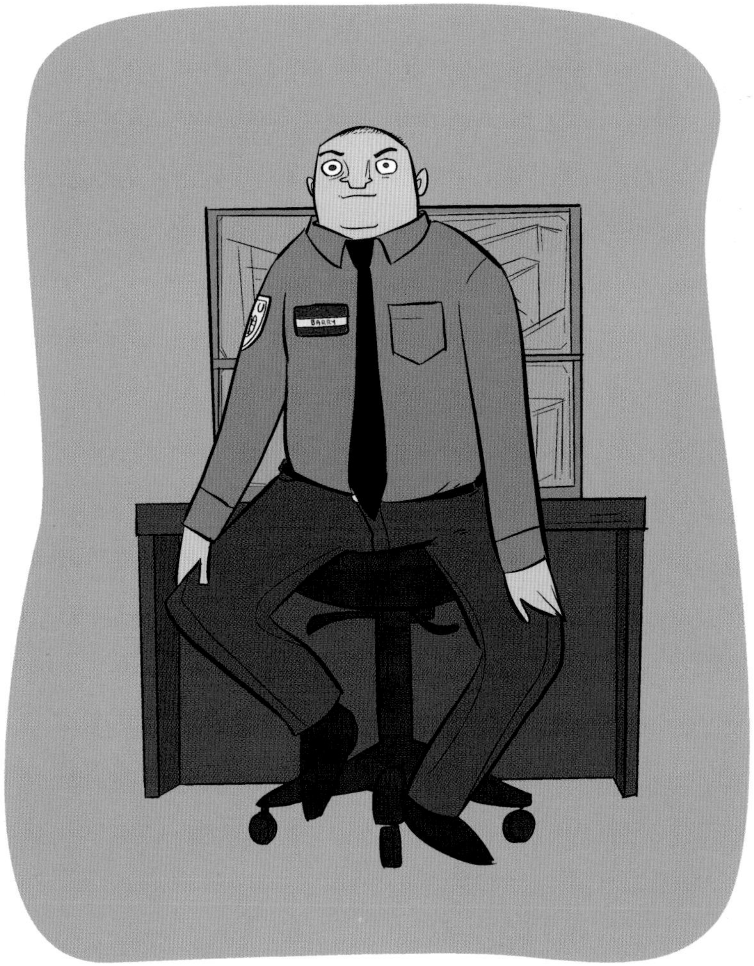
BARRY

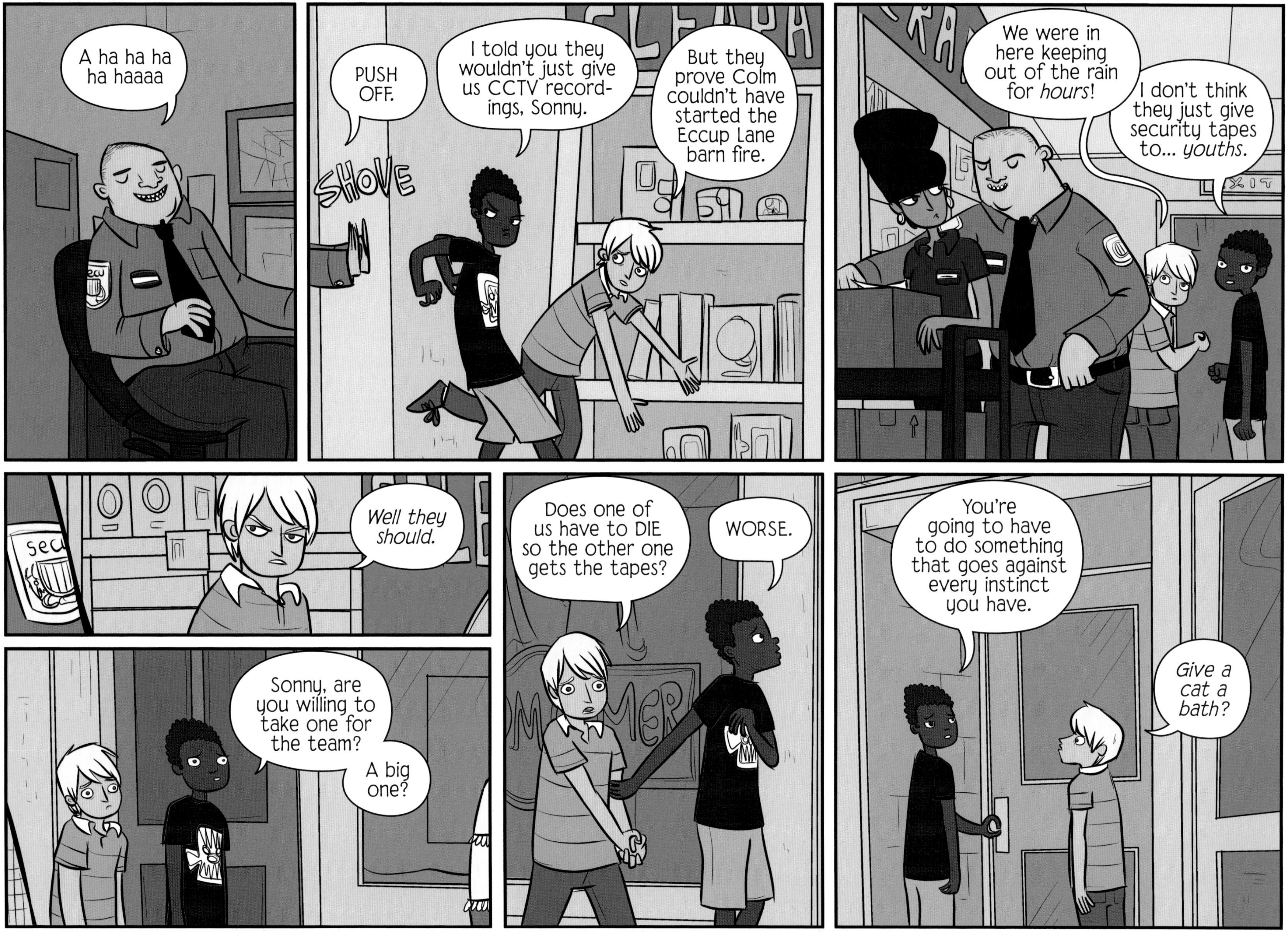
A ha ha ha ha haaaa
PUSH OFF.
SHOVE
I told you they wouldn't just give us CCTV recordings, Sonny.
But they prove Colm couldn't have started the Eccup Lane barn fire.
We were in here keeping out of the rain for *hours*!
I don't think they just give security tapes to... *youths*.
Well they should.
Sonny, are you willing to take one for the team?
A big one?
Does one of us have to DIE so the other one gets the tapes?
WORSE.
You're going to have to do something that goes against every instinct you have.
Give a cat a bath?

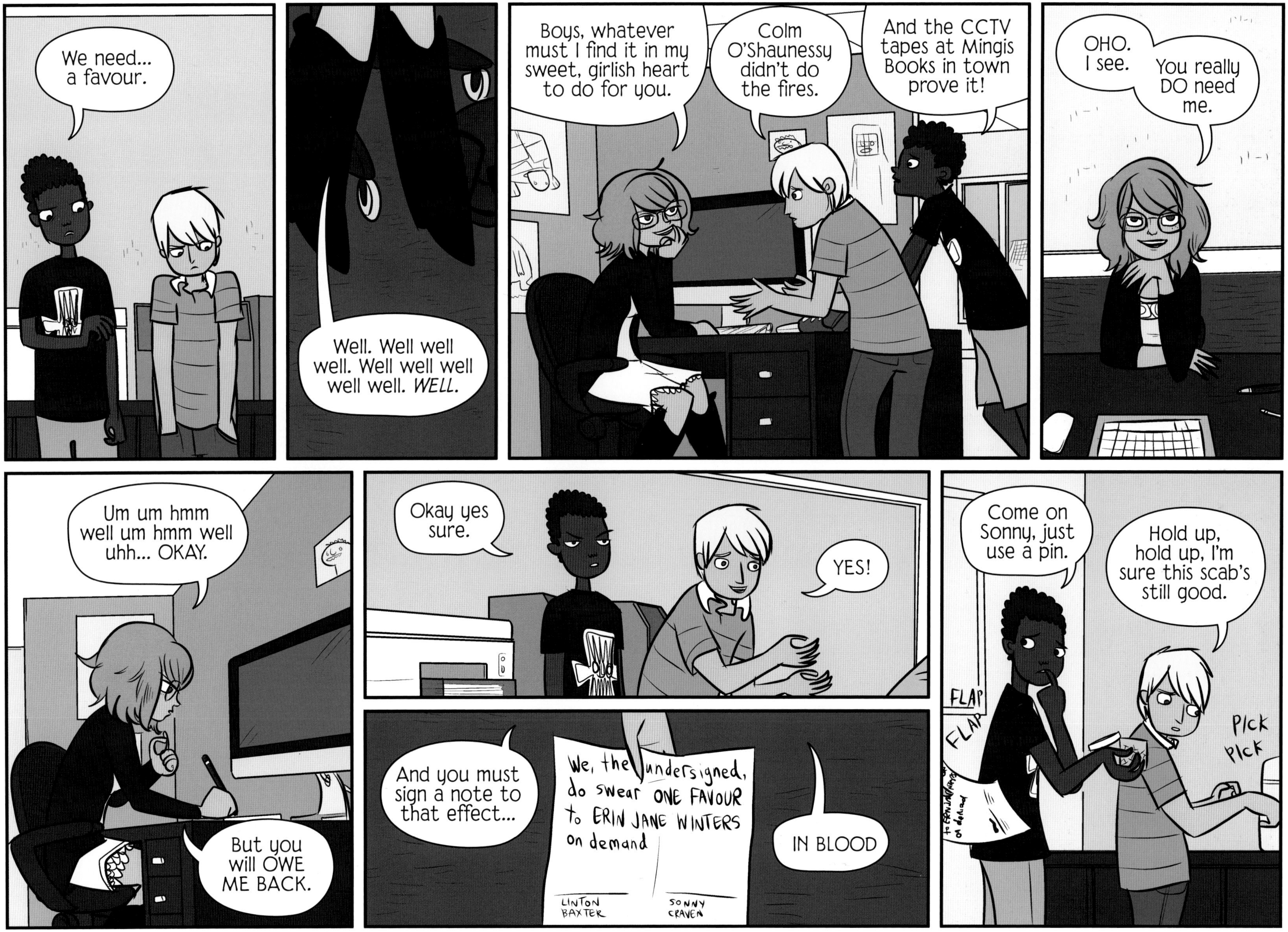
We need... a favour.
Well. Well well well. Well well well well well. WELL.
Boys, whatever must I find it in my sweet, girlish heart to do for you.
Colm O'Shaunessy didn't do the fires.
And the CCTV tapes at Mingis Books in town prove it!
OHO. I see.
You really DO need me.
Um um hmm well um hmm well uhh... OKAY.
But you will OWE ME BACK.
Okay yes sure.
YES!
And you must sign a note to that effect...
We, the undersigned, do swear ONE FAVOUR to ERIN JANE WINTERS on demand
LINTON BAXTER
SONNY CRAVEN
IN BLOOD
Come on Sonny, just use a pin.
Hold up, hold up, I'm sure this scab's still good.
FLAP
FLAP
PICK
PICK

Bad Machinery, Volume Three

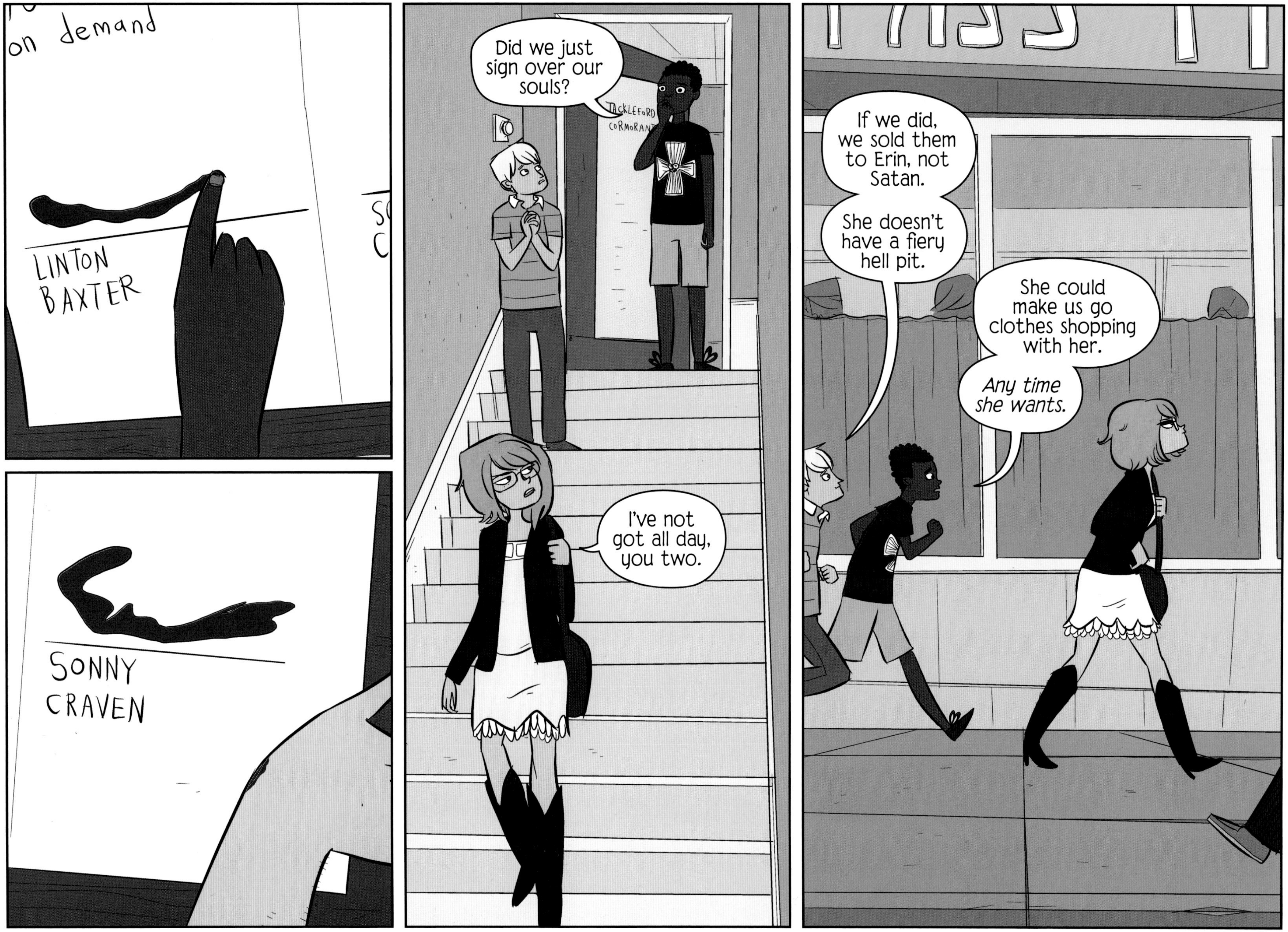
on demand
LINTON BAXTER
SONNY CRAVEN
Did we just sign over our souls?
TACKLEFORD CORMORANT
I've not got all day, you two.
If we did, we sold them to Erin, not Satan.
She doesn't have a fiery hell pit.
She could make us go clothes shopping with her.
Any time she wants.

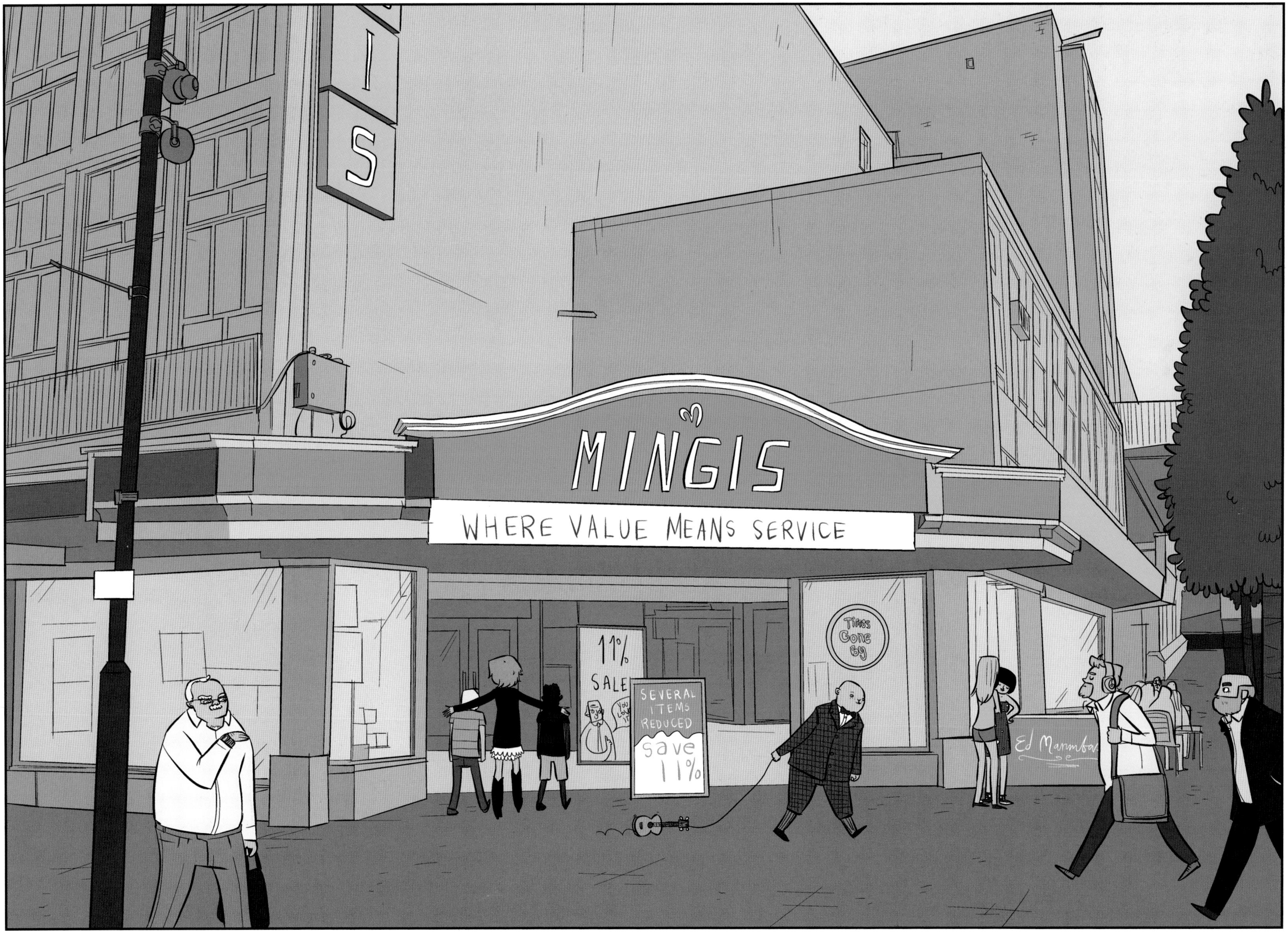
MINGIS
WHERE VALUE MEANS SERVICE
11% SALE
SEVERAL ITEMS REDUCED
save 11%
Times Gone By

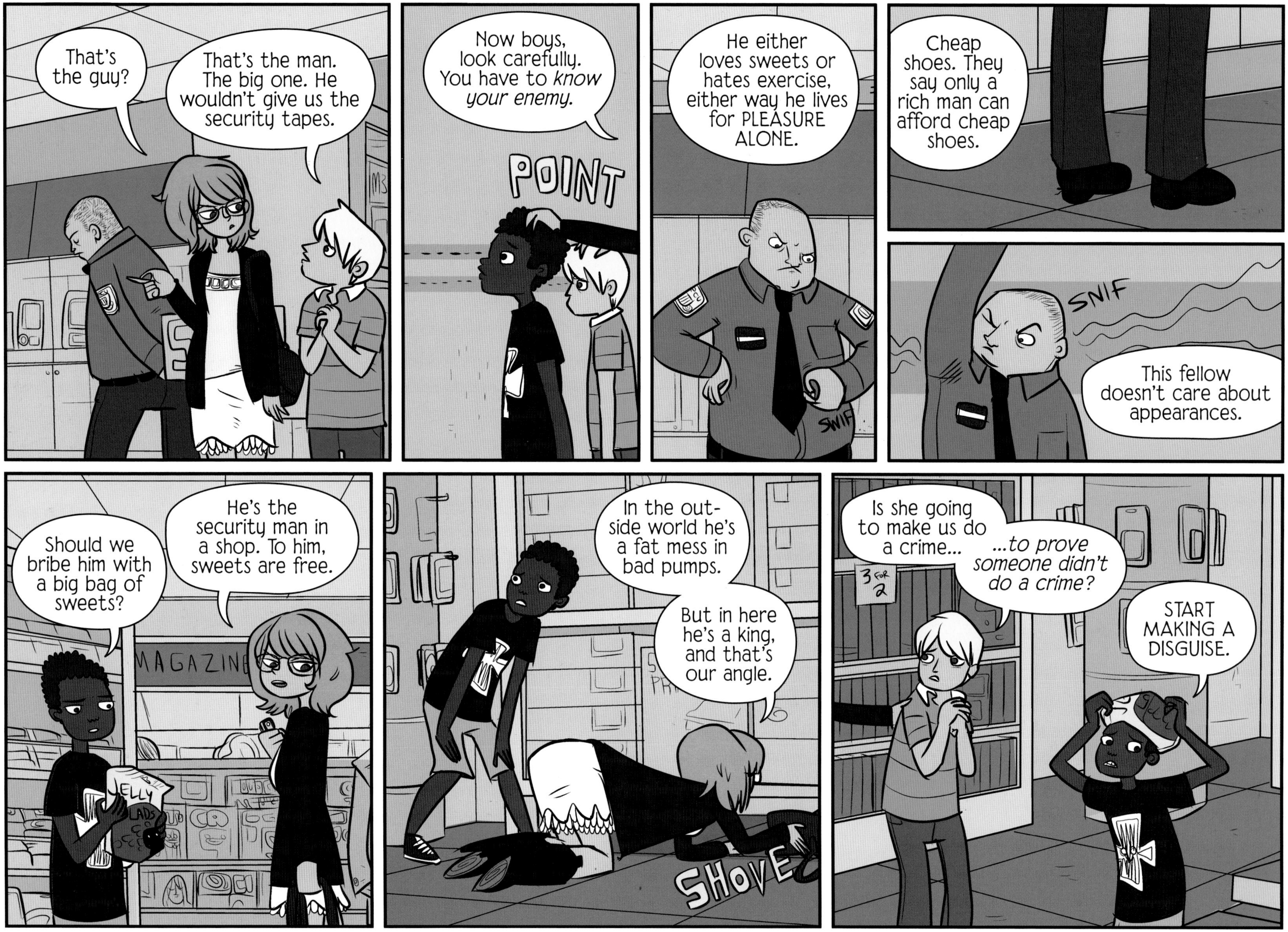
That's the guy?
That's the man. The big one. He wouldn't give us the security tapes.
Now boys, look carefully. You have to *know your enemy.*
POINT
He either loves sweets or hates exercise, either way he lives for PLEASURE ALONE.
SNIF
Cheap shoes. They say only a rich man can afford cheap shoes.
SNIF
This fellow doesn't care about appearances.
Should we bribe him with a big bag of sweets?
He's the security man in a shop. To him, sweets are free.
MAGAZINE
JELLY
In the out-side world he's a fat mess in bad pumps.
But in here he's a king, and that's our angle.
SHOVE
Is she going to make us do a crime...
...to prove someone didn't do a crime?
3 FOR 2
START MAKING A DISGUISE.

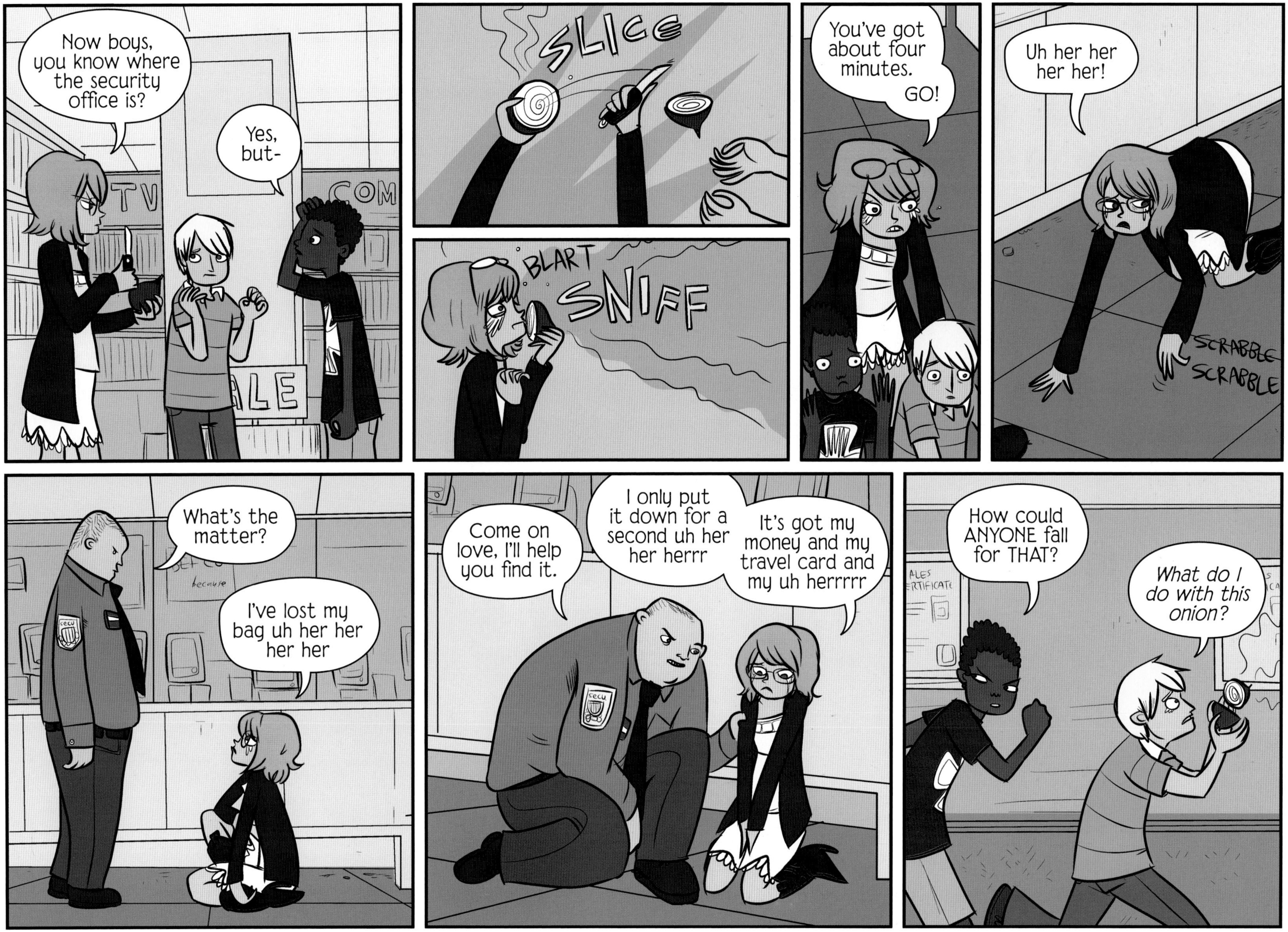
Now boys, you know where the security office is?
Yes, but-
TV
COM
ALE
SLICE
BLART
SNIFF
You've got about four minutes.
GO!
Uh her her her her!
SCRABBLE
SCRABBLE
What's the matter?
I've lost my bag uh her her her her
Come on love, I'll help you find it.
I only put it down for a second uh her her herrr
It's got my money and my travel card and my uh herrrrr
How could ANYONE fall for THAT?
What do I do with this onion?

Bad Machinery, Volume Three

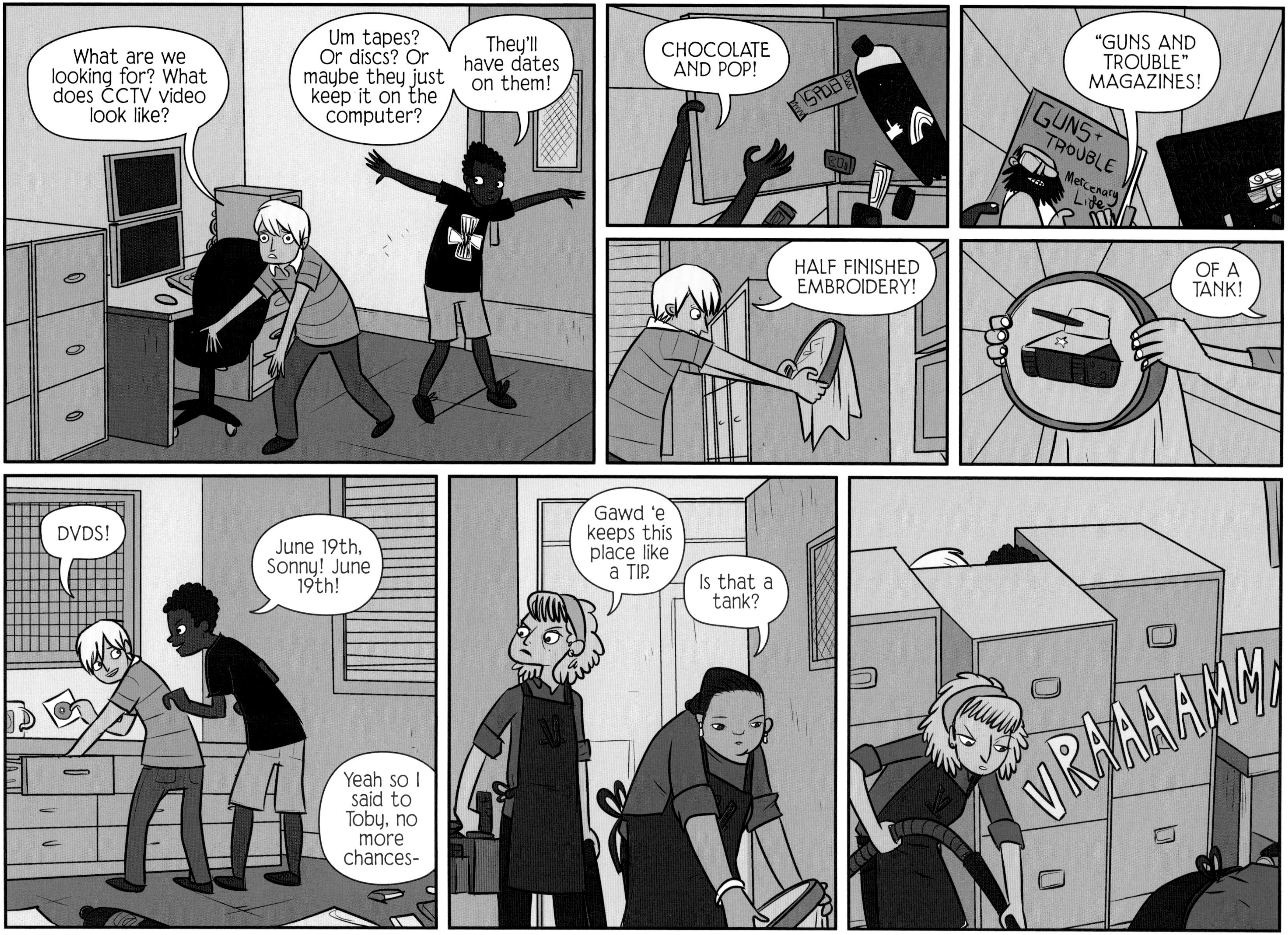
What are we looking for? What does CCTV video look like?
Um tapes? Or discs? Or maybe they just keep it on the computer?
They'll have dates on them!
CHOCOLATE AND POP!
"GUNS AND TROUBLE" MAGAZINES!
GUNS + TROUBLE
Mercenary Life
HALF FINISHED EMBROIDERY!
OF A TANK!
DVDS!
June 19th, Sonny! June 19th!
Yeah so I said to Toby, no more chances-
Gawd 'e keeps this place like a TIP.
Is that a tank?
VRAAAAMM

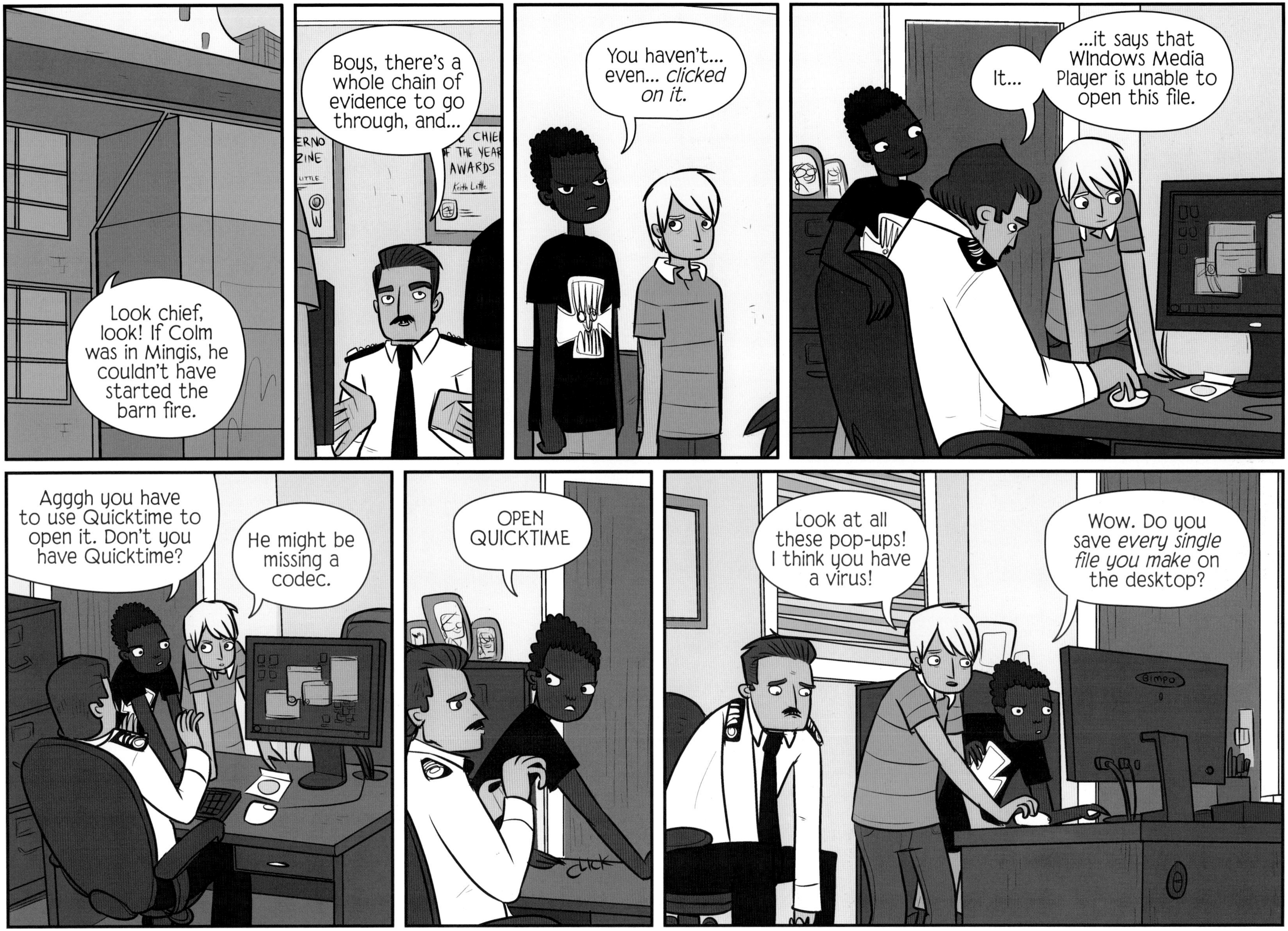
Look chief, look! If Colm was in Mingis, he couldn't have started the barn fire.
Boys, there's a whole chain of evidence to go through, and...
You haven't... even... *clicked on it.*
It...
...it says that WIndows Media Player is unable to open this file.
Agggh you have to use Quicktime to open it. Don't you have Quicktime?
He might be missing a codec.
OPEN QUICKTIME
CLICK
Look at all these pop-ups! I think you have a virus!
Wow. Do you save *every single file you make* on the desktop?

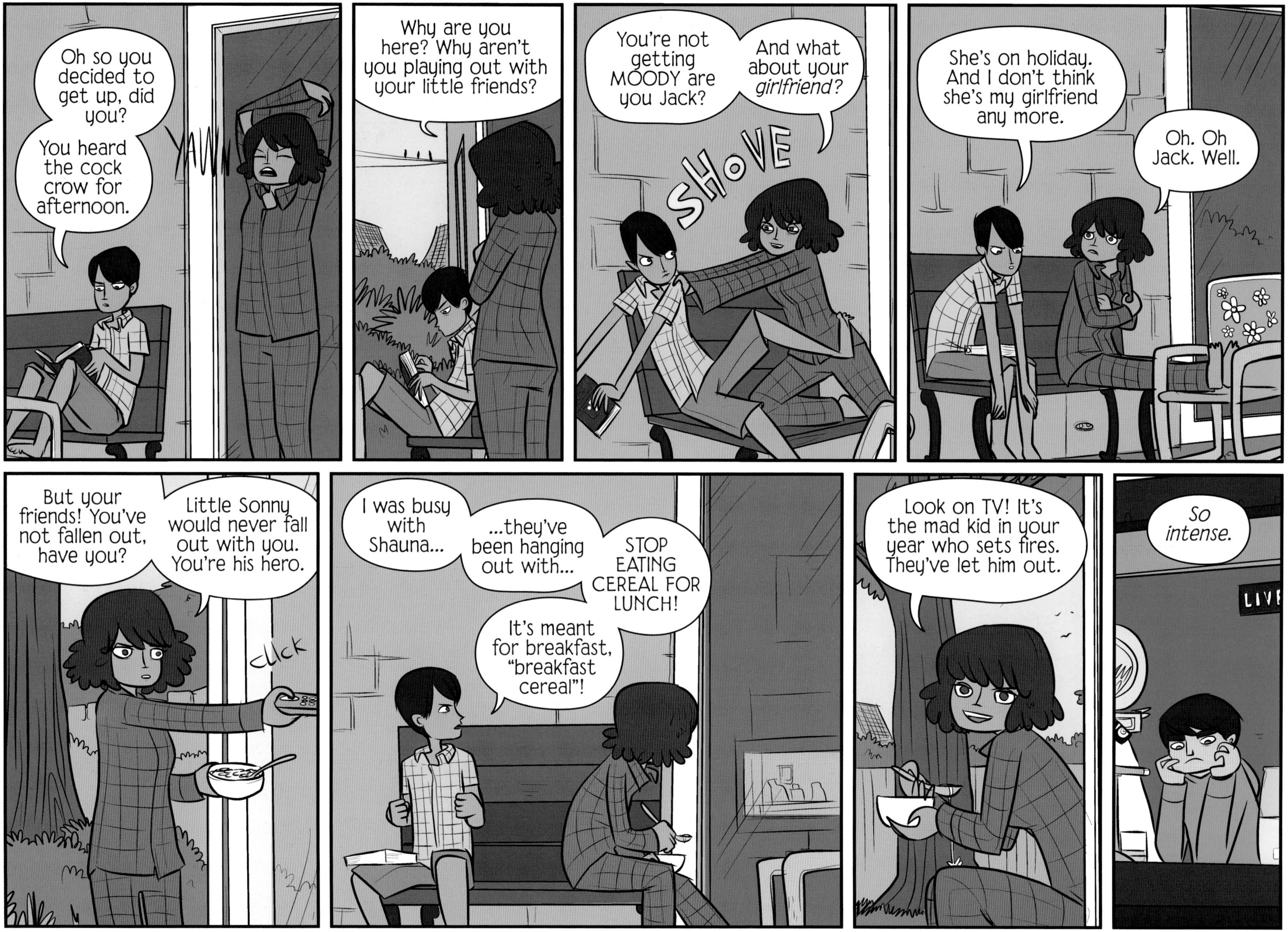
Oh so you decided to get up, did you?
You heard the cock crow for afternoon.
YAWN
Why are you here? Why aren't you playing out with your little friends?
You're not getting MOODY are you Jack?
And what about your *girlfriend?*
SHOVE
She's on holiday. And I don't think she's my girlfriend any more.
Oh. Oh Jack. Well.
But your friends! You've not fallen out, have you?
Little Sonny would never fall out with you. You're his hero.
click
I was busy with Shauna...
...they've been hanging out with...
STOP EATING CEREAL FOR LUNCH!
It's meant for breakfast, "breakfast cereal"!
Look on TV! It's the mad kid in your year who sets fires. They've let him out.
So intense.
LIVE

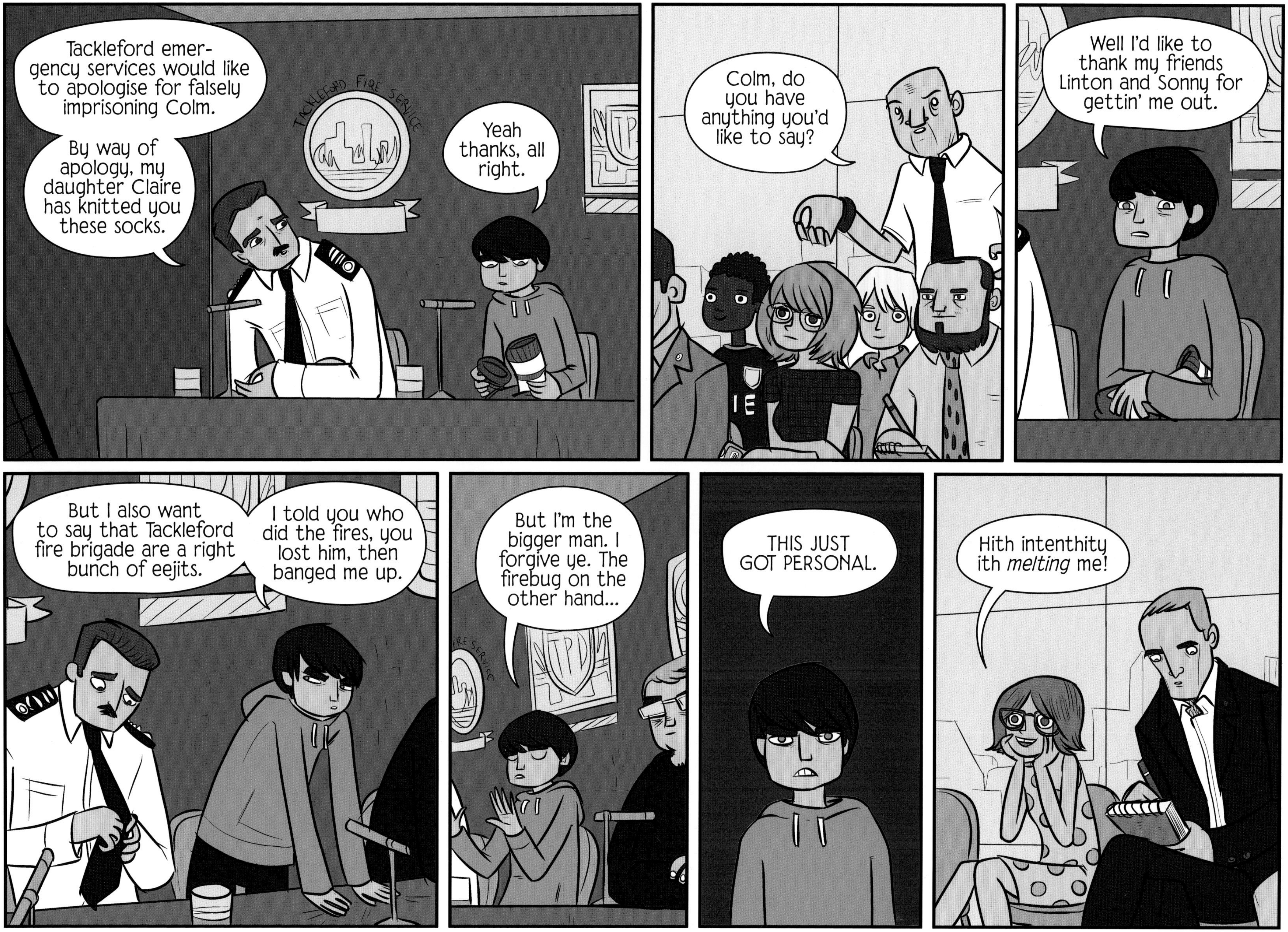
Tackleford emergency services would like to apologise for falsely imprisoning Colm.
By way of apology, my daughter Claire has knitted you these socks.
TACKLEFORD FIRE SERVICE
Yeah thanks, all right.
Colm, do you have anything you'd like to say?
Well I'd like to thank my friends Linton and Sonny for gettin' me out.
But I also want to say that Tackleford fire brigade are a right bunch of eejits.
I told you who did the fires, you lost him, then banged me up.
But I'm the bigger man. I forgive ye. The firebug on the other hand...
THIS JUST GOT PERSONAL.
Hith intenthity ith *melting* me!

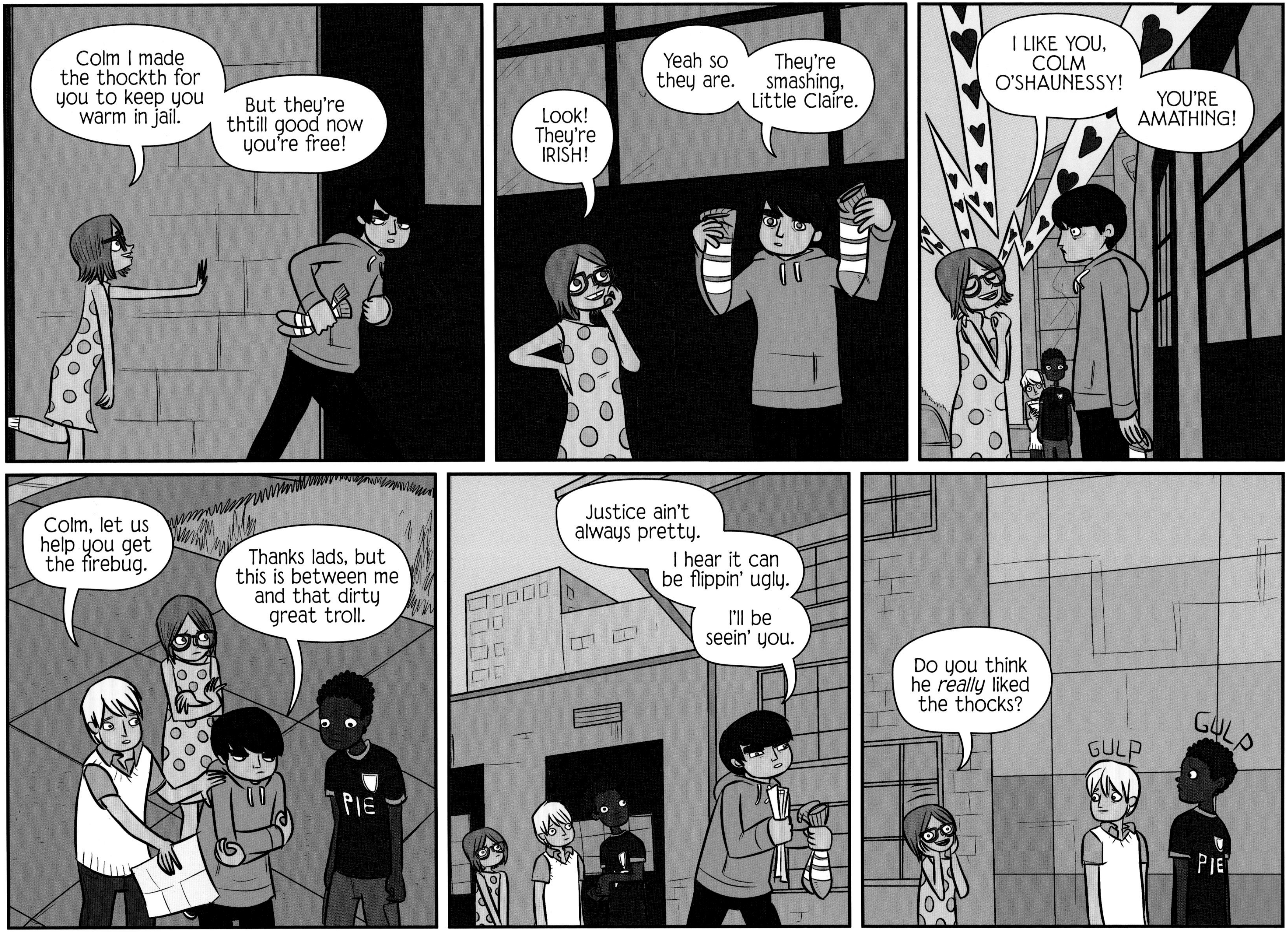
Colm I made the thockth for you to keep you warm in jail.
But they're thtill good now you're free!
Look! They're IRISH!
Yeah so they are.
They're smashing, Little Claire.
I LIKE YOU, COLM O'SHAUNESSY!
YOU'RE AMATHING!
Colm, let us help you get the firebug.
Thanks lads, but this is between me and that dirty great troll.
PIE
Justice ain't always pretty.
I hear it can be flippin' ugly.
I'll be seein' you.
Do you think he *really* liked the thocks?
GULP
GULP
PIE

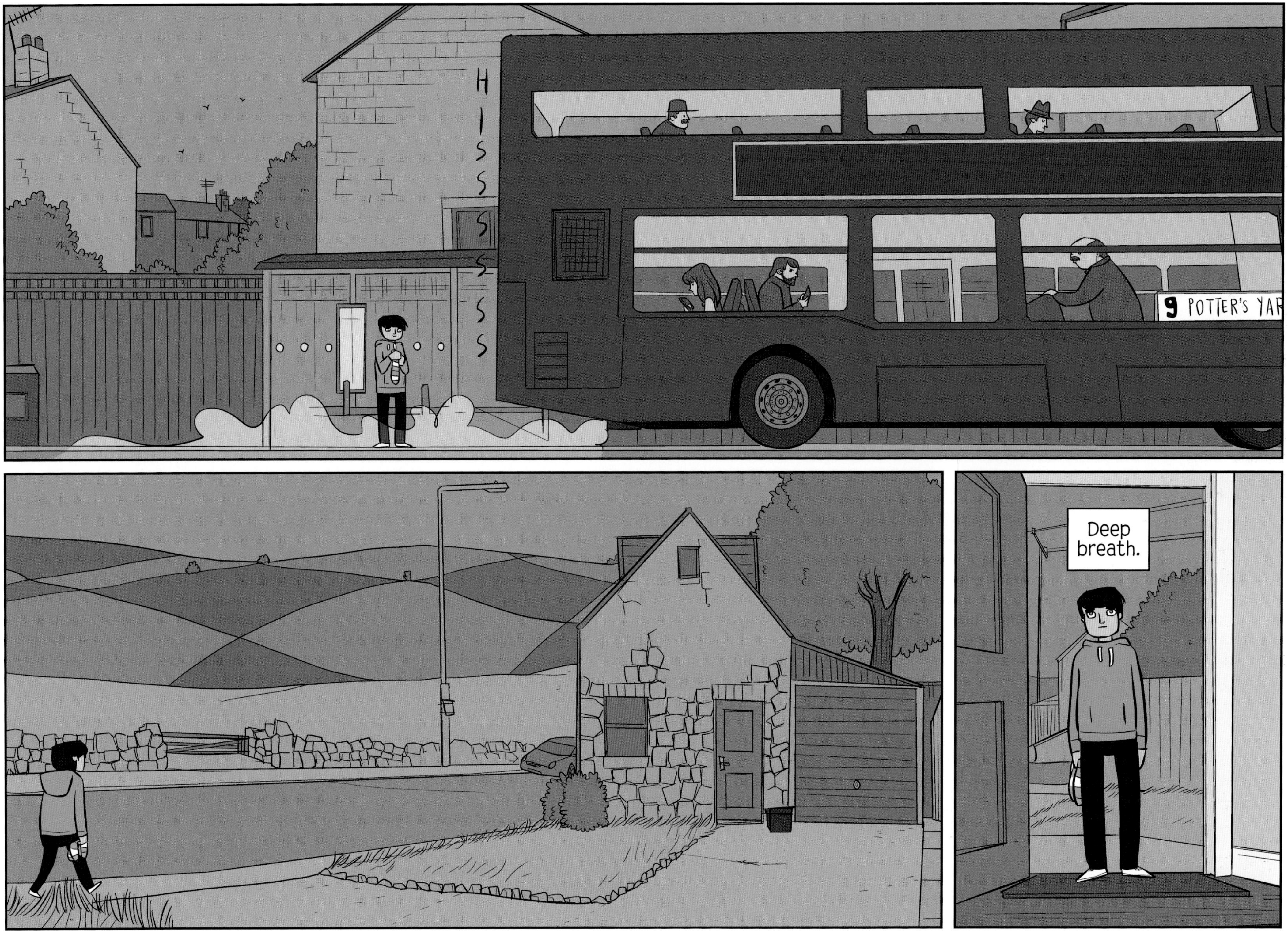
HISSSSS
9 POTTER'S YAR
Deep breath.

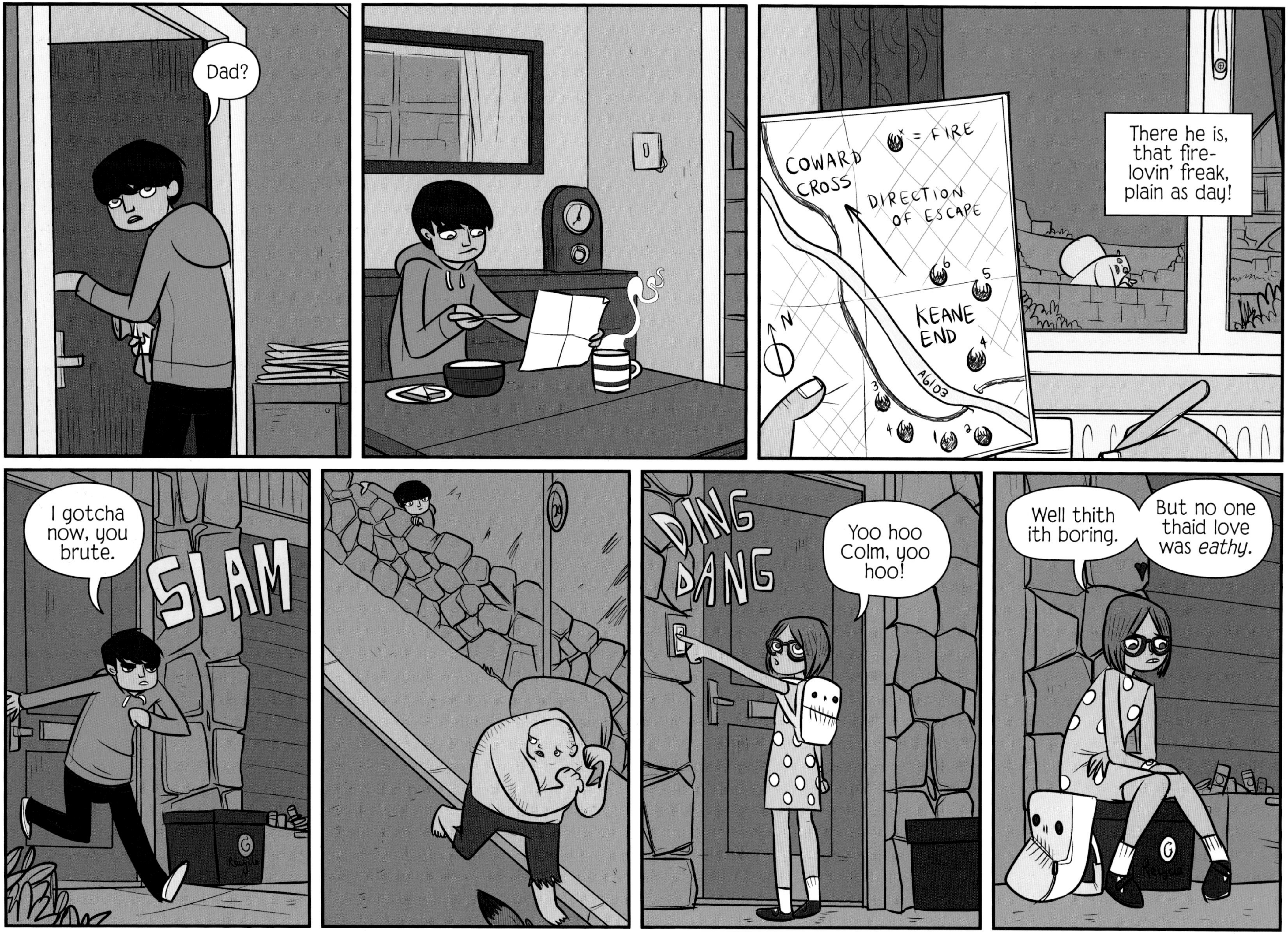
Dad?
COWARD CROSS
= FIRE
DIRECTION OF ESCAPE
KEANE END
N
A6103
There he is, that fire-lovin' freak, plain as day!
I gotcha now, you brute.
SLAM
DING DANG
Yoo hoo Colm, yoo hoo!
Well thith ith boring.
But no one thaid love was *eathy*.

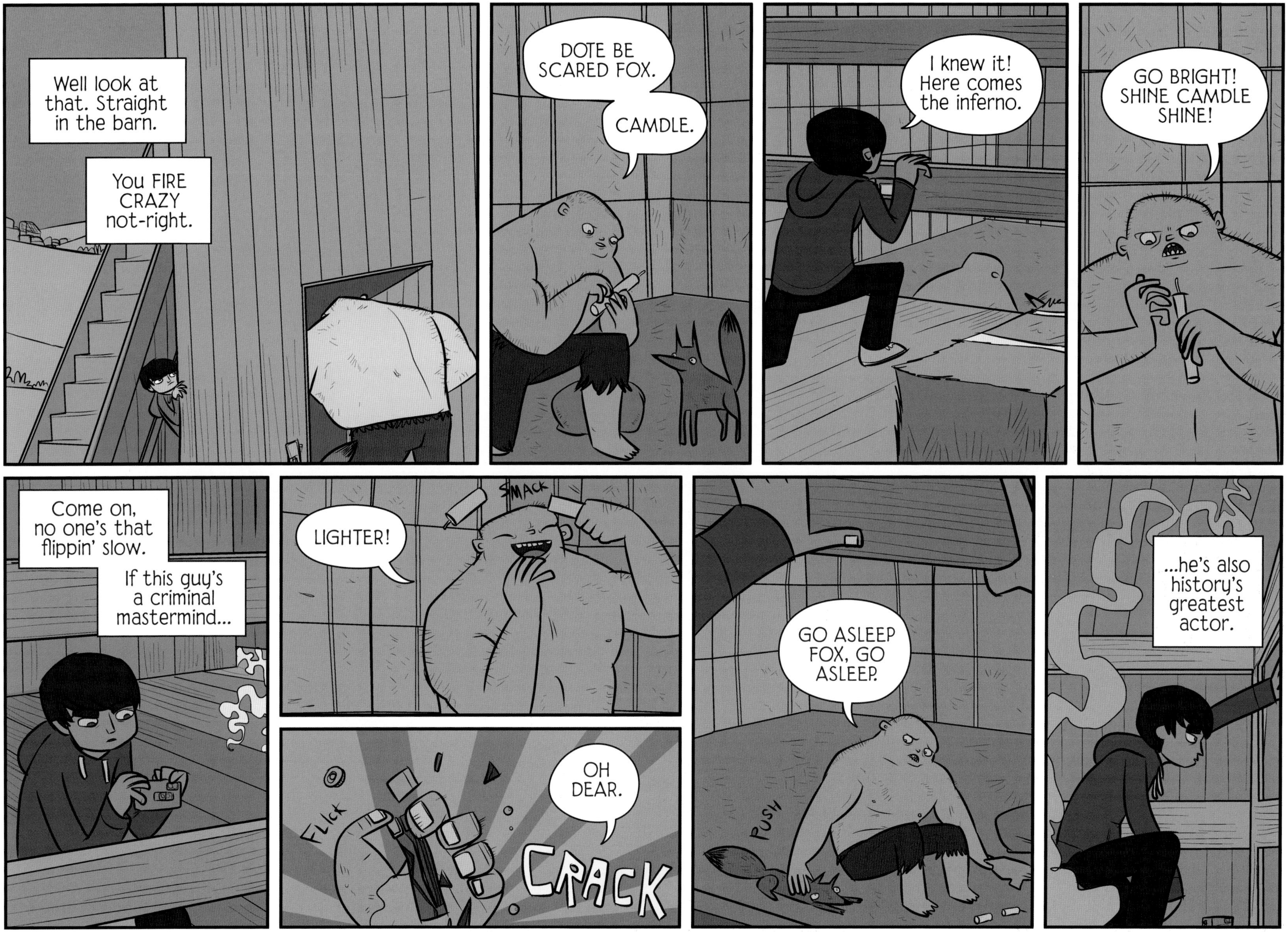
Well look at that. Straight in the barn.
You FIRE CRAZY not-right.
DOTE BE SCARED FOX.
CAMDLE.
I knew it! Here comes the inferno.
GO BRIGHT! SHINE CAMDLE SHINE!
Come on, no one's that flippin' slow.
If this guy's a criminal mastermind...
SMACK
LIGHTER!
FLICK
OH DEAR.
CRACK
GO ASLEEP FOX, GO ASLEEP.
PUSH
...he's also history's greatest actor.

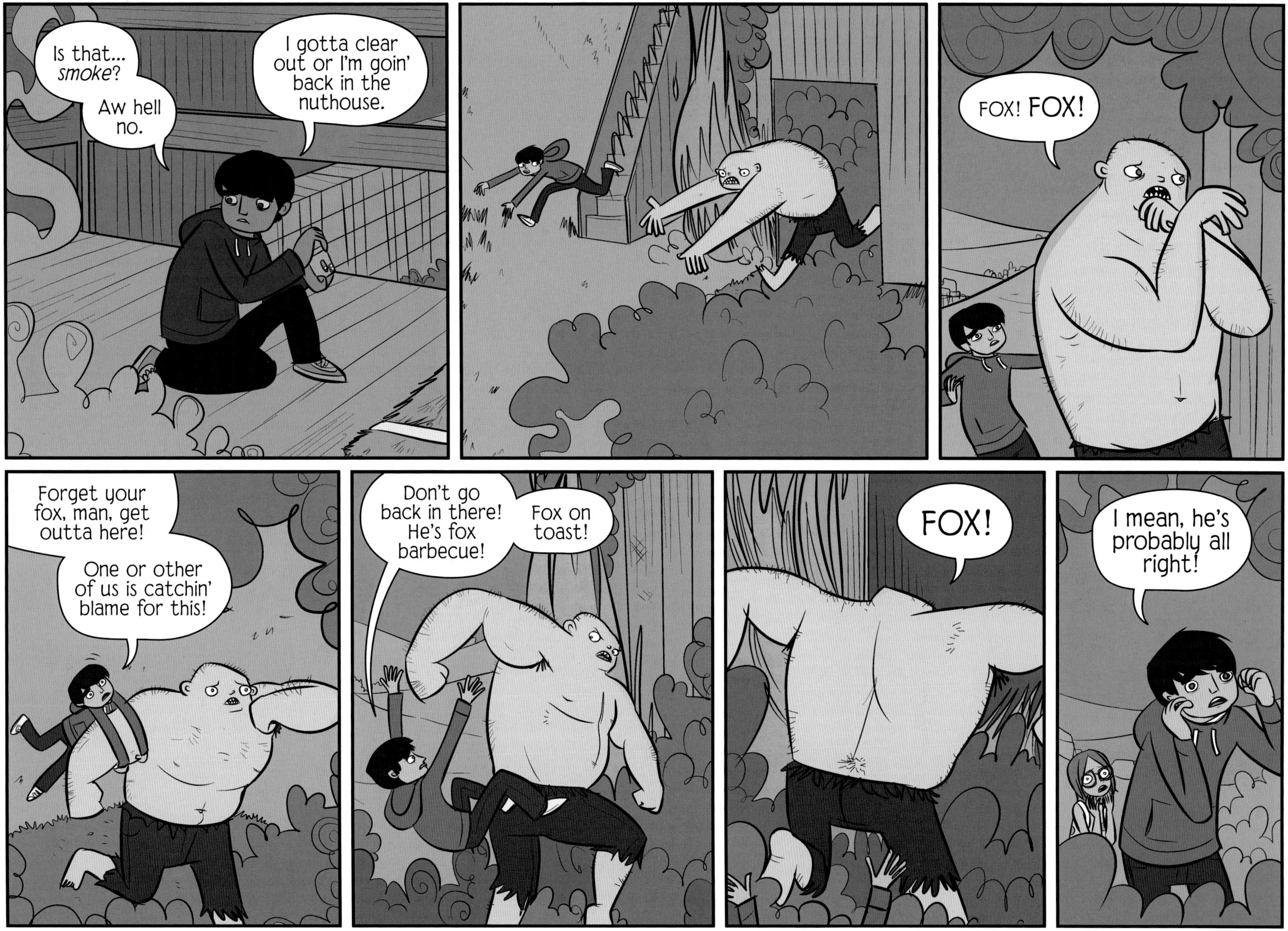
Is that... *smoke*?
Aw hell no.
I gotta clear out or I'm goin' back in the nuthouse.
FOX! FOX!
Forget your fox, man, get outta here!
One or other of us is catchin' blame for this!
Don't go back in there! He's fox barbecue!
Fox on toast!
FOX!
I mean, he's probably all right!

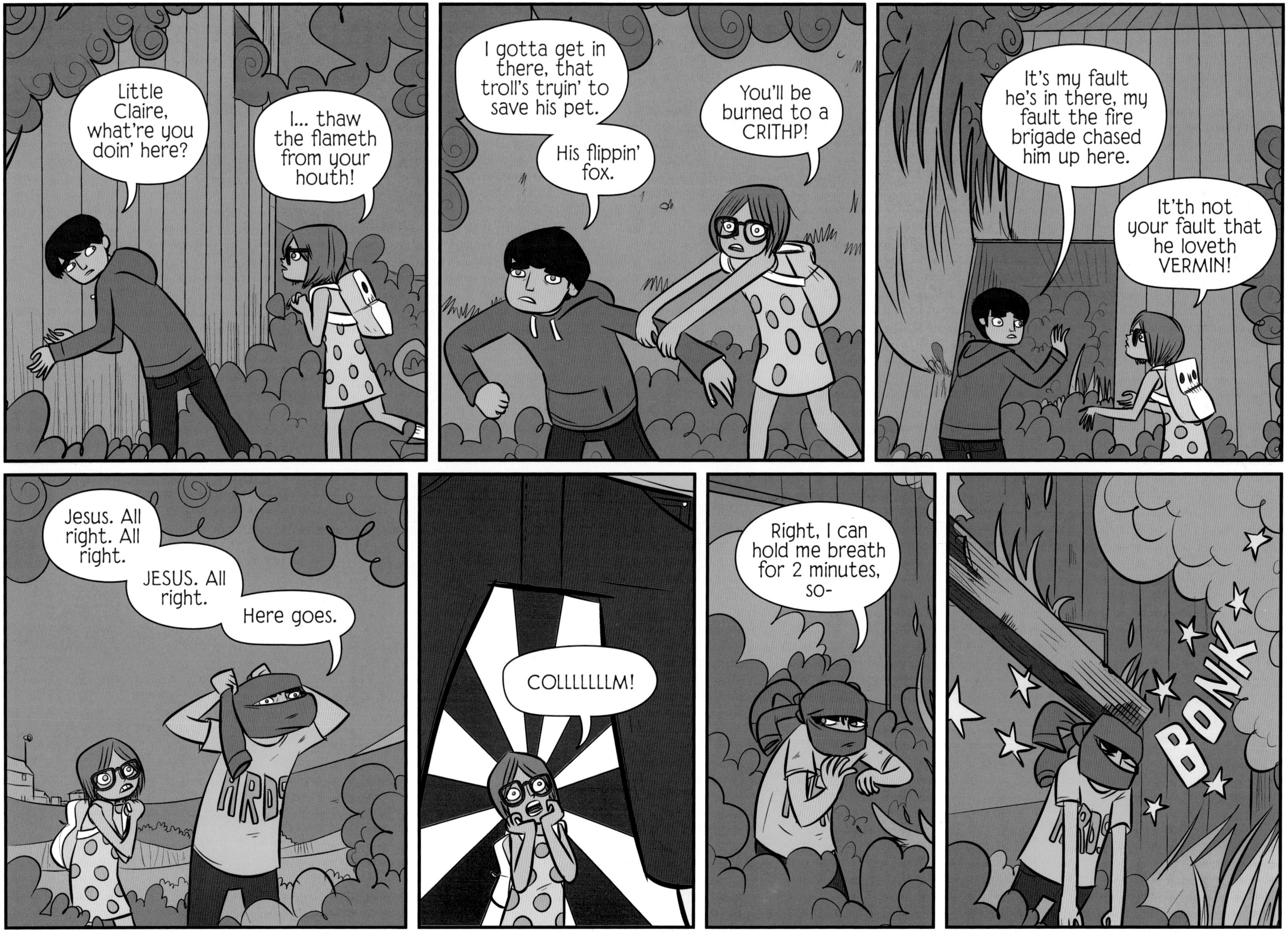
Little Claire, what're you doin' here?
I... thaw the flameth from your houth!
I gotta get in there, that troll's tryin' to save his pet.
His flippin' fox.
You'll be burned to a CRITHP!
It's my fault he's in there, my fault the fire brigade chased him up here.
It'th not your fault that he loveth VERMIN!
Jesus. All right. All right.
JESUS. All right.
Here goes.
COLLLLLLLLM!
Right, I can hold me breath for 2 minutes, so-
BONK

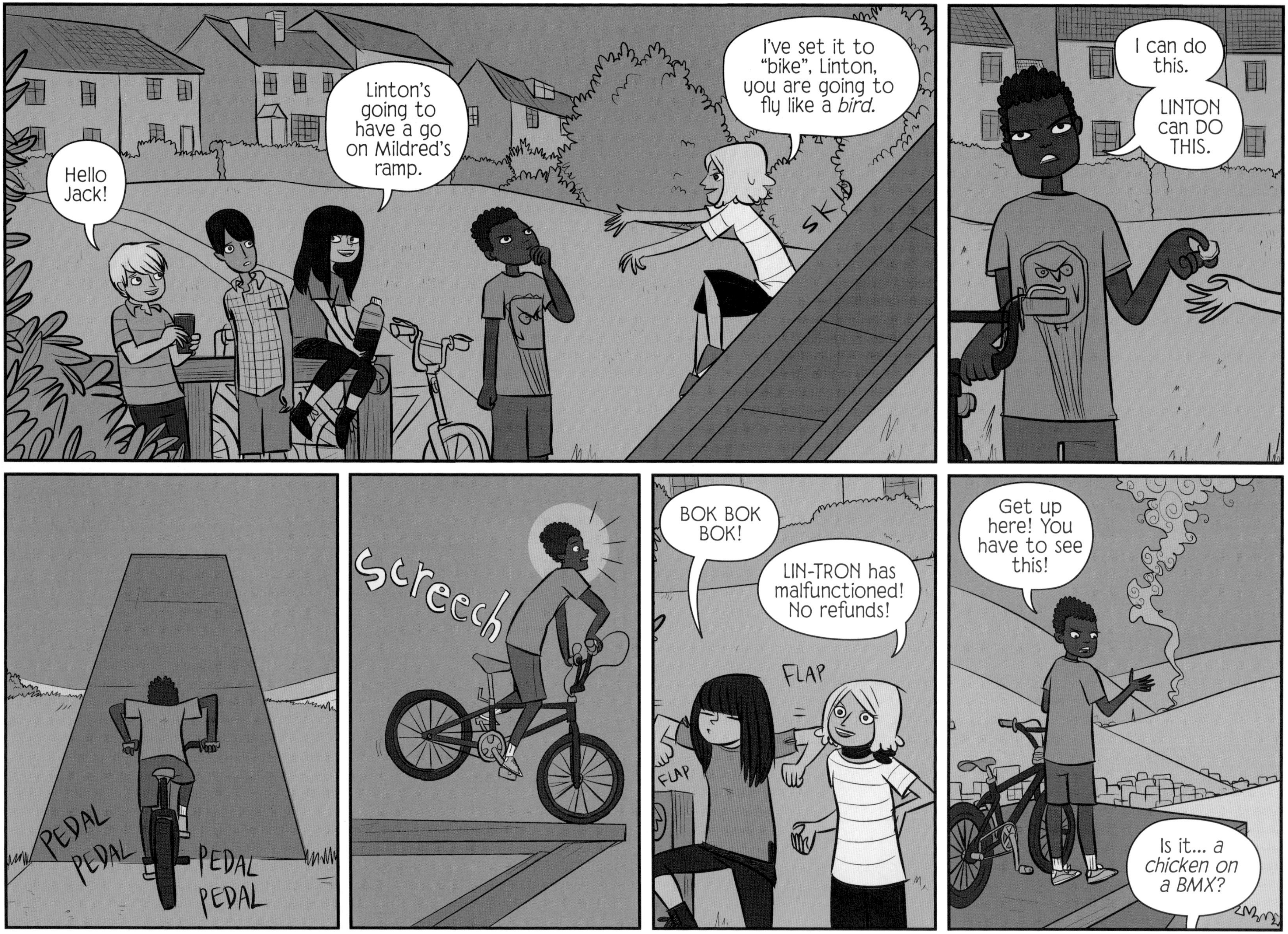
Hello Jack!
Linton's going to have a go on Mildred's ramp.
I've set it to "bike", Linton, you are going to fly like a *bird.*
SK
I can do this.
LINTON can DO THIS.
PEDAL PEDAL PEDAL PEDAL
Screech
BOK BOK BOK!
LIN-TRON has malfunctioned! No refunds!
FLAP
FLAP
Get up here! You have to see this!
Is it... *a chicken on a BMX?*

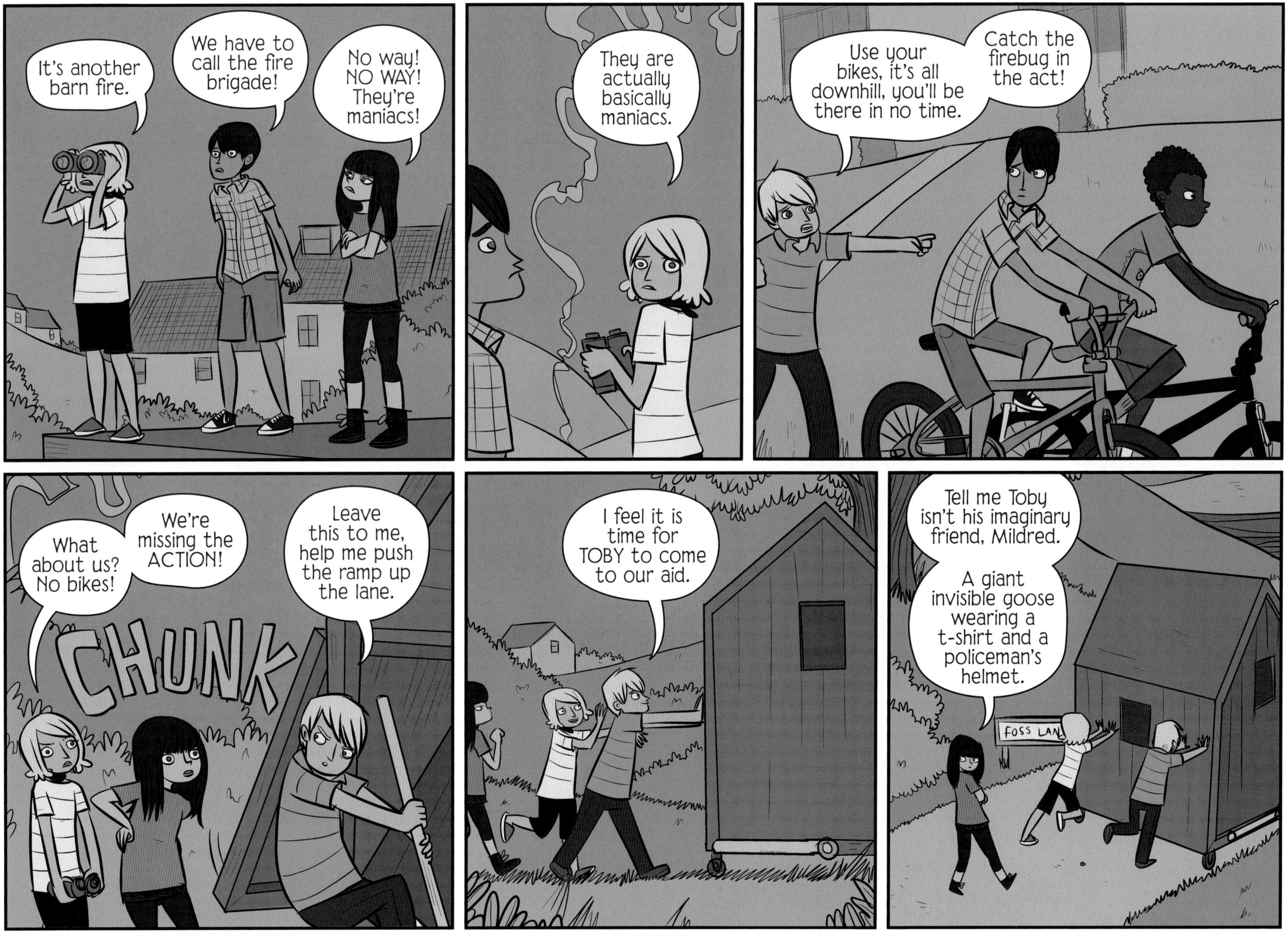
It's another barn fire.
We have to call the fire brigade!
No way! NO WAY! They're maniacs!
They are actually basically maniacs.
Use your bikes, it's all downhill, you'll be there in no time.
Catch the firebug in the act!
What about us? No bikes!
We're missing the ACTION!
Leave this to me, help me push the ramp up the lane.
CHUNK
I feel it is time for TOBY to come to our aid.
Tell me Toby isn't his imaginary friend, Mildred.
A giant invisible goose wearing a t-shirt and a policeman's helmet.
FOSS LAN

So how come you're not with *Shauna* today, Jack.

She's on holiday. But...

...I don't think we're going out any more.

Oh right, she chucked you.

No! She just wanted to do other things...

...er I mean WE wanted to do other things.

Oh yeah right! She was making you do girlie things all the time?

Well um no... she... I was missing adventure times....

So er I told her

we should

COOL IT. Yeah man. Take control.

I miss doing all the things I used to do.

Maybe we ought to just be friends for a bit.

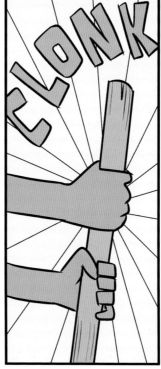

CLONK

The ramp turns into a BOAT! Toby is a BOAT!

This had better not sink.

It's hard to tell my swimmin' technique and drownin' technique apart.

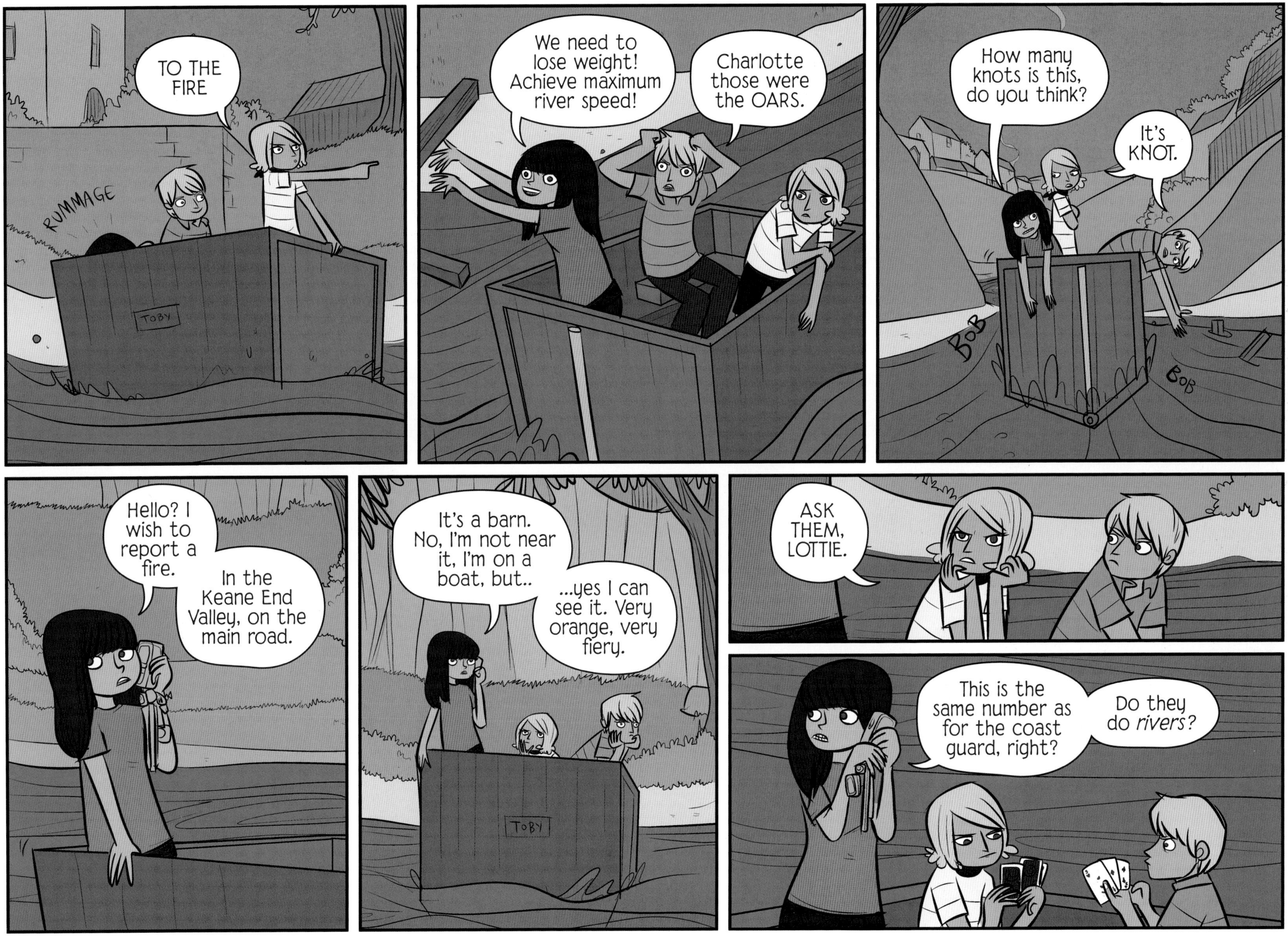
TO THE FIRE
RUMMAGE
TOBY
We need to lose weight! Achieve maximum river speed!
Charlotte those were the OARS.
How many knots is this, do you think?
It's KNOT.
BOB
BOB
Hello? I wish to report a fire.
In the Keane End Valley, on the main road.
It's a barn. No, I'm not near it, I'm on a boat, but..
...yes I can see it. Very orange, very fiery.
TOBY
ASK THEM, LOTTIE.
This is the same number as for the coast guard, right?
Do they do *rivers*?

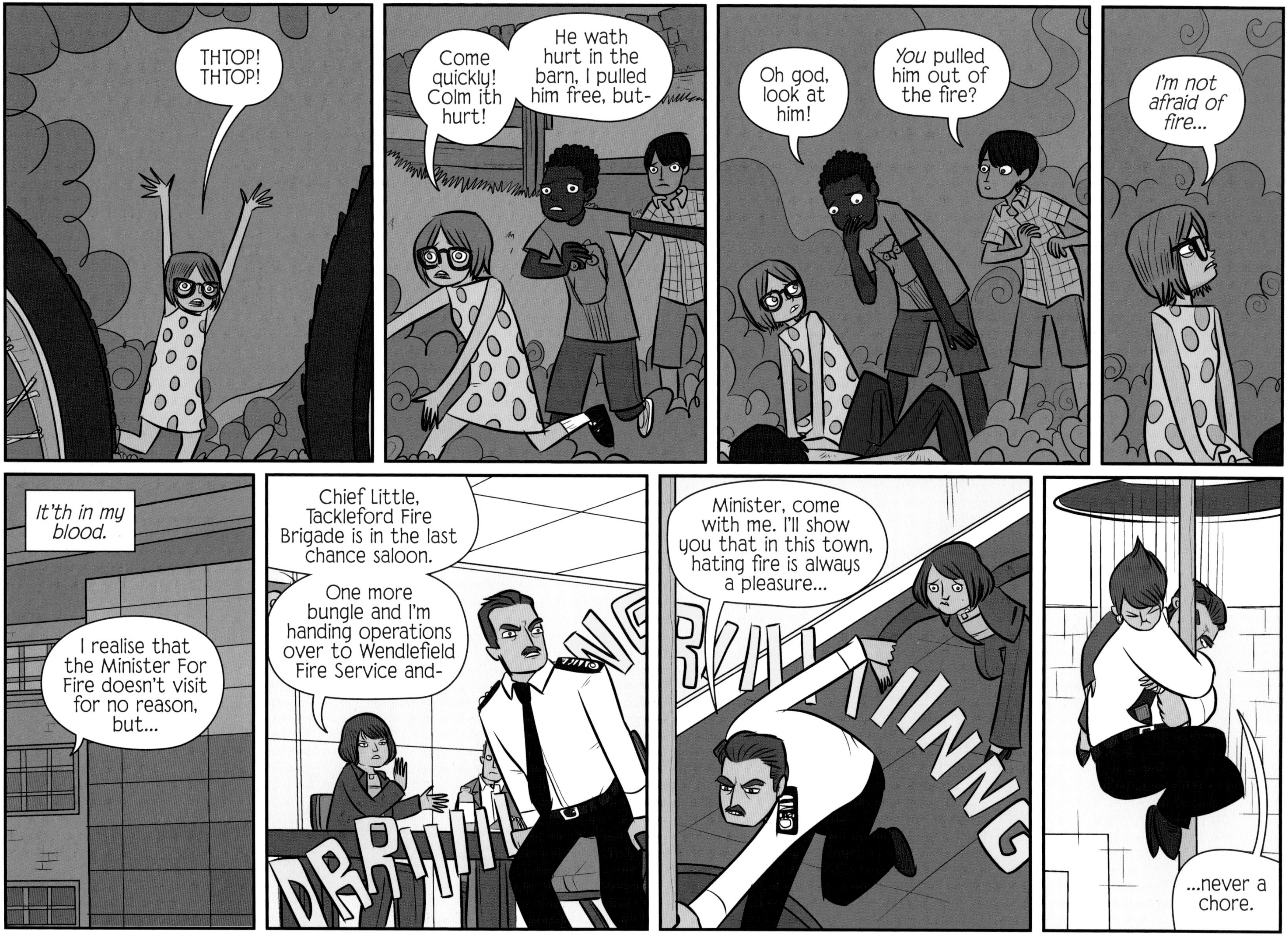
THTOP! THTOP!
Come quickly! Colm ith hurt!
He wath hurt in the barn, I pulled him free, but-
Oh god, look at him!
You pulled him out of the fire?
I'm not afraid of fire...
It'th in my blood.
I realise that the Minister For Fire doesn't visit for no reason, but...
Chief Little, Tackleford Fire Brigade is in the last chance saloon.
One more bungle and I'm handing operations over to Wendlefield Fire Service and-
DRRIIIII
Minister, come with me. I'll show you that in this town, hating fire is always a pleasure...
IIIIIINNG
...never a chore.

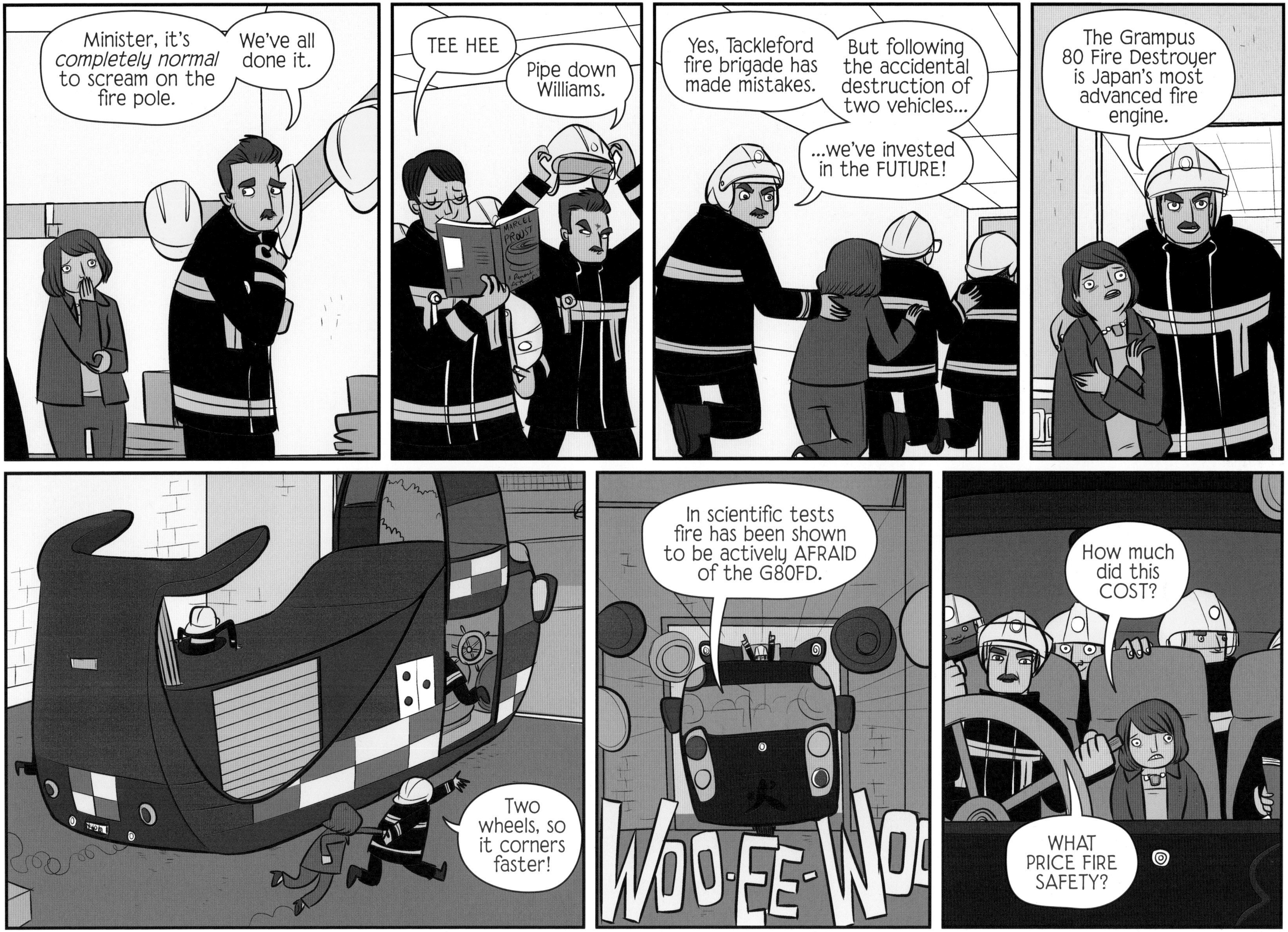
Minister, it's *completely normal* to scream on the fire pole.
We've all done it.
TEE HEE
Pipe down Williams.
MARCEL PROUST
Yes, Tackleford fire brigade has made mistakes.
But following the accidental destruction of two vehicles...
...we've invested in the FUTURE!
The Grampus 80 Fire Destroyer is Japan's most advanced fire engine.
Two wheels, so it corners faster!
In scientific tests fire has been shown to be actively AFRAID of the G80FD.
WOO-EE-WOO
How much did this COST?
WHAT PRICE FIRE SAFETY?

Bad Machinery, Volume Three

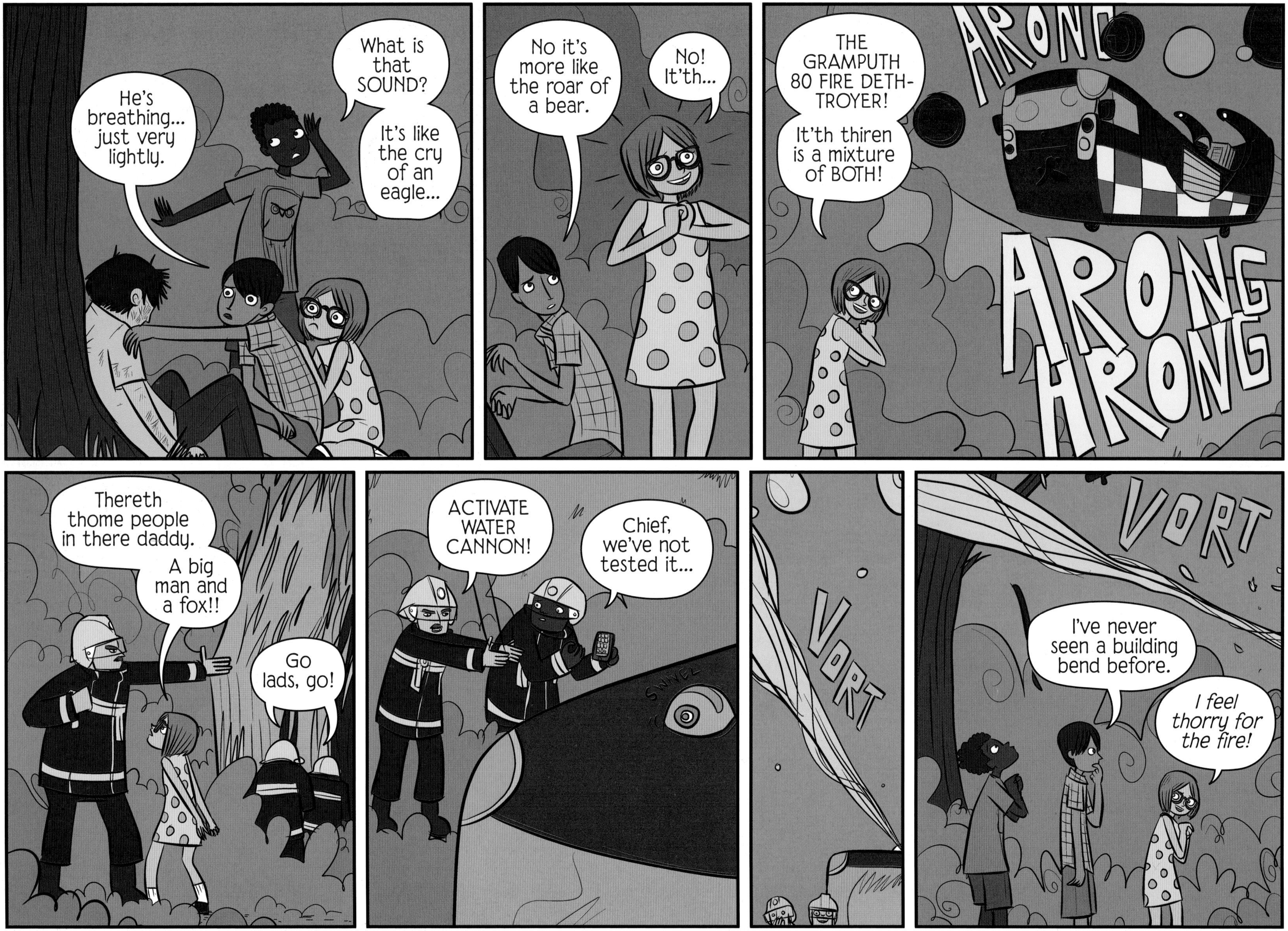
What is that SOUND?
He's breathing... just very lightly.
It's like the cry of an eagle...
No it's more like the roar of a bear.
No! It'th...
THE GRAMPUTH 80 FIRE DETH-TROYER!
It'th thiren is a mixture of BOTH!
ARONG
ARONG
HRONG
Thereth thome people in there daddy.
A big man and a fox!!
Go lads, go!
ACTIVATE WATER CANNON!
Chief, we've not tested it...
SWIVEL
VORT
VORT
I've never seen a building bend before.
I feel thorry for the fire!

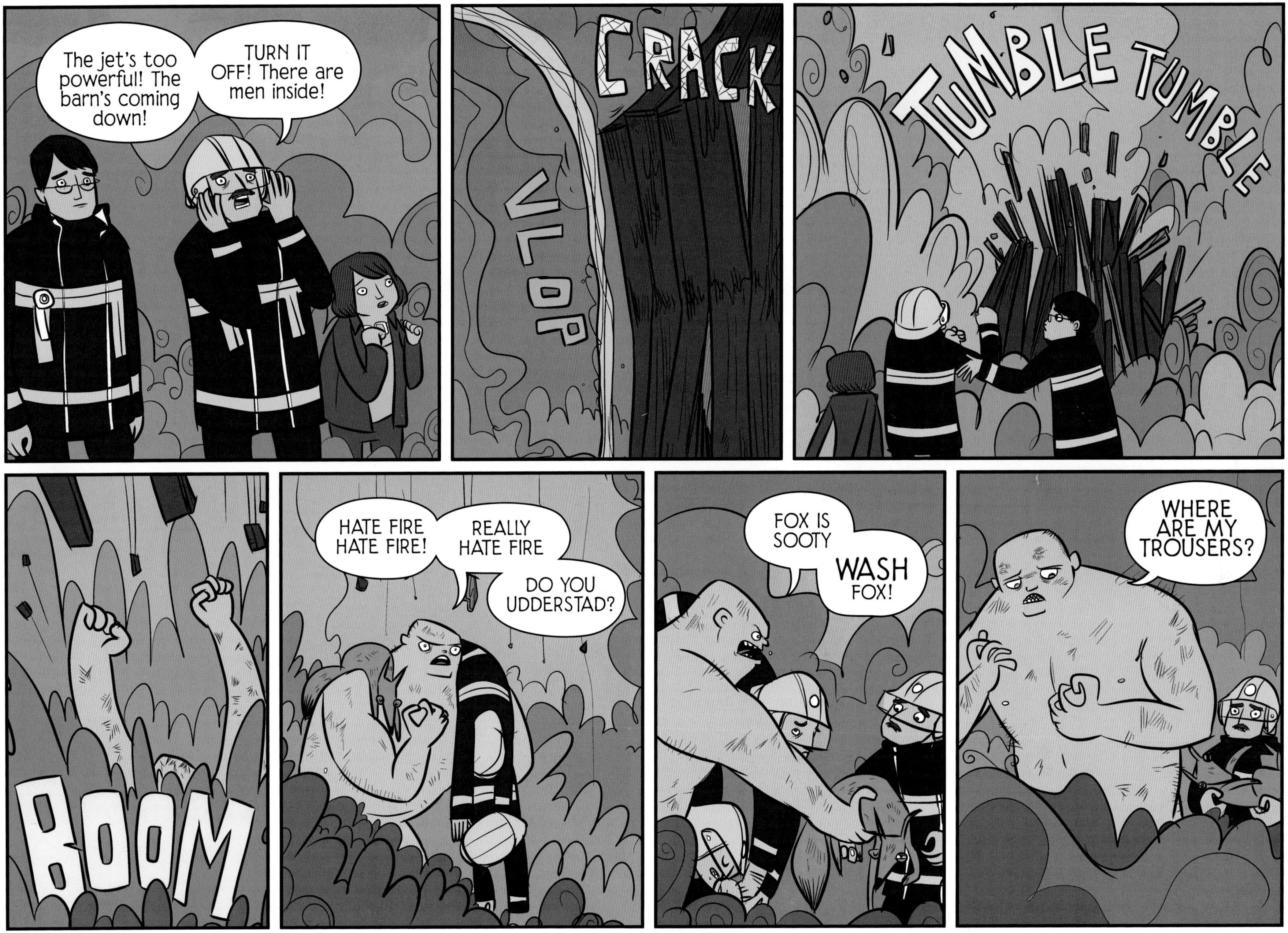
The jet's too powerful! The barn's coming down!
TURN IT OFF! There are men inside!
CRACK
VLOP
TUMBLE TUMBLE
BOOM
HATE FIRE HATE FIRE!
REALLY HATE FIRE
DO YOU UDDERSTAD?
FOX IS SOOTY
WASH FOX!
WHERE ARE MY TROUSERS?

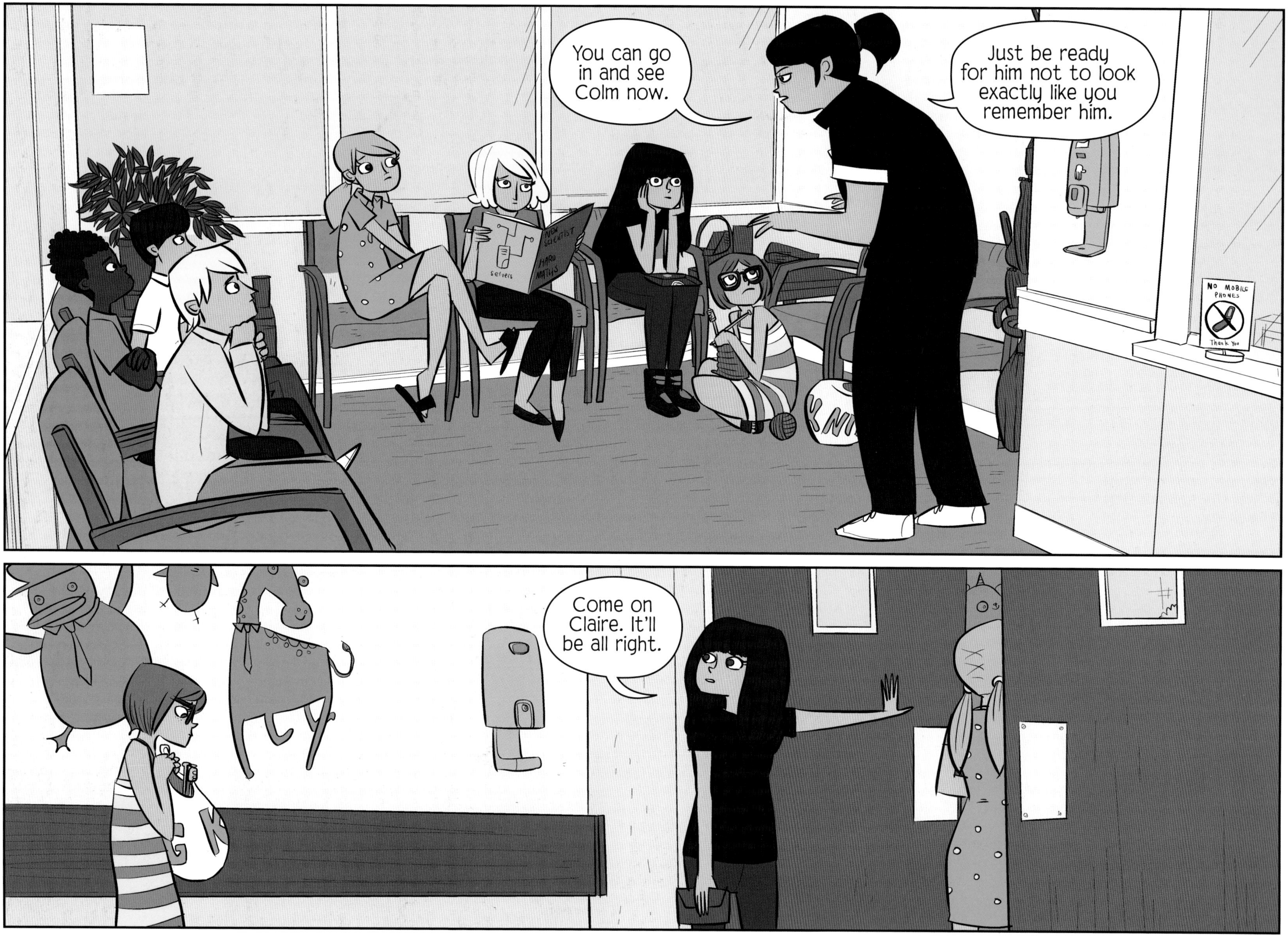
You can go in and see Colm now.
Just be ready for him not to look exactly like you remember him.
NEW SCIENTIST
HARD MATHS
NO MOBILE PHONES
Thank You
Come on Claire. It'll be all right.

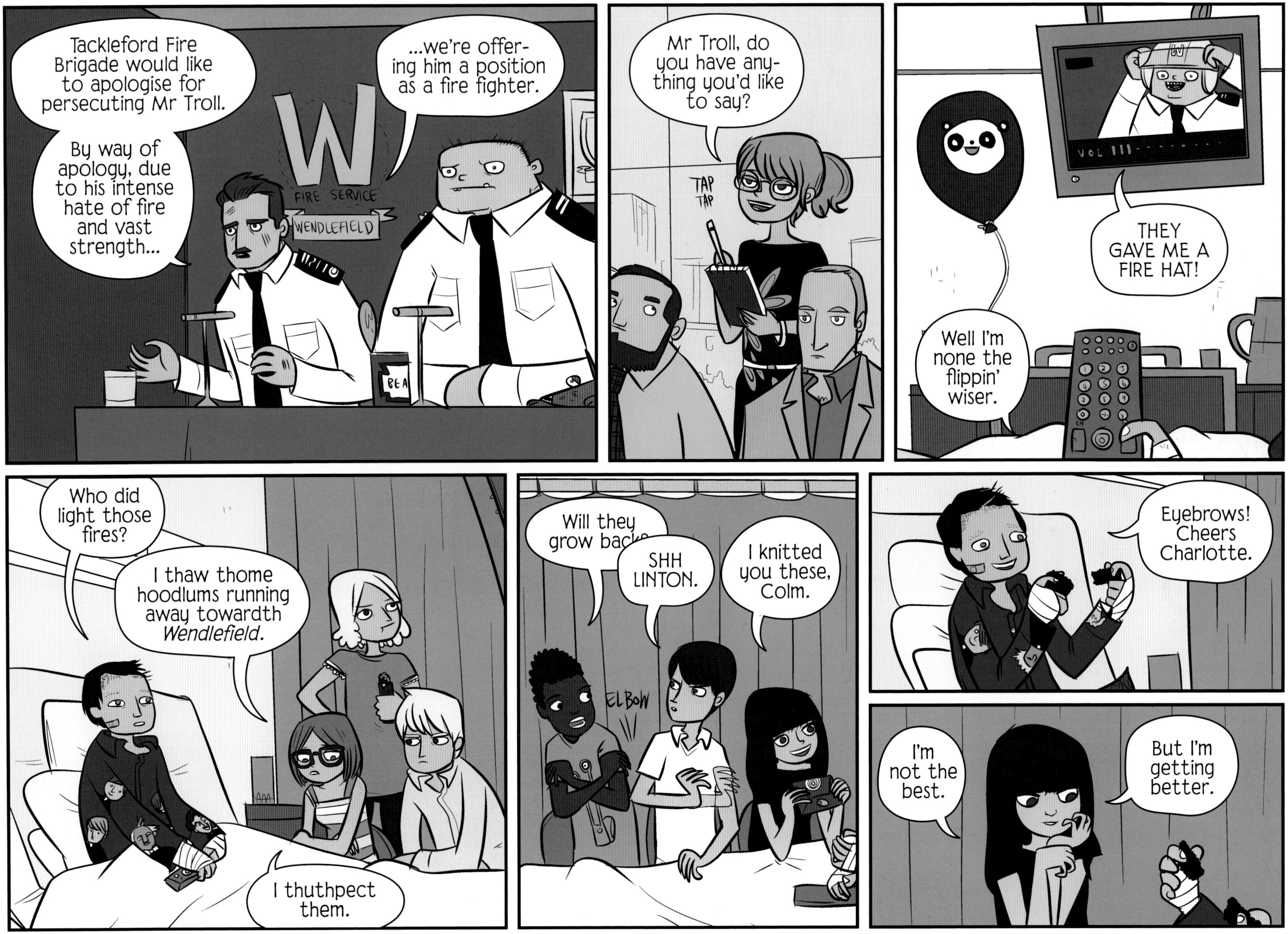
Tackleford Fire Brigade would like to apologise for persecuting Mr Troll.
By way of apology, due to his intense hate of fire and vast strength...
...we're offering him a position as a fire fighter.
W
FIRE SERVICE
WENDLEFIELD
Mr Troll, do you have anything you'd like to say?
TAP TAP
THEY GAVE ME A FIRE HAT!
Well I'm none the flippin' wiser.
Who did light those fires?
I thaw thome hoodlums running away towardth *Wendlefield.*
I thuthpect them.
Will they grow back
SHH LINTON.
ELBOW
I knitted you these, Colm.
Eyebrows! Cheers Charlotte.
I'm not the best.
But I'm getting better.

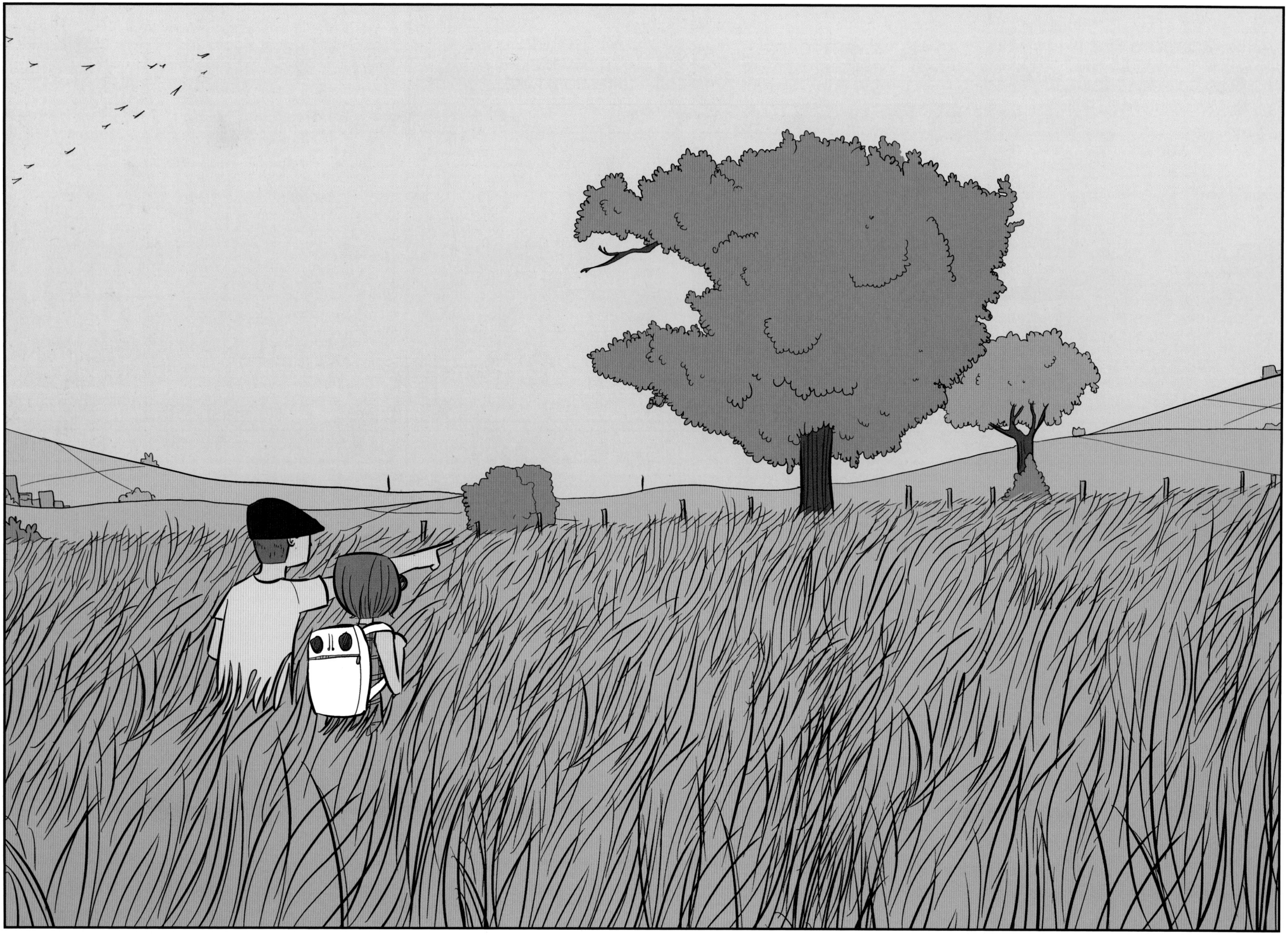

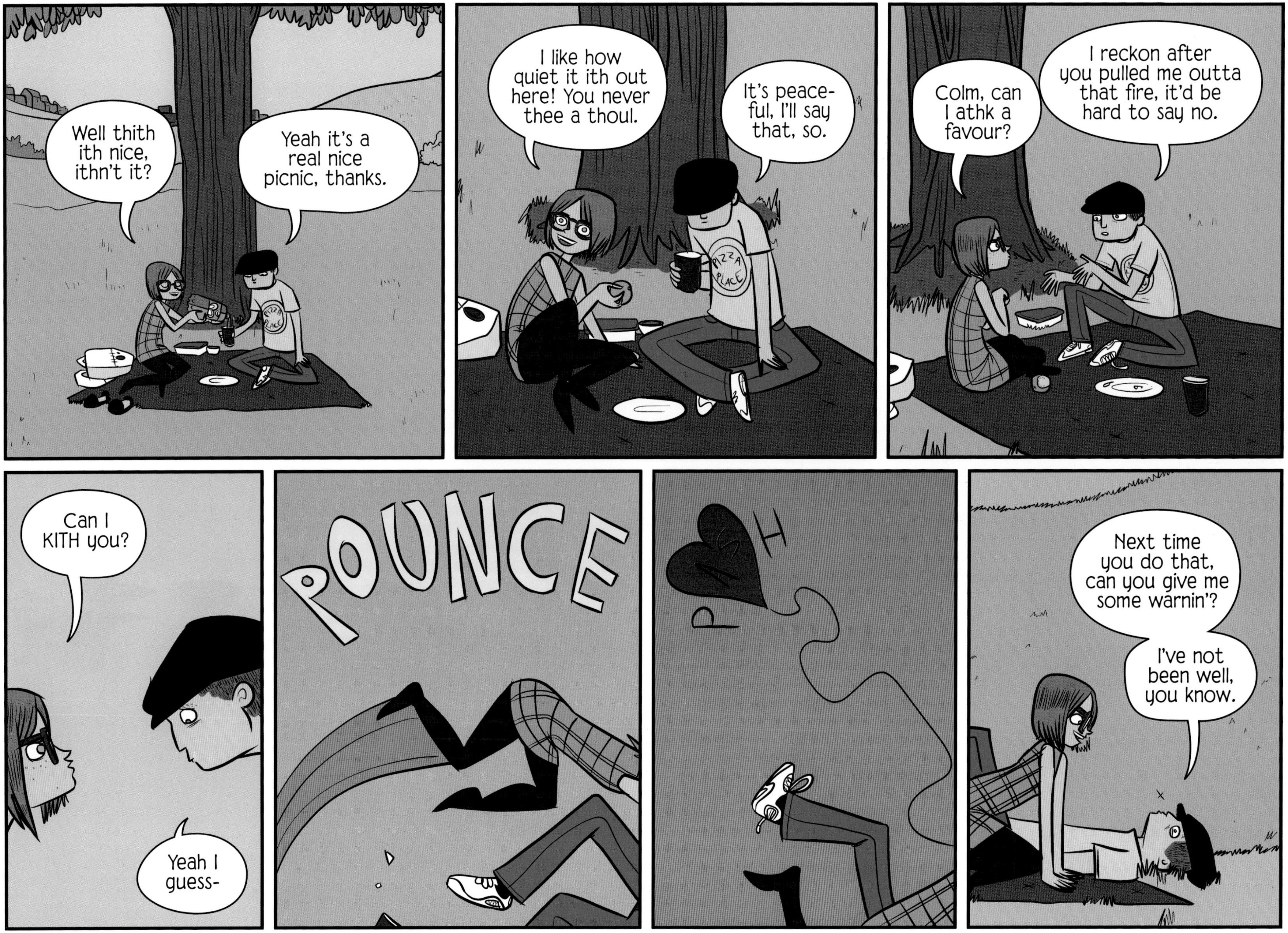

Well thith ith nice, ithn't it?
Yeah it's a real nice picnic, thanks.
I like how quiet it ith out here! You never thee a thoul.
It's peace-ful, I'll say that, so.
Colm, can I athk a favour?
I reckon after you pulled me outta that fire, it'd be hard to say no.
Can I KITH you?
Yeah I guess-
POUNCE
Next time you do that, can you give me some warnin'?
I've not been well, you know.

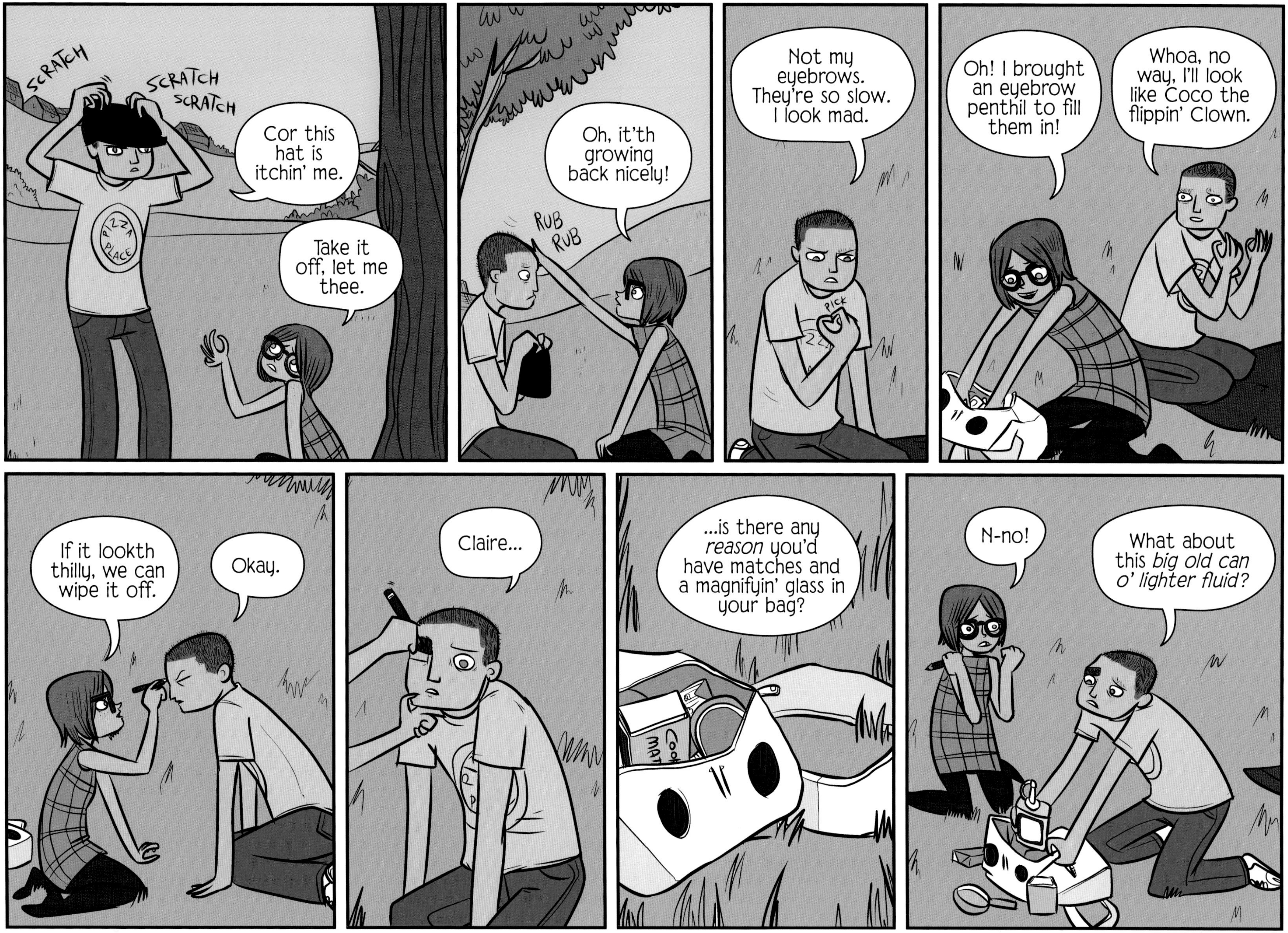
SCRATCH
SCRATCH
SCRATCH
Cor this hat is itchin' me.
Take it off, let me thee.
RUB RUB
Oh, it'th growing back nicely!
Not my eyebrows. They're so slow. I look mad.
PICK
Oh! I brought an eyebrow penthil to fill them in!
Whoa, no way, I'll look like Coco the flippin' Clown.
If it lookth thilly, we can wipe it off.
Okay.
Claire...
...is there any *reason* you'd have matches and a magnifyin' glass in your bag?
N-no!
What about this *big old can o' lighter fluid?*

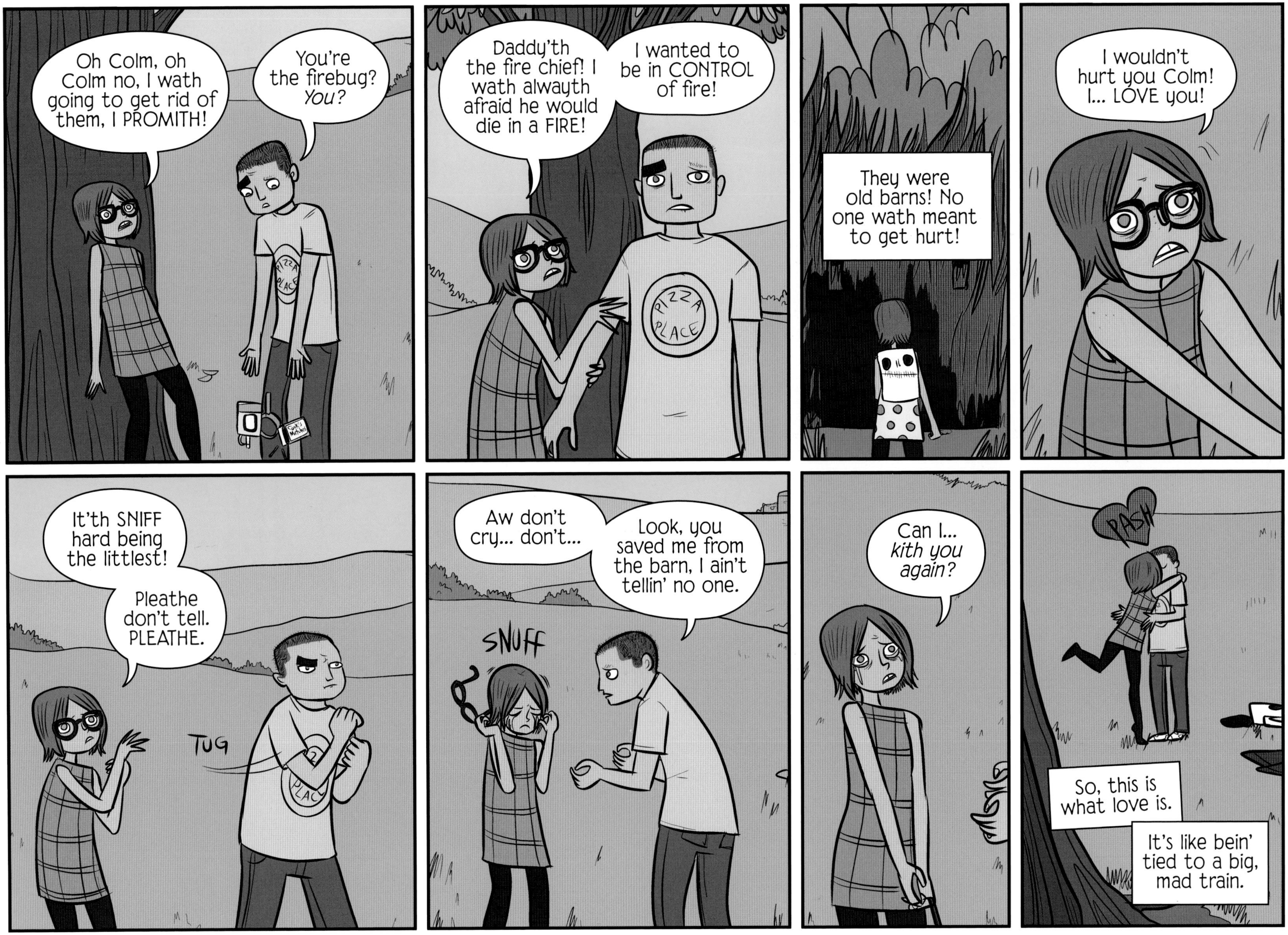
Oh Colm, oh Colm no, I wath going to get rid of them, I PROMITH!
You're the firebug? *You?*
PIZZA PLACE
Daddy'th the fire chief! I wath alwayth afraid he would die in a FIRE!
I wanted to be in CONTROL of fire!
PIZZA PLACE
They were old barns! No one wath meant to get hurt!
I wouldn't hurt you Colm! I... LOVE you!
It'th SNIFF hard being the littlest!
Pleathe don't tell. PLEATHE.
TUG
Aw don't cry... don't...
Look, you saved me from the barn, I ain't tellin' no one.
SNUFF
Can I... *kith you again?*
PASH
So, this is what love is.
It's like bein' tied to a big, mad train.

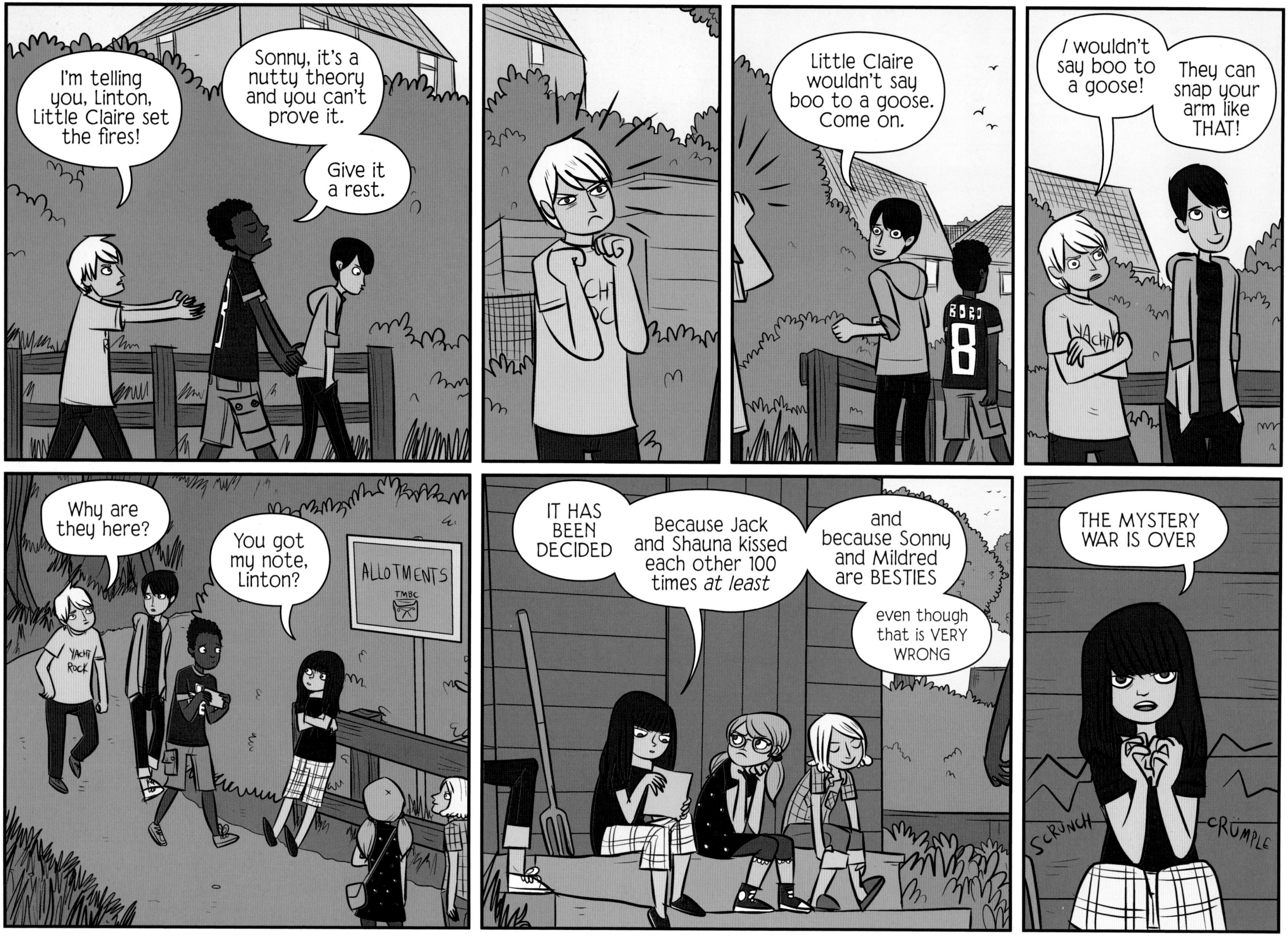
I'm telling you, Linton, Little Claire set the fires!
Sonny, it's a nutty theory and you can't prove it.
Give it a rest.
Little Claire wouldn't say boo to a goose. Come on.
BORO
8
I wouldn't say boo to a goose!
They can snap your arm like THAT!
YACHT
Why are they here?
YACHT ROCK
You got my note, Linton?
ALLOTMENTS
TMBC
IT HAS BEEN DECIDED
Because Jack and Shauna kissed each other 100 times *at least*
and because Sonny and Mildred are BESTIES
even though that is VERY WRONG
THE MYSTERY WAR IS OVER
SCRUNCH
CRUMPLE

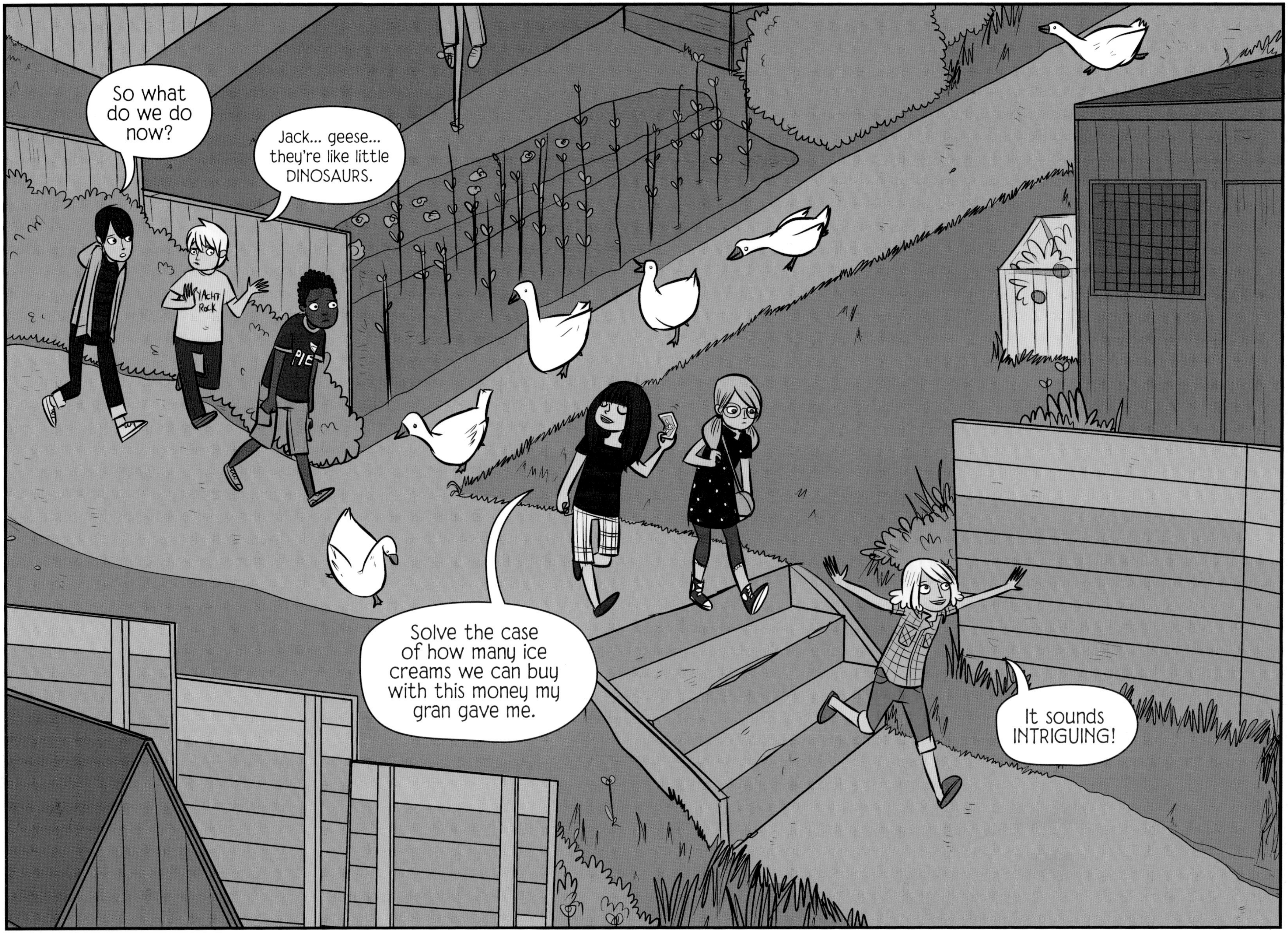
So what do we do now?
Jack... geese... they're like little DINOSAURS.
YACHT ROCK
PIE
Solve the case of how many ice creams we can buy with this money my gran gave me.
It sounds INTRIGUING!

GLOSSARY

Picts
KINGDOM OF THE SCOTTI
NORTHUMBRIA
ANGLO-SAXON KINGDOMS
IRISH KINGDOMS
MERCIA
Britons
EAST ANGLIA
London
Winchester
KINGDOM OF THE FRANKS

Great Britain is a comprised of four countries: England, Scotland, Wales, and Northern Ireland. Then there is Cornwall what has its own flag and language but is too obsessed with surfing to really be a country. They don't have a government but they do have "Surfers Against Sewage" which deals with probably 75% of their concerns as a nation. This mixture of people has created a lot of interesting phrases that you may wish to add to your international dictionary.

LOVE,
Charlotte
XXX

Mental: This is when your brainbox does not work quite right. Not to be confused with "The Mentalist" who is a man whose brain works maybe too well?

Parson: A holy man, a cleric. When picturing a parson as the people of Britane might think of him, imagine a priest in a cassock who has gone bright red because a lady in a short skirt just walked in. Maybe there is the sound of a swannee whistle at the same time.

Telly: Television. Please note, belly is not an abbreviation of "bellyvision" which is well a nightmare scenario.

SONEY
VOLUME

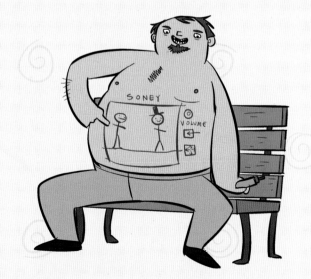

Potty: See "mental". I resent the implication that I do not have a fully working mind. I think eventually Potty Grote will be replaced by "Hottie Grote" or, among less shallow members of the school, "Polyglotty Grote", because of my great mastery of the Fronch long-uage.

FIG 1: NON-POTTY HOBBIES

FINANCIAL TIMES
BUY, YOU BUMS
I SAY SELL
RATES UP, FED STUMPED

Dinner lady: In America, "lunch lady". Any meal served by the school at lunchtime is referred to as "school dinner". School dinners are a Controversial Area because in the past schools were always trying to feed you meat they found at the town dump and childers liked that bad meat because the government had made it into a fun shape and put breadcrumbs on it. Then Jamie Oliver got involved.

They all use their knife and fork wrong: Cutlery skills are very important in the UK because for many years the food was not worth eating so you had to concentrate on something else.

The craic: Something Irish people say. Maybe it means "a good time", but that could be too simple, it can also mean gossip, fine entertainment or just some red hot chat. It is a catch-all term for anything that floats the Irish boat I reckon.

Sports Day: Day on which the whole school competes with each other in a load of track and field events. Well, most do. The kids with kind parents get notes written and enjoy pulling buttercups and daisies out of the living earth in the summer sun while watching Sonia Williams from 4B throw a "shot put".

107
SONIA WILLIAMS:
ASTOUNDING PHYSICAL POWER

Wendlefield: Tackleford's main enemy town. As soon as you go under the bridge to Wendlefield, there are no colours, milk goes sour, and a lad scratches your car with a coin while you're in the supermarket.

Property prices: If you listen carefully on any bus or train in our fine nation, this is what the adult humans are talking about.

TWITCH
TWITCH

The glad eye: When a lady has taken a shine to a man, she bestows upon him a loving and sen-sual gaze and that is the glad eye. See also: the skunk eye, the dead eye, the kill eye.

Bare nipples and back hair all showing: As soon as the sun is out, certain men head to the downtown zone with this look. The sun has confused them about how much we want to see their bare top halves. It is a national disgrace hem hem.

MUM
CHIVES

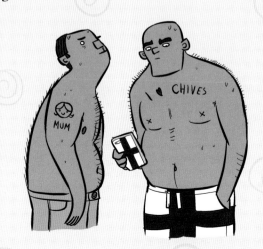

The nuthouse, nutters: It is important to be very respeckful of people who have mind problems, as it is not their fault. Sadly most boys have about as much respect for the feelings of the unwell as they do for an atmosphere untroubled by farts.

Wendy house: A little play house. The day you no longer fit in a Wendy house is the day you take on the cares and concerns of the adult world. Or, well, the concerns of the older than seven world. You will never own a house again *(see "property prices")*.

Tip: The town dump *(repository for old mattresses and future school dinner meats pre-breadcrumbing)*.

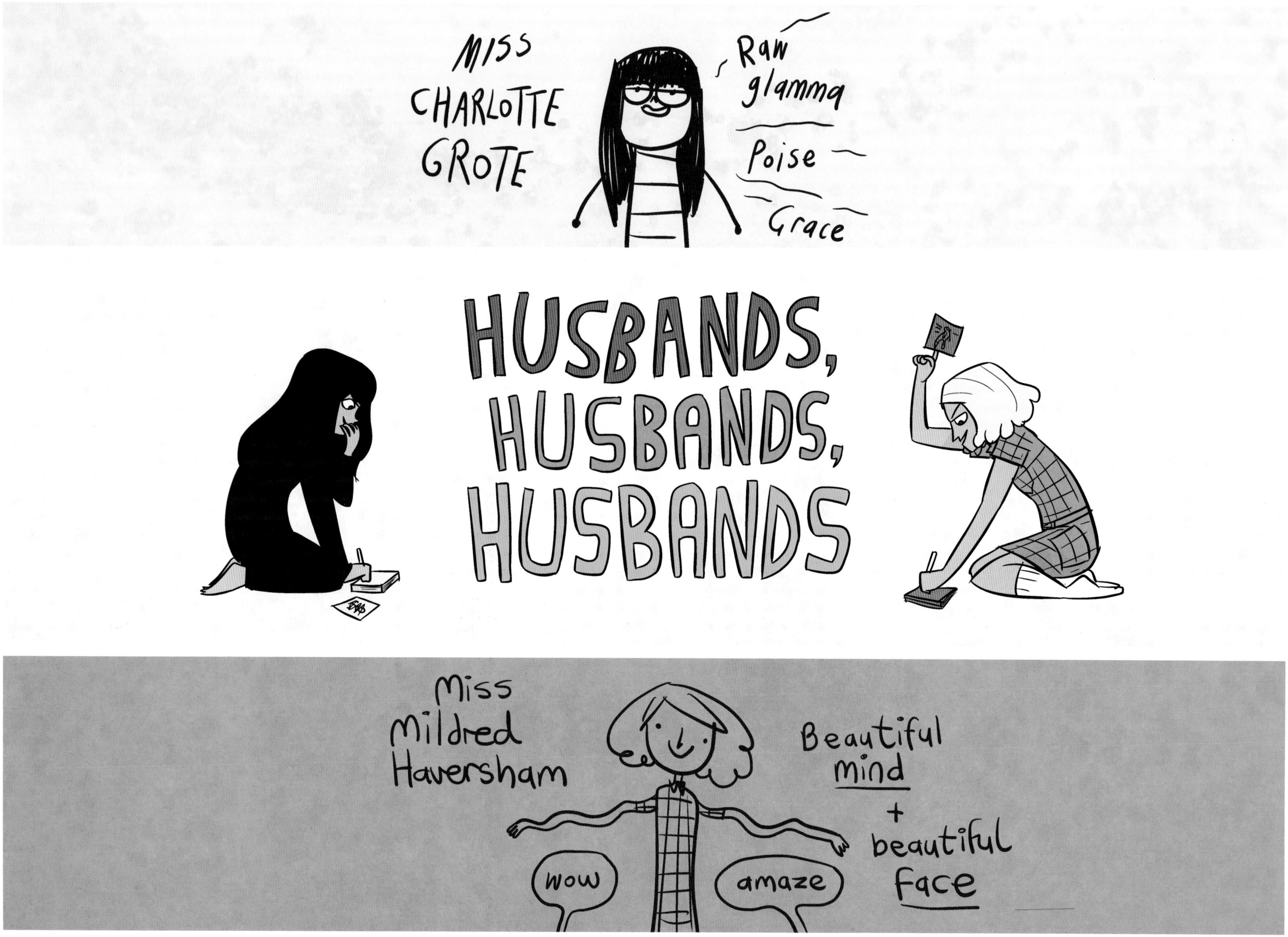
MISS CHARLOTTE GROTE
Raw glamma
Poise
Grace
HUSBANDS, HUSBANDS, HUSBANDS
Miss Mildred Haversham
Beautiful mind + beautiful face
wow
amaze

FOOTBALLER HUSBAND

YES: Great wealth + strong physique

BUT: 1% chance of mental agility

kick

PIE

VICAR HUSBAND

YES: free house, listening ear, good behaviour

BUT: might grass your sins up to GOD

DOCTOR HUSBAND

YES: "in-house" expert on dropsy, penicillin and mystery aches

BUT: carries a lady's handbag everywhere with him

(even to the toilet? CHECK)

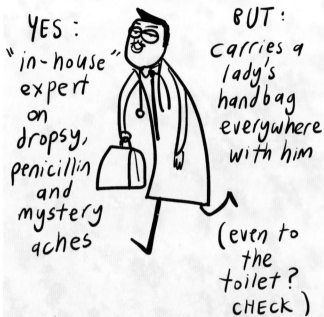

Builder husband

YES: willing participant in fancies such as bothy, gazebo, motte and bailey

BUT: hard hat leads to premature baldness, hat hair

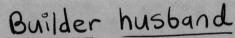
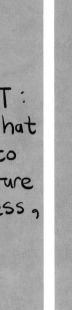

Architect husband

YES: all the benefits of a builder but cleaner

BUT: dangerous obsession with expensive spectacles + "FRANK GEHRY"

Actor husband

YES: handsome and charismatic

BUT: in love with own reflection + sensual danger of leading ladies

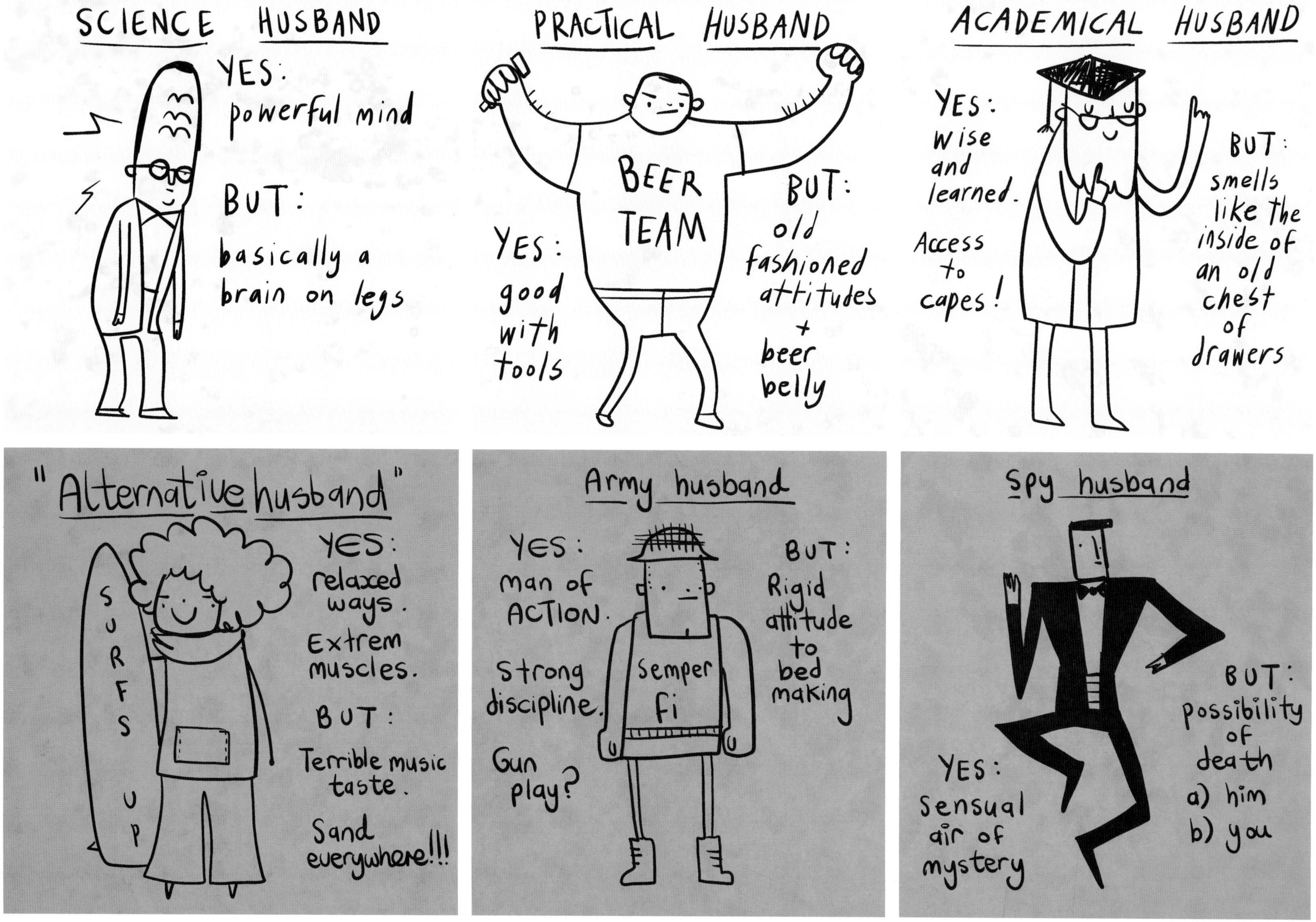
SCIENCE HUSBAND
YES: powerful mind
BUT: basically a brain on legs
PRACTICAL HUSBAND
BEER TEAM
YES: good with tools
BUT: old fashioned attitudes + beer belly
ACADEMICAL HUSBAND
YES: wise and learned.
Access to capes!
BUT: smells like the inside of an old chest of drawers
"Alternative husband"
SURFS UP
YES: relaxed ways. Extrem muscles.
BUT: Terrible music taste. Sand everywhere!!!
Army husband
YES: man of ACTION. Strong discipline. Gun play?
Semper Fi
BUT: Rigid attitude to bed making
Spy husband
YES: sensual air of mystery
BUT: possibility of death a) him b) you

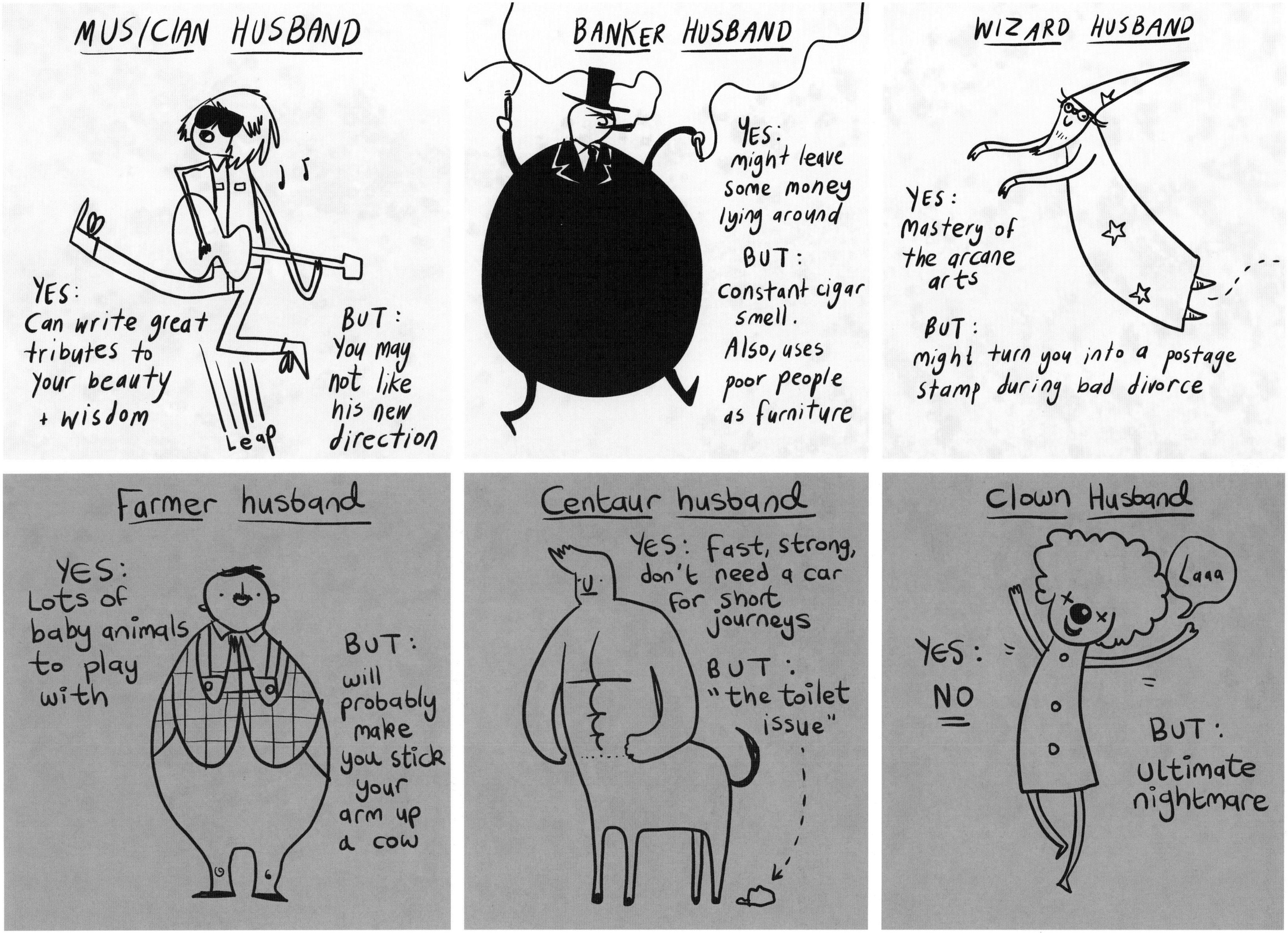
MUSICIAN HUSBAND
YES: Can write great tributes to your beauty + wisdom
BUT: You may not like his new direction
Leap
BANKER HUSBAND
YES: might leave some money lying around
BUT: constant cigar smell. Also, uses poor people as furniture
WIZARD HUSBAND
YES: Mastery of the arcane arts
BUT: might turn you into a postage stamp during bad divorce
Farmer husband
YES: Lots of baby animals to play with
BUT: will probably make you stick your arm up a cow
Centaur husband
YES: Fast, strong, don't need a car for short journeys
BUT: "the toilet issue"
Clown Husband
Laaa
YES: NO
BUT: ultimate nightmare

ALSO FROM JOHN ALLISON & ONI PRESS!

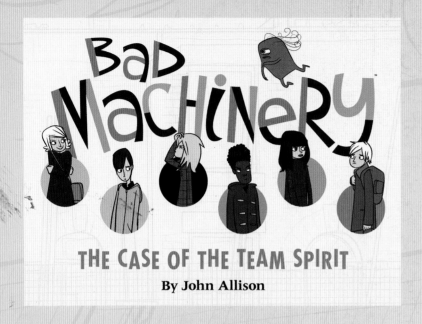

BAD MACHINERY
THE CASE OF THE TEAM SPIRIT
By John Allison

BAD MACHINERY
THE CASE OF THE GOOD BOY
By John Allison

BAD MACHINERY, VOLUME 1: THE CASE OF THE TEAM SPIRIT
By John Allison
136 pages, Softcover, Full Color
ISBN 978-1-62010-084-4

BAD MACHINERY, VOLUME 2: THE CASE OF THE GOOD BOY
By John Allison
144 pages, Softcover, Full Color
ISBN 978-1-62010-114-8

BAD MACHINERY
THE CASE OF THE LONELY ONE
Coming Soon!
UT ROWING CHAMPIONSHIP 1999